T0222295

Introduction to Deep Learning Business Applications for Developers

From Conversational Bots in Customer Service to Medical Image Processing

Armando Vieira
Bernardete Ribeiro

Apress®

Introduction to Deep Learning Business Applications for Developers

Armando Vieira
Linköping, Sweden

Bernardete Ribeiro
Coimbra, Portugal

ISBN-13 (pbk): 978-1-4842-3452-5
https://doi.org/10.1007/978-1-4842-3453-2

ISBN-13 (electronic): 978-1-4842-3453-2

Library of Congress Control Number: 2018940443

Managing Director, Apress Media LLC: Welmoed Spahr
Acquisitions Editor: Celestin John
Development Editor: Matthew Moodie
Coordinating Editor: Divya Modi

Cover designed by eStudioCalamar

Cover image designed by Freepik (www.freepik.com)

Distributed to the book trade worldwide by Springer Science+Business Media New York, 233 Spring Street, 6th Floor, New York, NY 10013. Phone 1-800-SPRINGER, fax (201) 348-4505, e-mail orders-ny@springer-sbm.com, or visit www.springeronline.com. Apress Media, LLC is a California LLC and the sole member (owner) is Springer Science + Business Media Finance Inc (SSBM Finance Inc). SSBM Finance Inc is a **Delaware** corporation.

For information on translations, please e-mail rights@apress.com, or visit www.apress.com/rights-permissions.

Apress titles may be purchased in bulk for academic, corporate, or promotional use. eBook versions and licenses are also available for most titles. For more information, reference our Print and eBook Bulk Sales web page at www.apress.com/bulk-sales.

Any source code or other supplementary material referenced by the author in this book is available to readers on GitHub via the book's product page, located at www.apress.com/978-1-4842-3452-5. For more detailed information, please visit www.apress.com/source-code.

Printed on acid-free paper

To my family.

—Bernardete Ribeiro

Table of Contents

About the Authors

Armando Vieira earned his PhD in physics in 1997 from the University of Coimbra and started working in artificial neural networks soon after. He pioneered research on deep neural networks in 2003 and more recently worked as a senior data scientist consultant for several companies and startups, ranging from image processing, drug discovery, and credit scoring to risk analysis. He has been a speaker at many events related to artificial intelligence and business. He is the founder of Alea.ai. You can find more information at `http://armando.lidinwise.com`.

Bernardete Ribeiro is full professor at the University of Coimbra, Portugal, where she teaches programming, pattern recognition, business intelligence, and other topics. She holds a PhD and habilitation in informatics engineering at the University of Coimbra (CISUC). She is also the director of the Center of Informatics and Systems at CISUC. Her research interests are in the areas of machine learning, pattern recognition, financial engineering, text classification, and signal processing, as well as their applications in a broad range of fields. She has been the founder and director of the Laboratory of Artificial Neural Networks (LARN) for more than 20 years. Bernardete is the president of the Portuguese Association of Pattern Recognition (APRP) and member of the governing board of the International Association for Pattern Recognition (IAPR).

About the Technical Reviewer

Jojo Moolayil is an artificial intelligence, deep learning, machine learning, and decision science professional with more than five years of industrial experience. He is the author of *Smarter Decisions: The Intersection of IoT and Decision Science* and has worked with several industry leaders on high-impact and critical data science and machine learning projects across multiple verticals. He is currently associated with General Electric and lives in Bengaluru—the Silicon Valley of India.

He was born and raised in Pune, India, and graduated from the University of Pune with a major in information technology engineering. He started his career with Mu Sigma Inc., the world's largest pure-play analytics provider and has worked with the leaders of many Fortune 50 clients. One of the early enthusiasts to venture into IoT analytics, he converged his learnings from decision science to bring the problem-solving frameworks and his learnings from data and decision science to IoT analytics.

To cement his foundations in data science for industrial IoT and scale the impact of the problem-solving experiments, he joined a fast-growing IoT analytics startup called Flutura based in Bangalore and headquartered in the valley. After a short stint with Flutura, Jojo moved on to work with the leaders of industrial IoT, General Electric, in Bangalore, where he focuses on solving decision science problems for industrial IoT use cases. As a part of his role in GE, Jojo also focuses on developing data science and decision science products and platforms for industrial IoT.

In addition to authoring books on decision science and IoT, Jojo has been the technical reviewer for various books on machine learning, deep learning, and business analytics with Apress and Packt publications. He is an active data science tutor and maintains a blog at `www.jojomoolayil.com/web/blog/`. You can reach him at `https://www.linkedin.com/in/jojo62000`.

Acknowledgments

We would like to thank all those who have contributed to bringing this book to publication for their help, support, and input. In particular, we appreciate all the support and encouragement from ContextVision AB, namely, Martin Hedlund and Mikael Rousson, for the inspiring conversations during the preparation of the book.

We also want to thank the Center of Informatics and Systems of the University of Coimbra (CISUC) and to the Informatics Engineering Department and the Faculty of Science and Technologies at the University of Coimbra (UC) for the support and means provided while researching and writing this book.

Our thanks also to Noel Lopes who reviewed the technical aspects of the book related to multicore processing and to Benjamin Auffarth for the careful reading of the manuscript.

A special thanks and appreciation to our editors, Celestin John and Divya Modi, at Springer for their essential encouragement.

Lastly, thank you to our families and friends for their love and support.

Armando Vieira and Bernardete Ribeiro
Coimbra, Portugal
February 2018

Introduction

Deep learning has taken artificial intelligence by storm and has infiltrated almost every business application. Because almost all content and transactions are now being recorded in a digital format, a vast amount of data is available for exploration by machine learning algorithms. However, traditional machine learning techniques struggle to explore the intricate relationships presented in this so-called Big Data. This is particularly acute for unstructured data such as images, voice, and text.

Deep learning algorithms can cope with the challenges in analyzing this immense data flow because they have a very high learning capacity. Also, deep neural networks require little, if any, feature engineering and can be trained from end to end. Another advantage of the deep learning approach is that it relies on architectures that require minimal supervision (in other words, these architectures learn automatically from data and need little human intervention). These architectures are the so-called "unsupervised" of weakly supervised learning. Last, but not least, they can be trained as generative processes. Instead of mapping inputs to outputs, the algorithms learn how to generate both inputs and outputs from pure noise (i.e., generative adversarial networks). Imagine generating Van Gogh paintings, cars, or even human faces from a combination of a few hundred random numbers.

Google language translation services, Alexa voice recognition, and self-driving cars all run on deep learning algorithms. Other emergent areas are heavily dependent on deep learning, such as voice synthesis, drug discovery, and facial identification and recognition. Even creative areas, such as music, painting, and writing, are beginning to be disrupted by this technology. In fact, deep learning has the potential to create such a profound transformation in the economy that it will probably trigger one of the biggest revolutions that humanity has ever seen.

Thanks to the dissemination of free, and powerful, computational frameworks and APIs such as Keras and TensorFlow, cheap cloud services to run the models, and the easy availability of data, anyone can run deep learning models in their home in a matter of hours. This democratization helps to explain the explosion of interest in the topic and the many breakthroughs being presented in an open format on Arxiv and in specialized top conferences like NIPS.

Introduction to Deep Learning Business Applications for Developers explores various deep learning algorithms by neatly abstracting the math skills. It gives an overview of several topics focused on the business applications of deep learning in computer vision, natural language processing, reinforcement learning, and unsupervised deep learning. It is targeted to mid-level and senior-level professionals as well as entry-level professionals with a basic understanding of machine learning. You can expect to understand the tangible depth of business applications and view use-case examples regarding future developments in each domain.

The book gives a short survey of the state-of-the-art algorithms of the whole field of deep learning, but its main purpose is more practical: to explain and illustrate some of the important methods of deep learning used in several application areas and in particular the impact on business. This book is intended for those who want to understand what deep learning is and how it can be used to develop business applications, with the aim of practical and successful deployment. The book filters out any overwhelming statistics and algebra and provides you with methods and tips on how to make simple hands-on tools for your business model.

First it introduces the main deep learning architectures and gives a short historical background of them. This is followed by examples of deep learning that are most advantageous and that have promising futures over traditional machine learning algorithms. Along these lines, the book covers applications of recommendation systems and natural language processing, including recurrent neural networks capable of capturing the richness of exhibiting language translation models. The book finishes by looking at the applications of deep learning models for financial risk assessment, control and robotics, and image recognition. Throughout the text, you will read about key companies and startups adopting this technology in their products. You will also find useful links and some examples, tricks, and insights on how to train deep learning models with some hands-on code examples in Keras and Python.

PART I

Background and Fundamentals

CHAPTER 1

Introduction

This chapter will describe what the book is about, the book's goals and audience, why artificial intelligence (AI) is important, and how the topic will be tackled.

Teaching computers to learn from experience and make sense of the world is the goal of artificial intelligence. Although people do not understand fully how the brain is capable of this remarkable feat, it is generally accepted that AI should rely on weakly supervised generation of hierarchical abstract concepts of the world. The development of algorithms capable of learning with minimal supervision—like babies learn to make sense of the world by themselves—seems to be the key to creating truly general artificial intelligence (GAI) [GBC16].

Artificial intelligence is a relatively new area of research (it started in the 1950s) that has had some successes and many failures. The initial enthusiasm, which originated at the time of the first electronic computer, soon faded away with the realization that most problems that the brain solves in a blink of an eye are in fact very hard to solve by machines. These problems include locomotion in uncontrolled environments, language translation, and voice and image recognition. Despite many attempts, it also became clear that the traditional (rule-based and descriptive) approach to solving complex mathematical equations or even proving theorems was insufficient to solve the most basic situations that a 2-year-old toddler had no difficulty with, such as understanding basic language concepts. This fact led to the so-called long AI winter, where many

© Armando Vieira, Bernardete Ribeiro 2018
A. Vieira and B. Ribeiro, *Introduction to Deep Learning Business Applications for Developers*,
https://doi.org/10.1007/978-1-4842-3453-2_1

researchers simply gave up creating machines with human-level cognitive capabilities, despite some successes in between, such as the IBM machine Deep Blue that become the best chess player in the world or such as the application of neural networks for handwritten digit recognition in late 1980s.

AI is today one of the most exciting research fields with plenty of practical applications, including autonomous vehicles, drug discovery, robotics, language translation, and games. Challenges that seemed insurmountable just a decade ago have been solved—sometimes with superhuman accuracy—and are now present in products and ubiquitous applications. Examples include voice recognition, navigation systems, facial emotion detection, and even art creation, such as music and painting. For the first time, AI is leaving the research labs and materializing in products that could have emerged from science-fiction movies.

How did this revolution become possible in such a short period of time? What changed in recent years that puts us closer to the GAI dream? The answer is more a gradual improvement of algorithms and hardware than a single breakthrough. But certainly *deep neural networks*, commonly referred to as *deep learning* (DL), appears at the top of the list [J15].

1.1 Scope and Motivation

Advances in computational power, big data, and the Internet of Things are powering the major transformation in technology and are powering productivity across all industries.

Through examples in this book, you will explore concrete situations where DL is advantageous with respect to other traditional (shallow) machine learning algorithms, such as content-based recommendation algorithms and natural language processing. You'll learn about techniques such as Word2vec, skip-thought vectors, and Item2Vec. You will also consider recurrent neural networks trained with stacked long short-term memory (LSTM) units and sequence2sequence models for language translation with embeddings.

A key feature of DL algorithms is their capability to learn from large amounts of data with minimal supervision, contrary to shallow models that normally require less (labeled) data. In this book, you will explore some examples, such as video prediction and image segmentation, with fully convolutional neural networks (FCNNs) and residual neural networks (ResNets) that have achieved top performance in the ImageNet image recognition competition. You will explore the business implications of these image recognition techniques and some active startups in this very active field.

The implications of DL-supported AI in business is tremendous, shaking to the foundations many industries. It is perhaps the biggest transformative force since the Internet.

This book will present some applications of DL models for financial risk assessment (credit risk with deep belief networks and options optimizations with variational auto-encoder). You will briefly explore applications of DL to control and robotics and learn about the DeepQ learning algorithm (which was used to beat humans in the game Go) and actor-critic methods for reinforcement learning.

You will also explore a recent and powerful set of algorithms, named *generative adversarial neural networks* (GANs), including the dcGAN, the conditional GAN, and the pixel2pixel GAN. These are very efficient for tasks such as image translation, image colorization, and image completion.

You'll also learn about some key findings and implications in the business of DL and about key companies and startups adopting this technology. The book will cover some frameworks for training DL models, key methods, and tricks to fine-tune the models.

The book contains hands-on coding examples, in Keras using Python 3.6.

1.2 Challenges in the Deep Learning Field

Machine learning, and deep learning in particular, is rapidly expanding to almost all business areas. DL is the technology behind well-known applications for speech recognition, image processing, and natural language processing. But some challenges in deep learning remain.

To start with, deep learning algorithms require large data sets. For instance, speech recognition requires data from multiple dialects or demographics. Deep neural networks can have millions or even billion of parameters, and training can be a time-consuming process—sometimes weeks in a well-equipped machine.

Hyperparameter optimization (the size of the network, the architecture, the learning rate, etc.) can be a daunting task. DL also requires high-performance hardware for training, with a high-performance GPU and at least 12Gb of memory.

Finally, neural networks are essentially black boxes and are hard to interpret.

1.3 Target Audience

This book was written for academics, data scientists, data engineers, researchers, entrepreneurs, and business developers.

While reading this book, you will learn the following:

- What deep learning is and why it is so powerful

- What major algorithms are available to train DL models

- What the major breakthroughs are in terms of applying DL

- What implementations of DL libraries are available and how to run simple examples

- Major areas of the impact of DL in business and startups

The book introduces the fundamentals while giving some practical tips to cover the information needed for a hands-on project related to a business application. It also covers the most recent developments in DL from a pragmatic perspective. It cuts through the buzz and offers concrete examples of how to implement DL in your business application.

1.4 Plan and Organization

The book is divided into four parts. Part 1 contains the introduction and fundamental concepts about deep learning and the most important network architectures, from convolutional neural networks (CNNs) to LSTM networks.

Part 2 contains the core DL applications, in other words, image and video, natural language processing and speech, and reinforcement learning and robotics.

Part 3 explores other applications of DL, including recommender systems, conversational bots, fraud, and self-driving cars.

Finally, Part 4 covers the business impact of DL technology and new research and future opportunities.

The book is divided into 11 chapters. The material in the chapters is structured for easy understanding of the DL field. The book also includes many illustrations and code examples to clarify the concepts.

## CHAPTER 2

Deep Learning: An Overview

Artificial neural networks are not new; they have been around for about 50 years and got some practical recognition after the mid-1980s with the introduction of a method (backpropagation) that allowed for the training of multiple-layer neural networks. However, the true birth of deep learning may be traced to the year 2006, when Geoffrey Hinton [GR06] presented an algorithm to efficiently train deep neural networks in an unsupervised way—in other words, data without labels. They were called *deep belief networks* (DBNs) and consisted of stacked restrictive Boltzmann machines (RBMs), with each one placed on the top of another. DBNs differ from previous networks since they are generative models capable of learning the statistical properties of data being presented without any supervision.

Inspired by the depth structure of the brain, deep learning architectures have revolutionized the approach to data analysis. Deep learning networks have won a large number of hard machine learning contests, from voice recognition [AAB+15] to image classification [AIG12] to natural language processing (NLP) [ZCSG16] to time-series prediction—sometimes by a large margin. Traditionally, AI has relied on heavily handcrafted features. For instance, to get decent results in image classification, several preprocessing techniques have to be applied, such as filters, edge detection, and so on. The beauty of DL is that most, if not

© Armando Vieira, Bernardete Ribeiro 2018
A. Vieira and B. Ribeiro, *Introduction to Deep Learning Business Applications for Developers*,
https://doi.org/10.1007/978-1-4842-3453-2_2

all, features can be learned automatically from the data—provided that enough (sometimes million) training data examples are available. Deep models have feature detector units at each layer (level) that gradually extract more sophisticated and invariant features from the original raw input signals. Lower layers aim to extract simple features that are then clumped into higher layers, which in turn detect more complex features. In contrast, shallow models (those with two layers such as neural networks [NNs] or support vector machine [SVMs]) present very few layers that map the original input features into a problem-specific feature space. Figure 2-1 shows the comparison between Deep Learning and Machine Learning (ML) models in terms of performance versus amount of data to build the models.

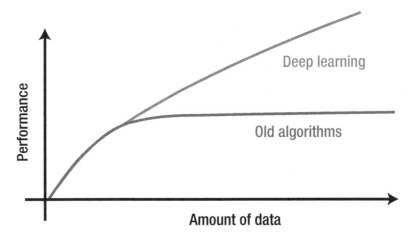

Figure 2-1. *Deep learning models have a high learning capacity*

Perfectly suited to do supervised as well as unsupervised learning in structured or unstructured data, deep neural architectures can be exponentially more efficient than shallow ones. Since each element of the architecture is learned using examples, the number of computational elements one can afford is limited only by the number of training samples—which can be of the order of billions. Deep models can be trained with hundreds of millions of weights and therefore tend to outperform shallow models such as SVMs. Moreover, theoretical results suggest that deep architectures are fundamental to learning the kind of complex functions that represent high-level abstractions (e.g., vision, language, semantics), characterized by many factors of variation that interact in nonlinear ways, making the learning process difficult.

2.1 From a Long Winter to a Blossoming Spring

Today it's difficult to find any AI-based technology that does not rely on deep learning. In fact, the implications of DL in the technological applications of AI will be so profound that we may be on the verge of the biggest technological revolution of all time.

One of the remarkable features of DL neural networks is their (almost) unlimited capacity to accommodate information from large quantities of data without overfitting—as long as strong regularizers are applied. DL is as much of a science as of an art, and while it's very common to train models with billions of parameters on millions of training examples, that is possible only by carefully selecting and fine-tuning the learning machine and sophisticated hardware. Figure 2-2 shows the trends in machine learning, pattern recognition and deep learning across the last decade/for more than one decade.

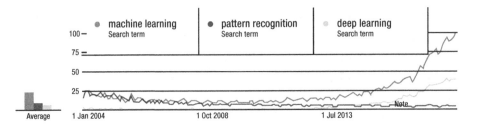

Figure 2-2. *Evolution of interest in deep learning (source: Google Trends)*

The following are the main characteristics that make a DNN unique:

- *High learning capacity*: Since DNNs have millions of parameters, they don't saturate easily. The more data you have, the more they learn.

- *No feature engineering required*: Learning can be performed from end to end—whether it's robotic control, language translation, or image recognition.

- *Abstraction representation*: DNNs are capable of generating abstract concepts from data.

- *High generative capability*: DNNs are much more than simple discriminative machines. They can generate unseen but plausible data based on latent representations.

- *Knowledge transfer*: This is one of the most remarkable properties—you can teach a machine in one large set of data such as images, music, or biomedical data and transfer the learning to a similar problem where less of different types data is known. One of the most remarkable examples is a DNN that captures and replicates artistic styles.

- *Excellent unsupervised capabilities*: As long as you have lots of data, DNNs can learn hidden statistical representations without any labels required.

- *Multimodal learning*: DNNs can integrate seamlessly disparate sources of high-dimensional data, such as text, images, video, and audio, to solve hard problems like automatic video caption generation and visual questions and answers.

- They are relatively easy to compose and embed domain knowledge - or prioris - to handle uncertainty and constrain learning.

The following are the less appealing aspects of DNN models[1]:

- They are hard to interpret. Despite being able to extract latent features from the data, DNNs are black boxes that learn by associations and co-occurrences. They lack the transparency and interpretability of other methods, such as decision trees.

- They are only partially able to uncover complex causality relations or nested structural relationships, common in domains such as biology.

---

[1]Regarding these points, note that this is an active area of research, and many of these difficulties are being addressed. Some of them are partially solved, while others (such as lack of interpretability) probably never will be.

- They can be relatively complex and time-consuming to train, with many hyperparameters that require careful fine-tuning.

- They are sensitive to initialization and learning rate. It's easy for the networks to be unstable and not converge. This is particularly acute for recurrent neural networks and generative adversarial networks.

- A loss function has to be provided. Sometimes it is hard to find a good one.

- Knowledge may not be accumulated in an incremental way. For each new data set, the network has to be trained from scratch. This is also called the *knowledge persistence problem*.

- Knowledge transference is possible for certain models but not always obvious.

- DNNs can easily memorize the training data, if they have a huge capacity.

- Sometimes they can be easily fooled, for instance, confidently classifying noisy images.

2.2 Why Is DL Different?

Machine learning (ML) is a somewhat vague but hardly new area of research. In particular, pattern recognition, which is a small subfield of AI, can be summarized in one simple sentence: finding patterns in data. These patterns can be anything from historical cycles in the stock market to distinguishing images of cats from dogs. ML can also be described as the art of teaching machines how to make decisions.

So, why all the excitement about AI powered by deep learning? As mentioned, DL is both quantitative (an improvement of 5 percent in voice recognition makes all the difference between a great personal assistant and a useless one) and qualitative (how DL models are trained, the subtle relations they can extract from high-dimensional data, and how these relations can be integrated into a unified perspective). In addition, they have had practical success in cracking several hard problems.

As shown in Figure 2-3, let's consider the classical iris problem: how to distinguish three different types of flower species (outputs) based on four measurements (inputs), specifically, petal and sepal width and length, over a data set of 150 observations. A simple descriptive analysis will immediately inform the user about the usefulness of different measurements. Even with a basic approach such as Naïve Bayes, you could build a simple classifier with good accuracy.

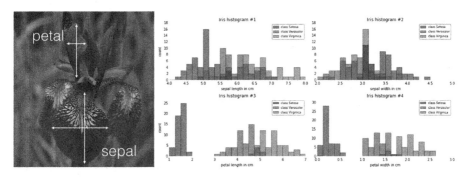

Figure 2-3. *Iris image and classification with Naïve Bayes (source: predictive modeling, supervised machine learning, and pattern classification by Sebastian Raschka)*

This method assumes independence of the inputs given a class (output) and works remarkably well for lots of problems. However, the big catch is that this is a strong assumption that rarely holds. So, if you want to go beyond Naïve Bayes, you need to explore all possible relations between inputs. But there is a problem. For simplicity, let's assume you have ten possible signal levels for each input. The number of possible

15

input combinations you need to consider in the training set (number of observations) will be $10^4 = 10000$. This is a big number and is much bigger than the 150 observations. But the problem gets much worse (exponentially worse) as the number of inputs increases. For images, you could have 1,000 (or more) pixels per image, so the number of combinations will be 10^{1000}, which is a number out of reach—the number of atoms in the universe is less than 10^{100}!

So, the big challenge of DL is to make tractable very high-dimensional problems (such as language, sound, or images) with a limited set of data and make generalizations on unseen input regions without using brute force to explore all the possible combinations. The trick of DL is to transform, or *map*, a high-dimensional space (discrete or continuous) into a continuous low-dimensional one (sometimes called the *manifold*) where you could find a simple solution to your problem. Here *solution* usually means optimizing a function; it could be maximizing the likelihood (equivalent of minimizing the classification error in problems like the iris problem) or minimizing the mean square error (in regression problems such as stock market prediction).

This is easier said than done. Several assumptions and techniques have to be used to approximate this hard inference problem. (*Inference* is simply a word to say "obtain the previously mentioned map" or the parameters of the model describing the posterior distribution that maximizes the likelihood function.) The key (somehow surprising) finding was that a simple algorithm called *gradient descent*, when carefully tuned, is powerful enough to guide the deep neural networks toward the solution. And one of the beauties of neural networks is that, after being properly trained, the mapping between inputs and outputs is smooth, meaning that you can transform a discrete problem, such as a language semantic, into a continuous or distributed representation. (You'll learn more about this when you read about Word2vec later in the chapter.)

That's the secret of deep learning. There's no magic, just some well-known numerical algorithms, a powerful computer, and data (lots of it!).

2.2.1 The Age of the Machines

After a long winter, we are now experiencing a blossoming spring in artificial intelligence. This fast-moving wave of technology innovations powered by AI is impacting business and society at such a velocity that it is hard to predict its implications. One thing is sure, though: cognitive computing powered by AI will empower (sometimes replace) humans in many repetitive and even creative tasks, and society will be profoundly transformed. It will impact jobs that had seemed impossible to automate, from doctors to legal clerks.

A study by Carl B. Frey and M. Osborne, from 2013, states that 47 percent of jobs in the United States were at risk of being replaced in the near future. Also, in April 2015, the McKinsey Global Institute published an essay that states AI is transforming society at a rate that will happen 10 times faster and at 300 times the scale (or roughly 3,000 times the impact) of the Industrial Revolution.

We may try to build a switch-off button or hard-coded rules to prevent machines from doing any harm to humans. The problem is that these machines learn by themselves and are not hard-coded. Also, even if there were a way to build such a "safety exit," how could someone code ethics into a machine? By the way, can we even agree on ethics for ourselves, humans?

Our opinion is that because AI is giving machines superhuman cognitive capabilities, these fears should not be taken lightly. For now, the apocalypse scenario is a mere fantasy, but we will eventually face dilemmas where machines are no longer deterministic devices (see `https://www.youtube.com/watch?v=nDQztSTMnd8`).

The only way to incorporate ethics into a machine is the same as in humans: through a lengthy and consistent education. The problem is that machines are not like humans. For instance, how can you explain the notion of "hungry" or "dead" to a nonliving entity?

Finally, it's hard to quantify, but AI will certainly have a huge impact on society, to an extent that some, like Elon Musk and Stephen Hawking, fear that our own existence is at risk.

2.2.2 Some Criticism of DL

There has been some criticism of DL as being a brute-force approach. We believe that this argument is not valid. While it's true that to train DL algorithms many samples are needed (for image classification, for instance, convolutional neural networks may require hundreds of thousands of annotated examples), the fact is that image recognition, which people take for granted, is in fact complex. Furthermore, DNNs are universal computing devices that may be efficient, especially the recurrent ones.

Another criticism is that networks are unable to reuse the accumulated knowledge to quickly extend it to other domains (the so-called knowledge transfer, compositionability, and zero-shot learning), which is something humans do very well. For instance, if you know what a bike is, you almost instantaneously understand the concept of motorbike and do not need to see millions of examples.

A common issue is that these networks are black boxes and therefore impossible for a human to understand their predictions. However, there are several ways to mitigate this problem. See, for instance, the recent work "PatternNet and PatternLRP: Improving the interpretability of neural networks." Furthermore, zero-shot learning (learning in unseen data) is already possible, and knowledge transfer is widely used in biology and art.

These criticisms, while valid, have been addressed in recent approaches; see [LST15] and [GBC16].

2.3 Resources

This book will guide you through the most relevant landmarks and recent achievements in DNNs from a practical point of view. You'll also explore the business applications and implications of the technology. The technicalities will be kept to a minimum so you can focus on the essentials. The following are a few good resources that are essential to understand this exciting topic.

2.3.1 Books

These are some good books on the topic:

- A recent book on deep learning from Yoshua Bengio et al. [GBC16] is the best and most updated reference on DNNs. It has a strong emphasis on the theoretical and statistical aspects of deep neural networks.

- *Deep Learning with Python* by Francois Chollet (Manning, 2017) was written by the author of Keras and is a must for those willing to get a hands-on experience to DL.

- The online book *Neural Networks and Deep Learning* is also a good introductory source for those interested in understanding the fundamentals of DL.

- *Fundamentals of Deep Learning* (O'Reilly, 2017) is a book that explains step-by-step the fundamental concepts of ANNs and DL.

- *Deep Learning with Python* (2016) is a hands-on e-book using Python libraries (Keras.io and TensorFlow).

- *Deep Learning Mastery* is an online book with an excellent step-by-step tutorial using Keras.

2.3.2 Newsletters

Here are some good newsletters:

- jack-clark.net is a good weekly review of deep learning and AI.

- Dataelixir.com is a weekly newsletter of curated data science news and resources from around the web.

- www.getrevue.co/profile/nathanbenaich from Nathan Benaich is a monthly review of artificial intelligence news, research, investments, and applications.

- Wildml.com is a good blog maintained by Denny Britz for tutorials on DL, and it has a weekly newsletter.

- Data Machina is a weekly newsletter on big data and machine learning.

- The Exponent View at www.getrevue.co/profile/azeem contains news about AI-based technology and its impact on society.

- Datascienceweekly.org is a weekly summary of new relevant aspects for machine learning and data science.

- CognitionX is a daily briefing on data science, AI, and machine learning.

2.3.3 Blogs

Here are some relevant blogs:

- The Andrew Karpathy blog is a great source of inspiration for those who want to get hands-on experience with deep learning tools, from image processing to recurrent neural networks.

- KDnuggets is a good blog covering a diversity of topics on ML and AI.

- Data Science Central provides interesting posts on the business implications of ML, and it has a daily newsletter.

- CreativeAI.net is an excellent blog showcasing works in the confluence of AI and art.

- Arxiv.org is the best repository of open publications in many areas, including computer science.

- Gitxiv.com is a blog combining publications on Arxiv, with the respective code on GitHub.

- Arxiv-sanity.com is a site made by A. Karpathy that curates content from Arxiv.

2.3.4 Online Videos and Courses

Here are some relevant videos and courses:

- Coursera has an excellent online course from the grandfather of ANN, G. Hinton (`https://www.coursera.org/learn/neural-networks`).

- This is the classic and pioneering course from Stanford professor Andrew Ng (`https://www.coursera.org/learn/machine-learning`).

- Udacity also has a good course about deep learning by Google.

- Re-Work summits are excellent events organized in London, New York, S. Francisco, and Shanghai on AI and deep learning.

- Data Science Summit organizes events for intense training. Internships are organized within the companies that support the initiative.

- General Assembly has some online courses and boot camps around the world.

- Science 2 Data Science is an intensive training program to prepare data scientists for companies.

- Jason Brownlee has some excellent tutorials and e-books to start understanding machine learning and deep learning models in Python using the Keras framework.

- Videolectures.net has good video content and lectures, for example, from ICML 2015 and the Deep Learning Summer School of 2016.

- Ian Goodfellow has an excellent tutorial on GANs.

2.3.5 Podcasts

Here are some podcasts:

- This Week in Machine Learning and AI gives an overview of the recent developments and applications of AI and always features a guest.

- Talking Machines is a podcast featuring a guest in each episode.

- Data Skeptic is a weekly podcast with interviews of experienced data scientists.

- Learning Machines is a gentle introduction to Artificial Intelligence and Machine Learning (http://www.learningmachines101.com/).

- The O'Reilly Data Show Podcast delves into the techniques behind Big Data, Data Science and AI `https://www.oreilly.com/topics/oreilly-data-show-podcast`.

- The A16Z podcast by Andreessen Horowitz is an excellent resource for topics related to data science and technology.

2.3.6 Other Web Resources

Here are some other web resources:

- `www.deeplearning.net` is the pioneer web site on deep learning. It's still a reference.

- `https://github.com/terryum/awesome-deep-learning-papers` is a list of the most cited and important papers in several DL domains.

- Image Completion with Deep Learning in TensorFlow (`http://bamos.github.io/2016/08/09/deep-completion/`) is a good tutorial on DNN for image completion.

- `https://github.com/kjw0612/awesome-deep-vision` is a list of resources of DL for computer vision.

- Machine Learning & Deep Learning Tutorials is a repository that contains a topic-wise curated list of Machine Learning and Deep Learning tutorials, articles and other resources (`https://github.com/ujjwalkarn/Machine-Learning-Tutorials`).

- Machine Learning Is Fun by Adam Geitgey is a website with an easy introduction to Machine Learning in more than 15 languages (`https://medium.com/@ageitgey/machine-learning-is-fun-80ea3ec3c471`).

- Approaching (Almost) Any Machine Learning Problem by Abhishek Thakur is a realistic overview of most machine learning pipelines.

- Kaggle.com promotes several challenging machine learning contests with prizes up to $100,000 USD. But more than the money, it's about creating a reputation as a true data scientist.

- `https://a16z.com/2016/06/10/ai-deep-learning-machines/` is a good overview of deep learning evolution from Andresseen Horowitz.

- These two AMA ("Ask Me Anything") at Reddit are extremely helpful in understanding the history behind ANN, narrated by some of their "grandparents," J. Schmidhuber (`https://www.reddit.com/r/MachineLearning/comments/2xcyrl/i_am_j%C3%BCrgen_schmidhuber_ama/`) and Geoffrey Hinton (`https://www.reddit.com/r/MachineLearning/comments/2lmo0l/ama_geoffrey_hinton/`).

2.3.7 Some Nice Places to Start Playing

Try these for hands-on experience:

- Great tutorials on Tensorflow using Google collaborative Jupyter notebooks (no code installation necessary) `https://www.tensorflow.org/get_started/eager`.

- Awesome TensorFlow has many examples to start playing with TensorFlow.

- `http://keras.github.com` is a Keras repository and has several examples to start working with DNNs.

- `http://research.baidu.com/warp-ctc/` open sources their code, Deep Speech 2, for end-to-end voice recognition and translation.

- `http://playground.tensorflow.org/` is a TensorFlow playground.

- H20.ai is a good API for R users, although the models available are quite limited.

- `https://aiexperiments.withgoogle.com` has experiments including playing pictionary against Google.

- `https://artsexperiments.withgoogle.com` has several very interesting experiments on art.

- `www.creativeai.net` is a space to share CreativeAI Projects from machine learning, music, writing, art, fashion to industrial design and architecture, among others.

2.3.8 Conferences

The following five conferences are considered to be the most relevant in Deep Learning:

- NIPS - considered the most important conference on DL with a focus on both theoretical and practical applications.

- ICML - International Conference on Machine Learning, one of the most prestigious conference on Machine Learning.

- ICLR - International Conference on Learning Representation, a more recent conference focused on deep learning.

- KDD - a widely recognised conference on machine learning and knowledge discovery.

- IJCNN an IEEE conference that covers a broad range of neural network concepts and applications.

2.3.9 Other Resources

The Deep RL Bootcamp cohosted by OpenAI and UC Berkeley features lectures about reinforcement learning basics as well as state-of-the-art research.

The Stanford course called Convolutional Neural Networks for Visual Recognition is a must, as is the Natural Language Processing with Deep Learning course.

Coursera has a deep learning specialization, and the University of Montreal offers the Deep Learning and Reinforcement Summer School. Also, check out UC Berkeley's Deep Reinforcement Learning from the fall of 2017 and the TensorFlow Dev Summit with presentations on DL fundamentals and TensorFlow APIs.

2.3.10 DL Frameworks

DL can be straightforward and fun, and you can start with the many tutorials available online. You can train a model with a few dozen lines of code. However, it is rarely the case that a real problem fits exactly into a category of the available academic benchmarks. In fact, training DL models can be hard and frustrating—depending on the problem you want to solve, the preprocessing required, the data available, and your willingness to understand the intricacies behind the learning algorithms.

It definitely requires a lot of Bayesian statistics, graphical models, nonparametric estimation, statistical inference (either deterministic [such as variational estimation] or approximations [such as Markov chain Monte Carlo]). You don't need to know them all, but you will encounter these concepts in the journey of becoming a specialist.

One of the remarkable things about DL research is that most of the work (papers, data, and even code) are open source, either from academia or from companies, so anyone can play and learn with it.

Many open source libraries and frameworks are available to work with DL. The most common are Caffe, TensorFlow, Keras, Theano, or Torch. A brief description follows:

- TensorFlow is a recent project open sourced by Google that is becoming popular because of its support for several types of architectures, including convolutional neural networks, stacked auto-encoders, deep belief networks, and recurrent neural networks. In TensorFlow, a network is specified as a symbolic graph of vector operations, such as matrix add/multiply or convolution, and each layer is a composition of those operations. TensorFlow uses a high-level scripting language that is useful for the fast deployment of models. The interface is accessible through Python or C++, and it has a useful browser interface for debugging, called TensorBoard.

- Keras.io is a great framework that can run on top of either Theano or TensorFlow; it's simple and intuitive to use.

- Torch provides a high-level scripting interface (much like Matlab), with excellent performance for convolutional neural networks and recurrent neural networks. It gives less flexibility if the user wants to navigate at a more granular level. Torch runs on Lua, which allows for fast executions compared with other implementations. The recent Pytorch is a Python package that provides high-level features for Tensor computation (like Numpy) with strong GPU acceleration and deep neural networks built on a tape-based autograd system.

- MxNet, from Microsoft, was recently adopted by Amazon as its deep learning platform. It was recently included as one of the backends in Keras.

- Gluon is an open source deep learning interface recently released from Amazon and Microsoft. Gluon is a high-level framework for designing and defining machine learning models. According to Amazon, "Developers who are new to machine learning will find this interface more familiar to traditional code, since machine learning models can be defined and manipulated just like any other data structure." Gluon will initially be available within Apache MXNet (Amazon) and soon in CNTK (Microsoft).

- Caffe was one of the first deep learning toolkits, mainly used for convolutional neural networks. However, it doesn't support recurrent networks and NLP models. Its interface is also not user friendly.

- Theano is one of the most versatile and powerful toolkits for implementing deep learning models and is being used in recent research such as attentive mechanism and bidirectional recurrent networks. Theano uses symbolic graphs and has implementations for most state-of-the-art networks, sometimes presented as a high-level framework, such as Keras. io. It has good performance and supports single and multiple GPUs. The flip side is that it has a steep learning curve and is somewhat hard to debug.

2.3.11 DL As a Service

All big players (Amazon, IBM, Google, Facebook, Twitter, Baidu, Yahoo, and Microsoft) are creating their own DL platforms and open sourcing (some of) their core algorithms. We are entering in the age of AI-as-a-service. Table 2-1 summarizes the principal services offered by these companies.

Table 2-1. *Main Machine Learning Platforms*

Company	Cloud-Based ML Platform	DL Technology (Open Source)
Amazon	Amazon Machine Learning	DSSTNE
Baidu	Deep Speech 2	Paddle
Facebook	TorchNet, Pytorch	FastText
Google	NEXT Cloud	TensorFlow
IBM	Watson	IBM System
Microsoft	Azur	CNTK
Twitter	Cortex	

Figure 2-4 compares the different DL platforms.

	Languages	Tutorials and training materials	CNN modeling capability	RNN modeling capability	Architecture: easy-to-use and modular front end	Speed	Multiple GPU support	Keras compatible
Theano	Python, C++	++	++	++	+	++	+	+
Tensor-Flow	Python	+++	+++	++	+++	++	++	+
Torch	Lua, Python (new)	+	+++	++	++	+++	++	
Caffe	C++	+	++		+	+	+	
MXNet	R, Python, Julia, Scala	++	++	+	++	++	+++	
Neon	Python	+	++	+	+	++	+	
CNTK	C++	+	+	+++	+	++	+	

Figure 2-4. *Comparison of different Deep Learning frameworks (source: www.kdnuggets.com/2017/03/getting-started-deep-learning.html)*

Deep learning is moving to open source and to the cloud. Google, Facebook, IBM, Amazon, and Microsoft are trying to establish ecosystems around AI services provided in the cloud. Deep learning is a transversal technology that will be applied to every industry, so the competition is strong, and all players are trying to win through cloud services and integrated platforms. Forrester Research recently estimated $10.8 billion in cloud revenues for Amazon in 2016, $10.1 billion for Microsoft, and $3.9 billion for Google.

Probably the scarcest resource for these companies will be talent, which may justify a frenetic M&A activity with the "acquire" of deep learning startups. Furthermore, talented AI experts are mostly from academia, and they demand openness and engagement in active open source communities. That's why acceptance of any platform by the Apache Institute is a major source of credibility. That helps explain why Apple is lagging with respect to other big players, and its closed culture does not help.

Hardware is also key. Most DL algorithms demand huge computational power, local or on the cloud. Specifically, they require graphical processing units (GPUs) as in gaming consoles and field programmable gate arrays (FPGAs), which are chips that can be configured for special-purpose operations. Most of the statistical inference performed by DL involves intractable problems (for instance, evaluating complex integrals) that are possible only through approximations that are computational expensive. DL may soon become more a hardware problem than an algorithm problem. NVIDIA and Intel are launching new processors specific to cope with deep learning computational demands.

OpenAI, founded by Elon Musk as a nonprofit organization, is adding a new angle to the DL community. Motivated by the fears that society may be threatened by AI, OpenAI set up a long-term plan to make AI safe and is pushing the technology to be as open source and transparent as possible. It is interesting how fast OpenAI is growing its talented team, which may be a sign of how real (and serious) the problem is.

Google announced a new open source system in June 2017 to speed the process for creating and training machine learning models with TensorFlow. The library Tensor2Tensor (T2T) enables the creation of deep learning models. T2T can be used to build models for processes such as text translation or parsing, as well as image captioning, and allows you to speed up the creation and testing of models, thus lowering the barrier of entry for users looking to experiment with DL. It utilizes a standard interface including data sets, models, optimizers, and different sets of hyperparameters, so users can swap versions of these components and test them on the fly.

The market for machine learning platforms, according to Forrester, will grow at a rate of 15 percent annually through 2021. Figure 2-5 compares the major platforms available.

Cloud machine learning vendor comparison

	AMAZON MACHINE LEARNING	GOOGLE CLOUD MACHINE LEARNING	IBM WATSON MACHINE LEARNING	MICROSOFT AZURE MACHINE LEARNING
Overview	Largely automated platform that applies machine learning algorithms to data stored in the popular Amazon Web Services platform.	Gives users access to state-of-the-art algorithms used by Google in search and other industry-leading application. Users can also build their own models.	Most focused on getting models into production through REST API connectors.	Offers long list of predefined algorithms that users can apply to their own data. Less automated than other options.
Interface	▪Amazon Machine Learning Console ▪Amazon Command Line Interface	▪Command-line interface using gcloud mi-engine to control TensorFlow processes.	▪IBM's graphical analytics software SPSS can be used as a front end. ▪API connectors enable users to build models in third-party data science applications.	▪Azure Machine Learning Studio drag-and-drop environment. ▪Packages for R and Python coding.
Algorithms and modeling methods	Users can bring their data to prebuilt algorithms, including: ▪Regression ▪Binary classification ▪Multiclass classification	Users can build their own models from scratch or use pretrained models supporting these applications: ▪Video analysis ▪Image analysis ▪Speech recongnition ▪Text analysis ▪Translation	Users can build their own algorithms in any language through REST API connectors. Links to Apache Spark's MLlib library of machine learning algorithms are planned via IBM's Data Science Experience workbench platform (implementation currently in a closed beta).	Users can bring their data to prewritten algorithms, including: ▪Scalable boosted decision tree ▪Bayesian recommendation systems ▪Deep neural networks ▪Decision jungles ▪Classification The service also supports these algorithms: ▪Multiclass and binary classification ▪Regression clustering
Automatic algorithm suggestion?	Yes	Yes	No	No
Data location requirements	Data must be in an Amazon Web Services store before being used in Machine Learing service.	Data must be stored and models must be staged in Google Cloud Storage.	Data must be stored and models must be staged in IBM Bluemix.	Small data sets can be imported from third parties like AWS, but sets larger than a couple gigabytes must live in Azure.
Pricing	▪For data analysis and model building: $0.42 per hour. ▪Prediction fees: $0.10 per thousand batch predictions, rounded up to the next thousand; $0.0001 per real-time prediction, rounded up to the nearest penny, plus a reserved capacity charge of $0.001 per hour for each 10 MB of provisioned memory.	▪For model training: $0.49 per hour, per machine learning training unit (a measure of compute resources) in the U.S. $0.54 in Europe and Asia. ▪Prediction fees: $0.10 per thousand predictions, plus $0.40 per node hour in the U.S. $0.11/$0.44 in Europe and Asia. ▪Pricing varies significantly for API calls to pretrained models depending on features used.	▪$10.00 per service instance (running 20 models each). ▪For analysis and model building: $0.45 per compute hour. ▪Prediction fees: $0.50 per thousand real-time or batch predictions. ▪A free version is available with one service instance supporting up to two models, 5,000 predictions per month and five hours of compute time.	▪$9.99 per user.per month for Azure Machine Learning Studio.plus $1.00 per Studio experimentation hour (a measure of compute resources). ▪A free version with limited capabilities is also available for development and personal use. ▪Predictive analytics applications can be deployed as web services at a tiered price of $100, $1,000 and $10,000 per month.
Extras	Extra fees for data stored in Amazon Web Services billed separately.	Google Cloud Platform account required.	IBM SPSS Modeler or Data Science Experience required for authoring new models. Bluemix account required.	Azure account required with the paid version; the free one requires only a Microsoft account.
Other considerations	Includes an automatic data transformation tool.	Very little abstraction means coders agin control, but less techy users may face learning curve.	The service is mainly geared toward building machine learning-backed applications through API connections.	Visual interface may give users limited insight into how models operate under the hood.

Figure 2-5. *Comparison of different DL platforms (source:* http://searchbusinessanalytics.techtarget.com/feature/Machine-learning-platforms-comparison-Amazon-Azure-Google-IBM)

2.4 Recent Developments

Here are some recent developments in the field.

2.4.1 2016

The year of 2016 recorded a tremendous number of breakthroughs in DL, either in research, applications, projects, or funding and platforms. According to Yann LeCunn, generative adversarial networks are probably the most important idea in machine learning in the last decade. Although introduced in 2014 by Ian Goodfellow, only recently GANs have started to show their potential. Improved techniques for helping training and better architecture designs (deep convolutional GANs), introduced recently, have fixed some of the previous limitations and opened the doors to new applications. GANs work by having a discriminative network (D) playing with a generative network (G) that tries to trick the D network with faked representations of data. As the game evolves, the G network learns how to build examples that are close to the real ones. The nice part is that you don't need to have an explicit loss function to minimize.

2.4.2 2017

The year of 2017 was characterized by several breakthroughs in deep learning. One of the hottest areas was reinforcement learning applied to games and robotics. AlphaGo was probably the most notorious case of reinforcement learning because it was able to beat the world's best Go player.

AlphaGo Zero took the algorithm a step further by learning to play Go without human training data; see the reference paper at https://arxiv.org/abs/1705.08439. It was so good that it beat the first version of AlphaGo. A generalization of this algorithm, called AlphaZero, was proposed by Deepmind and was able to master chess and shogi.

Libratus, a system developed by researchers from CMU, managed to beat the top poker players in a 20-day, heads-up, no-limit Texas hold 'em tournament. Research in reinforcement learning has now shifted to harder multiplayer games. DeepMind is working on Starcraft 2 and releasing a research environment, and an OpenAI demonstrated initial success in 1v1 game matches under standard tournament rules with Dota 2 bot. The bot learned the game from scratch in complex and messy goals. The idea is to compete in a near future with the full 5v5 game.

Google's Tacotron 2 text-to-speech system produced good audio samples from text, based on WaveNet, an autoregressive model that is also deployed in the Google Assistant and has seen massive speed improvements in the past year. WaveNet had previously been applied to machine translation, resulting in faster training times in recurrent architectures.

The effort to use less expensive recurrent architectures is a trend in machine translation. In Attention Is All You Need, researchers get rid of recurrence and convolutions and use a more sophisticated attention mechanism to achieve state-of-the-art results at a fraction of the training costs.

Another area of active research is drug discovery. The potential of deep learning to effectively search for new molecules in the huge search spaces of all possible chemical arrangements is being proved quite successful. See, for example, the recent work using generative recurrent networks for De Novo Drug Design or the review of applications of deep learning on biomedical data [MVPZ16].

Waymo's self-driving cars had their first real riders in April 2017 and later completely took out the human operators. Lyft announced that it is building its own autonomous driving hardware and software, and a pilot project in Boston is now underway. There are a few novelties from Tesla Autopilot, while Apple confirmed that is working on software for self-driving cars.

2.4.3 Evolution Algorithms

In 2017 Evolution Strategies (ES) became a popular alternative to train ANNs. The exploration of the search space does not rely on gradients and can be effective for reinforcement learning. The advantage is that Evolution Strategies (ES) do not need differentiable loss function. In addition, evolutionary algorithms can scale linearly to thousands of machines for fast parallel training and do not require expensive GPUs.

Researchers from OpenAI demonstrated that ES can achieve performance comparable to standard reinforcement learning algorithms such as deep Q-learning. A team from Uber released a blog post that makes the case for the potential of genetic algorithms to optimize neural networks. With a simple genetic algorithm, Uber was able to teach a machine to play complex Atari Games.

2.4.4 Creativity

Generative models were pervasive in creating, modeling, and improving images, music, sketches, and even videos. The NIPS 2017 conference inclusively organized a Machine Learning for Creativity and Design workshop.

GANs made significant progress in 2017. New models such as CycleGAN, DiscoGAN, and StarGAN achieved astonishing results in generating images, particularly faces. See, for example, pix2pixHD.

A recent project for Manga colorization claims to be the best available automatic colorization tool for Manga.

A generative model to create female Manga characters from noise using a GAN is also available. If you want to play with improving image quality using GANs, try Letsenhance.io.

The year 2017 was also remarkable for applications of DL in biology. For example, there was work on generating and designing DNA with deep generative models, which opens the door to create synthetic DNA from scratch. Another example is work from Google Research Deep Variant where the team showed a great boost in identifying DNA variants in genome sequencing.

CHAPTER 3

Deep Neural Network Models

The concept of deep learning originated from artificial neural networks research, in which feed-forward neural networks or multilayer perceptrons (MLPs) with many hidden layers are often referred as *deep neural networks* (DNNs).

The MLP networks are generally trained by a gradient descent algorithm, designated by backpropagation (BP). The idea of BP is simple: for each set of input/output, you compare the signal from the last layer of the neural network (output layer) with the real output in the data; the difference is the error. Since you can compute the signal in the network from input to output, you can correct the weights connecting neurons in the layers so that the error is reduced in the next iteration. To do so, you update the weights by a measure proportional to the error.

For training deep networks, BP alone has several problems, including local optima traps in the nonconvex objective function and vanish gradients (the output signal decreases exponentially as information is backpropagated through layers). To understand how this problem was solved, first you will explore some history of artificial neuron networks (ANNs).

© Armando Vieira, Bernardete Ribeiro 2018
A. Vieira and B. Ribeiro, *Introduction to Deep Learning Business Applications for Developers*,
https://doi.org/10.1007/978-1-4842-3453-2_3

3.1 A Brief History of Neural Networks

ANNs started with a work by McCullogh and Pitts who showed that sets of simple units (artificial neurons) could perform all possible logic operations and thus be capable of universal computation. This work was concomitant to Von Neumann and Turing who first dealt with statistical aspects of the information processing of the brain and how to build a machine capable of reproducing them. Frank Rosembalt invented the perceptron machine to perform simple pattern classification. However, this new learning machine was incapable of solving simple problems, like the logic XOR. In 1969 Minsky and Papert showed that perceptrons had intrinsic limitations that could not be transcended, thus leading to a fading enthusiasm for ANNs.

In 1983 John Hopfield proposed a special type of ANNs (the Hopfield networks) and proved that they had powerful pattern completion and memory properties.

The backpropagation algorithm was first described by Linnainmaa, S. (1970) as the representation of the cumulative rounding error of an algorithm (as a Taylor expansion of the local rounding errors), without reference to neural networks. In 1985, Rumelhart, McClelland, and Hinton rediscovered this powerful learning rule that allowed them to train ANNs with several hidden units, thus surpassing the Minsk criticism.

Table 3-1 presents an overview of the evolution of neural networks.

Table 3-1. *Some Milestones in Neural Networks*

Year	Contributor	Contribution
1949	Donald Hebb	Hebbian learning rule
1958	Frank Rosenblatt	Introduced the first perceptron
1965	Ivakhnenko and Lapa	Introduces the predecessor of MLP, the group method data handling (GMDH)
1970	Seppo Linnainmaa	Proposed the backpropagation algorithm
1980	Teuvo Kohonen	Self-organizing map
	Kunihiko Fukushima	Published the neocognitron, the precessor of CNNs
1982	John Hopfield	Hopfield recurrent networks
1985	Hinton and Sejnowski	Boltzmann machine
1986	Rulmelhart and Hinton	Popularized the backpropagation to train MLP
1990	Yann LeCun	Introduced LeNet, demonstrating the possibility of deep neural networks in practice
1991	Sepp Hochreiter	Explored the problems of vanishing and exploding gradients in the BP algorithm
1997	Schuster and Paliwal	Bidirectional recurrent neural network
	Hochreiter and Schmidhuber	LSTM; solved the problem of vanishing gradient in recurrent neural networks
2006	Geoffrey Hinton	Deep belief networks; introduced layer-wise pretraining and opened current deep learning era
2009	Salakhutdinov and Hinton	Deep Boltzmann machines

(*continued*)

Table 3-1. (*continued*)

Year	Contributor	Contribution
2012	Geoffrey Hinton	Dropout, an efficient way of training neural networks
2013	Kingma and Welling	Introduced variational auto-encoder (VAE), which may bridge the fields of deep learning and Bayesian probabilistic graphic models
2014	Bahdanau et al.	Introduced attention models
	Ian J. Goodfellow	Introduced generative adversarial network
2015	Srivastava and Schmidhuber	Introduced the highway networks
	He et al.	Introduced residual block and residual network, which are currently the state of the art for vision problems
2016	Wang et al.	Introduced select-additive network, which may bridge the field of deep learning and the field of causal inference
2017	Mnih et al.	Introduced RL DNN, Q-learning, and A3C

3.1.1 The Multilayer Perceptron

The multilayer perceptron was proposed to solve problems that were not linearly separable. In other words, you cannot separate categories with a set of straight lines. Figure 3-1 shows an example of a multilayered perceptron.

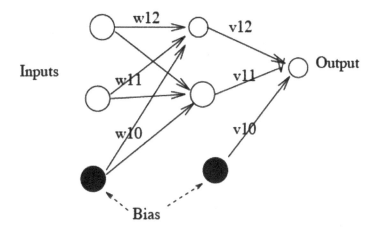

Figure 3-1. *The MLP, with inputs, a hidden layer, and outputs. Training consists of finding the best weights, W and v, and bias.*

An ANN consists of a set of inputs, connected to a set of hidden unities through weights, *w*. The hidden unities are connected to the output through weights, *v*. Initially, all the weights and the bias term are set to random numbers. The activity in the network is propagated forward via weights from the input layer to the hidden layer where some function of the net activation is calculated. Normally the transfer functions are sigmoid, tanh, or, more recently, rectified linear unities (ReLU). Then the activity is propagated via more weights to the output neurons.

Two sets of weights must be updated, namely, those between the hidden and output layers and those between the input and hidden layers. The error because of the first set of weights is calculable by the least mean square rule. To propagate backward that part of the error because of the errors in the second set of weights (*W*), the backpropagation algorithm is often used. This simply states the errors should be proportional to the weight contribution. The algorithm has two main parameters: learning rate and momentum (to avoid traps in local minima). Also, the number of unities in the hidden layer is an important input (more hidden unities will increase the computational power, but it could also compromise the generalization capabilities).

The choice of the network parameters is normally performed by k-fold cross validation, fixing k–1 parts of the training data for training and the remaining for testing and then swapping these segments.

The *stochastic gradient descent* (SGD) algorithm is a technique used to accelerate the training of a neural network. Contrary to gradient descent, where the optimization is performed through all training samples, in SGD only a subset of the training sample is used. SGD is faster in convergence since it uses only a fraction of the training samples at each epoch.

3.2 What Are Deep Neural Networks?

It has long been known that ANNs with more hidden layers (deeper) could have a higher computational power and be better suited to solve classification or regression problems [AV03, YAP13, BLPL06]. The challenge was how to train them, in other words, learn the weights or connections that link a layer of neurons to the others. The backpropagation algorithm worked fine for ANNs with a single hidden layer, but it strives to generalize for deeper architectures because of the so-called vanish gradient problem. In other words, the correction signal from the output dissipates as it travels to lower layers.

In 2006, Hinton et al. [GR06] proposed an unsupervised learning algorithm using a method called *contrastive divergence* (CD), which was successful in training deep generative models known as *deep belief networks* (DBNs) [HOT06]. A CD is a layer-by-layer learning algorithm as illustrated in Figure 3-2. It is normally used for unsupervised tasks but can be fine-tuned to perform supervised learning by attaching a softmax layer to the top layer.

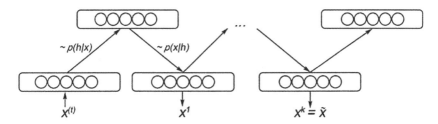

Figure 3-2. *Contrastive divergence (CD) simulated as an MCMC process with k steps. CD-1 stops in stage 1 and ignores further iterations, as the input x is nicely reconstructed as x_1.*

There are many DL approaches and architectures, but most of the DNNs can be classified into five major categories.

- Networks for unsupervised learning, designed to capture high-order correlation of data by capturing jointly statistical distributions with the associated classes when available. The Bayes rule can later be used to create a discriminative learning machine.

- Networks for supervised learning, designed to provide maximal discriminative power in classification problems and trained only with labeled data. All the outputs should be tagged.

- Hybrid or semisupervised networks, where the objective is to classify data using the outputs of a generative (unsupervised) model. Normally, data is used to pretrain the network weights to speed up the learning process prior to the supervision stage. Figure 3-2 shows that knowing the structure of the unlabeled data x, or in statistical terms the distribution $P(x)$, can be more efficient than a pure supervised learning in labeled data.

- Reinforcement learning, where the agent interacts and changes the environment and receives feedback only after a set of actions is completed. This type of learning is normally used in the field of robotics and games.

- Generative neural networks, where deep generative models are a powerful approach to unsupervised and semisupervised learning and the goal is to discover the hidden structure within data without relying on labels. Since they are generative, such models can form a rich imagery of the world in which they are used. This imagination can be harnessed to explore variations in data, to reason about the structure and behavior of the world, and, ultimately, to make decisions. A great advantage of these models is that there is no need to supplement an external loss function because they learn the structure of the data autonomously.

Despite all the hype around deep learning, traditional models still play an important role in solving machine learning problems, especially when the amount of data is not very large and the input features are relatively "clean." Also, if the number of variables is large compared with the number of training examples, support vector machines (SVMs) or ensemble methods such as random forest or extreme gradient boosting trees (XGBoost) may be simpler, faster, and better options.

The most popular types of DNN architectures are stacked denoising auto-encoders (SdAEs), deep belief networks, convolutional neural networks (CNNs), and recurrent neural networks (RNNs). Many advances in machine vision were achieved using CNNs, making this DNN type the standard for image processing. However, there are many flavors of DNNs that are applicable to the various business applications, depending on the architecture, connectivity, initialization, training method, and loss functions being used.

Figure 3-3 summarizes these popular DNN architectures. The following sections offer some guideline for the terminology used and the most popular types of deep neural networks.

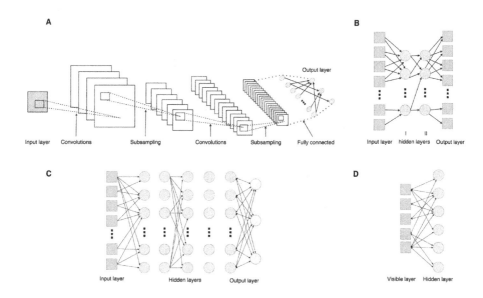

Figure 3-3. *Four of the most popular classes of deep learning architectures in data analysis. A. A CNN has several levels of convolutional and subsampling layers optionally followed by fully connected layers with deep architecture. B. The stacked auto-encoder consisting of multiple sparse auto-encoders. C. A DBN is trained layer-wise by freezing previous layer weights and feeding the output to the next layer. D. The RBM architecture includes one visible layer and one layer of hidden units.*

3.3 Boltzmann Machines

The Boltzmann machine [AHS85] is a stochastic version of the Hopfield network [Mac03, SA08] with hidden unities; it received its name from the Boltzmann distribution.

The energy function of the Boltzmann machine is defined in a similar way to the Hopfield network, except that visible units, v, and hidden units, h, have distinct labels.

$$E(v,h) = -\sum_i v_i b_i - \sum_k h_k b_k - \sum_{i,j} v_i v_j w_{ij} - \sum_{i,k} v_i h_k w_{ik} - \sum_{k,l} h_k h_l w_{k,l} \quad (3.1)$$

Here, v refers to visible units, h refers to hidden units, b is the bias, and w_{ij} are the weights between units i and j.

Given this energy function, the probability of a joint configuration over both the visible unit and the hidden unit is as follows:

$$p(v,h) = \frac{e^{-E(v,h)}}{\sum_{m,n} e^{-E(m,n)}} \quad (3.2)$$

The probability of visible/hidden units is determined by marginalization of this joint probability. For example, by marginalizing out hidden units, you can get the probability distribution of visible units.

$$p(v) = \frac{\sum_h e^{-E(v,h)}}{\sum_{m,n} e^{-E(m,n)}} \quad (3.3)$$

This can now be utilized to sample visible units.

When a Boltzmann machine is fully trained and has reached the so-called thermal equilibrium, the probabilies distribution, $p(v,h)$, remains constant since the distribution of energy itself a constant. However, the probability for each visible, or hidden, unit may vary, and its energy may not be at its minimum.

A Boltzmann machine is trained by obtaining the parameters that maximize the likelihood of the observed data. Gradient descent on the logarithm of the likelihood function is the usual objective function.

The algorithm runs as described. First, you calculate the log likelihood function of visible units.

$$l(v;w) = \log p(v;w) = \log \sum_h e^{-E_{v,h}} - \log \sum_{m,n} e^{-E_{m,n}} \tag{3.4}$$

Now you take the derivative of log likelihood function as a function of w and simplify it.

$$\frac{\partial l(v;w)}{\partial w} = -\sum_h p(h|v)\frac{\partial E(v,h)}{\partial w} + \sum_{m,n} p(m,n)\frac{\partial E(m,n)}{\partial w} \tag{3.5}$$

$$= -\mathbb{E}_{p(h|v)}\frac{\partial E(v,h)}{\partial w} + \mathbb{E}_{p(m,n)}\frac{\partial E(m,n)}{\partial w} \tag{3.6}$$

Here, $\mathbb{E}$ denotes expectation. The gradient is composed of two parts. The first part is the expected gradient of the energy function with respect to the conditional distribution $p(h|v)$. The second is the expected gradient of the energy function with respect to the joint distribution over all states.

Computing these expectations is in general an intractable problem as it involves summing over a huge number of possible states/configurations. The general approach for solving this problem is to use Markov chain Monte Carlo (MCMC) to approximate these quantities.

$$\frac{\partial l(v;w)}{\partial w} = - <s_i,s_j>_{p(h_{data}|v_{data})} + <s_i,s_j>_{p(h_{model}|v_{model})} \tag{3.7}$$

Here, $<\cdot>$ denotes expectation.

Equation 3.7 is the difference between the expectation value of the product of states while the data is fed into visible states and the expectation of the product of states while no data is fed. The first term is calculated by taking the average value of the energy function gradient when the visible and hidden units are being driven by observed data samples.

The first term is easy to calculate, but the second one is harder as it involves running a set of Markov chains over all possible states until they reach the current model's equilibrium distribution, finally taking the average energy function gradient. This complexity led to the invention of the restricted Boltzmann machine.

3.3.1 Restricted Boltzmann Machines

The restricted Boltzmann machine (RBM) was invented by Smolensky [Smo86]. It is a Boltzmann machine with no connections either between visible units or between hidden units.

Figure 3-4 shows how the restricted Boltzmann machine is achieved based on the Boltzmann machine. The connections between hidden units, as well as the connections between visible units, are removed, and the model becomes a bipartite graph. With this restriction introduced, the energy function of the RBM is much simpler.

$$E(v,h) = -\sum_i v_i b_i - \sum_k h_k b_k - \sum_{i,k} v_i h_k w_{ik} \tag{3.8}$$

Hidden units

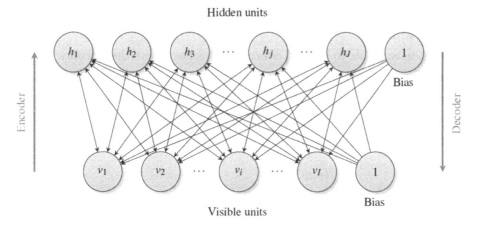

Visible units

Figure 3-4. *Illustration of restricted Boltzmann machine. With the restriction that there are no connections between hidden units ($h_j = 1 \cdots J$ nodes) and no connections between visible units ($v_i = 1 \cdots I$ nodes), the Boltzmann machine turns into a restricted Boltzmann machine. The model now is a bipartite graph.*

Contrastive Divergence

The RBM can still be trained in the same way as a Boltzmann machine is trained. Since the energy function of the RBM is much simpler, the sampling method used to infer the second term in Equation 3.7 becomes easier. Despite this relative simplicity, this learning procedure still requires a large amount of sampling steps to approximate the model distribution.

To emphasize the difficulties of such a sampling mechanism, as well as to simplify the follow-up introduction, you can rewrite Equation 3.7 with a different set of notations, as follows:

$$\frac{\partial l(v;w)}{\partial w} = - <s_i, s_j>_{p_0} + <s_i, s_j>_{p_\infty} \tag{3.9}$$

Here you use p_0 to denote data distribution and p_∞ to denote model distribution. The other notations remain unchanged. Therefore, the difficulty of the mentioned methods to learn the parameters is that they require potentially "infinitely" many sampling steps to approximate the model distribution.

Hinton was able to [Hin02] overcome this issue with the introduction of a method named *contrastive divergence*. Empirically, he found that one does not have to perform "infinite" sampling steps to converge to the model distribution; a finite k number of steps of sampling is enough. Therefore, Equation 3.9 is effectively rewritten like this:

$$\frac{\partial l(v;w)}{\partial w} = -<s_i,s_j>_{p_0} + <s_i,s_j>_{p_k}$$

Hinton et al. [Hin02] proved that using $k=1$ is sufficient for the learning algorithm to converge. This is the so-called CD1 algorithm.

3.3.2 Deep Belief Nets

Deep belief networks were introduced by [GR06], which showed that RBMs can be stacked layer-wise and trained in a greedy manner.

Figure 3-5 shows the structure of a three-layer deep belief network. Contrary to the stacking RBM, a DBN only allows bidirectional connections (top-down and bottom-up) at the top layer. All the remaining lower layers have only unidirectional connections. You can consider a DBN to be a multistage generative model where each neuron is a stochastic cell.

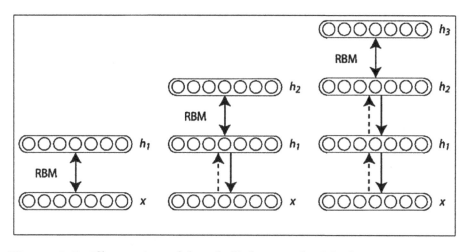

Figure 3-5. *Illustration of deep belief networks. The bottom layers (all layers except the top one) do not have the bidirectional connections, but only connections from the top down.*

Therefore, the model only needs to sample for the thermal equilibrium at the upper layer and then retrospectively pass the information to the visible states.

DBNs are trained using a two-step process: a layer-wise pretraining and a parameter fine-tuning.

Layer-wised pretraining consists of training one layer at a time. After the first layer is trained, you freeze the connections and add a new layer on top of the first one. The second layer is trained in the same way as the initial one, and the process continues with as many layers as needed. This pretraining can be seen as an effective weights initialization [BLPL06, EBC⁺10, RG09].

Fine-tuning is performed to further optimize the network using one of two different fine-tuning strategies.

- *Fine-tuning for a generative model*: Fine-tuning for a generative model is achieved with a contrastive version of wake-sleep algorithm [HDFN95], a process inspired by neuroscience. In the wake phase, the information flows from the bottom to upper layer to adjust down-up weights in order to create a representation in the upper layer. In the sleep phase, the inverse occurs; the information is propagated downward to adjust the top-bottom connections.

- *Fine-tuning for a discriminative model*: For this case, fine-tuning a DBN is simply done by applying standard backpropagation to a pretrained network using the labels of the data on the higher layer.

Apart from providing good initialization of the network, the DBN also has other important properties. First, all data can be used, even unlabeled data sets. Second, it can be seen as a probabilistic generative model, which is useful within the Bayesian framework. Third, the over-fitting problem can be effectively alleviated by the pretraining step and other strong regularizers, like dropout.

A DBN, however, suffers from the following problems:

- Inference in DBNs is a problem because of the "explaining away" effect.

- A DBN can only use greedy retraining and no joint optimization over all layers.

- Approximate inference is feed-forward; there is no bottom-up and top-down information flow.

3.3.3 Deep Boltzmann Machines

The deep Boltzmann machine was introduced by [RG09]. Figure 3-6 shows a three-layer deep Boltzmann machine. The distinction between DBM and DBN from the previous section is that DBM information flows on bidirectional connections in the bottom layers.

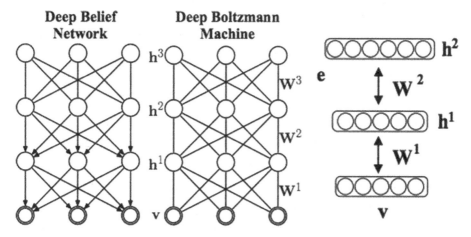

Figure 3-6. *Illustration of deep Boltzmann machine (DBM). The deep Boltzmann machine is more like stacking RBMs together. Connections between every two layers are bidirectional (source:* www.cs.toronto.edu/~rsalakhu/DBM.jpg*).*

The energy function is defined as an extension of the energy function of an RBM (Equation 3.8), as shown in the following for a DBM with N hidden layers:

$$E(v,h) = -\sum_i v_i b_i - \sum_{n=1}^{N}\sum_k h_{n,k} b_{n,k} - \sum_{i,k} v_i w_{ik} h_k - \sum_{n=1}^{N-1}\sum_{k,l} h_{n,k} w_{n,k,l} h_{n+1,l} \quad (3.10)$$

Because of the similarity of energy functions, you can also train a DBM using contrastive divergence (CD1).

DBN and DBM do have some similarities because both of them are deep neural networks inspired by the restricted Boltzmann machine. But the bidirectional structure of the DBM provides the ability to learn more complex patterns in data.

3.4 Convolutional Neural Networks

A CNN is composed of several blocks with different types of stacked layers. Each block consists of a convolutional layer and a pooling layer, normally the max pooling [SMB10]. These modules are often stacked up with one on top of another, or with a softmax logistic layer on top of it, to form a deep model. CNNs use several tricks that make them well suited for image processing, such as weight sharing, adaptive filters, and pooling. Pooling takes subsamples of the convolutional layer to feed the next layer, acting as a powerful regularizer. Weight sharing and pooling schemes (most usually a max pooling) allow the CNN to generate conservation properties like translation invariance. CNNs are highly effective and have been commonly used in computer vision and image recognition [AIG12].

CNNs operate on what should be considered a signal stream rather than a feature vector. That is, fully connected neural nets consist of activation units bound to all inputs of the feature vector. Every unit has a weight specific to each feature in the input. Convolutional layers, on the other hand, utilize weight sharing by sliding a small (trainable) filter of weights across the input vector (or the 2D input map, as CNNs are often used on images) and convolving each overlaid region of input with the filter.

CNNs with max pooling are powerful enough to mimic low-level stages of a primate's visual cortex and have biologically plausible feature detectors, such as Gabor filters [CHY+14]. However, once trained, the CNN acts as a simple feed-forward machine with frozen weights. Recently Stollenga et al. proposed an iterative version of CNNs with post-processing behavior, called *deep attention selective networks* (dasNet) [SMGS15].

This architecture is capable of modeling selective attention in CNNs by allowing each layer to influence all other layers on successive passes over an image through special connections (both bottom-up and top-down) that modulate the activity of the convolutional filters. The weights of these special connections implement a control policy that is learned through reinforcement learning after the CNN has been trained in the usual way via supervised learning. Given an input image, the attentional policy can enhance or suppress features over multiple passes to improve the classification of difficult cases not captured by the initially supervised training. The dasNet architecture allows to inspect automatically the internal CNN filters preventing manual checking.

3.5 Deep Auto-encoders

An *auto-encoder* is a DNN having as output the input data itself. If they are trained with some added noise, these architectures can act as generative models and are called *denoising auto-encoders*. An auto-encoder can be trained with a greedy layer-wise mode, much like the DBNs, to form a deep model [VLBM08].

Auto-encoders can be stacked to form a deep network by forwarding the outputs of the auto-encoder in the layer below as input to the layer above. The unsupervised pretraining is done one layer at a time, and each layer is trained to minimize errors in reconstructing of its input. After being pretrained, the network can be fine-tuned by adding a softmax layer and applying supervised backpropagation, as if they were multilayer perceptrons.

A stacked denoising auto-encoder (SdAE) is a stochastic version of AE obtained by adding noise to the input in order to prevent learning of the identity map. They you try to encode the input while undoing the effect of a corruption capturing the statistical dependencies in the inputs.

3.6 Recurrent Neural Networks

Traditional ML methods, like support vector machines, logistic regression, and feed-forward networks, have proved useful without explicitly modeling time in the temporal process by projecting time as space. This assumption, however, is incapable of modeling long-range dependencies and has limited usability in complex temporal patterns. Recurrent neutral networks are a rich family of models differentiable from end to end, thus amenable to gradient-based training, later regularized via standard techniques, such as dropout or noise injection. Recurrence is key to solving hard problems, like language, as it seems to be present in most brain mechanisms. Figure 3-7 gives a chart illustration of several types of neural networks including the recurrent networks.

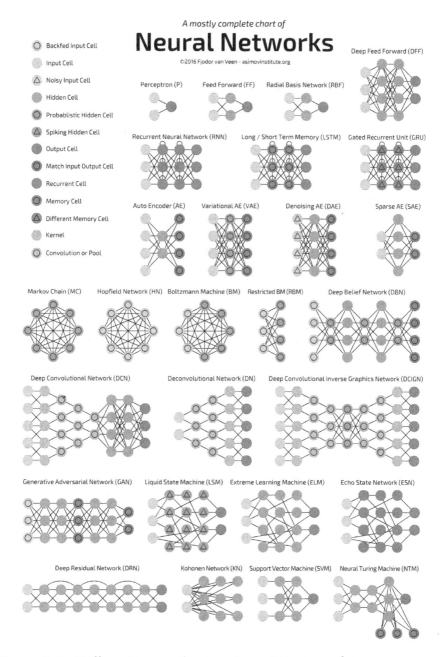

Figure 3-7. *Different types of networks architectures (source:*
`http://www.asimovinstitute.org/neural-network-zoo/)`

The first structures of RNNs were introduced by Jordan [Jor90] as feed-forward networks with a single hidden layer extended with special units. Output node values are fed to the special units, which then feed these values to the hidden nodes at the following time step. If the output values are actions, the special units allow the network to remember actions taken at previous time steps. Additionally, the special units in a Jordan network are self-connected.

The architecture introduced by Elman [Elm90] is simpler. Associated with each unit in the hidden layer is a context unit. Each such unit takes as input the state of the corresponding hidden node at the previous time step, along an edge of fixed weight. This value then feeds back into the same hidden node j along a standard edge. This architecture is equivalent to a simple RNN in which each hidden node has a single self-connected recurrent edge. The idea of fixed-weight recurrent edges that make hidden nodes self-connected is fundamental in the subsequent work on LSTM networks [HS97].

RNNs are a class of unsupervised or supervised architectures to learn temporal, or sequential, patterns. An RNN can be used to predict the next data point in a sequence using the previous data samples. For instance, in text, a sliding window over previous words is used to predict the next word or set of words in the sentence. RNNs are generally trained with the long short-term memory (LSTM) algorithm proposed by Schmidhuber et al. [HS97] or gated recurrent units (GRUs). The flip side is that they are difficult to train in capturing long-term dependencies because of the well-known gradient vanishing or gradient explosion problems and because of the great care required in optimizing hyperparameters.

RNN have become recently very popular, especially with the introduction of several tricks, such as bidirectional learning (forward and backward sequence prediction) and attentive mechanisms that allow the use of dynamic size sliding windows, especially useful to build language models.

Figure 3-8 depicts several RNNs operating over sequences of vectors in the input and output. Each rectangle is a vector; from bottom up, the input vectors are at bottom, output vectors are at top, and in-between rectangles hold the RNN's state.

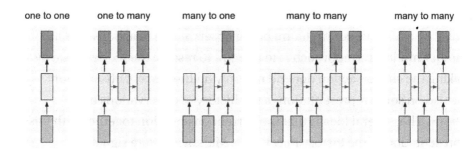

Figure 3-8. *Topologies of recurrent networks (source:*
http://karpathy.github.io/2015/05/21/rnn-effectiveness/)

A nice tutorial can be accessed at http://blog.echen.me/2017/05/
30/exploring-lstms/?utm_content=buffer1bdf8 about visualizing
LSTMs. Also, see the video tutorial by Andrej Karpathy on training RNNs
at https://skillsmatter.com/skillscasts/6611-visualizing-and-
understanding-recurrent-networks.

3.6.1 RNNs for Reinforcement Learning

Reinforcement learning (RL) works by using delayed reward signals to
adjust the parameters of the learning machine. The hardest challenges for
RL are tasks where the state of the environment is only partially observable
and hidden states have to be considered—the so-called non-Markovian
tasks or partially observable Markov decision processes. Many real-world
tasks follow in this category, such as maze navigation tasks. Hidden states,
however, make the problem more difficult because the agents not only
learn the mapping from environmental states to actions but also need to
determine, at each position, which environmental state they are in.

RNNs trained with LSTM are particularly adequate to handle these
complex tasks, particularly when no a priori model of the environment
is available. One could build a model online that learns to predict
observations and rewards, thus learning to infer the environment or

decompose it into a set of Markovian subtasks, each of which can be solved by a reactive controller mapping observations to actions [WS98]. Another model-free approach is to attempt to resolve the hidden state by making the chosen action depend not only on the current observation but also on some representation of the history of observations and actions. The general idea is that the current observation together with this representation of the history may yield a Markovian state signal.

If there are long-term dependencies between events, all these methods may face difficulties for a maze navigation task where T-junctions look identical and the only way to distinguish them is considering previous sequence of events. For these cases, there is no straightforward way to decompose the task into Markovian subtasks, and the agent must remember the relevant information. LSTM units were proposed by Schmidhuber to help solve this problem by incorporating a memory state and a forgetting term that are learned from data [HS97]; see Figure 3-9.

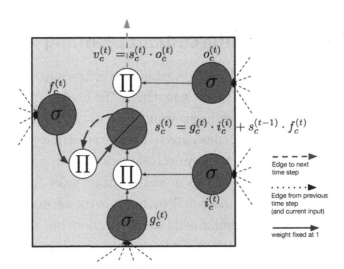

Figure 3-9. *An LSTM cell with forgetting memory gate (source:* `https://arxiv.org/pdf/1506.00019.pdf`*)*

Reinforcement learning, where an agent learns actions it should take in a given environment to maximize a cumulative reward, has seen progress by leveraging deep learning for feature representations.

In a recent work at `https://arxiv.org/pdf/1604.06778.pdf` [DCH+16], the authors present a new standardized and challenging test bed for evaluating algorithms in the continuous control domain, where data is high-dimensional and model-free methods are often used. The framework consists of 31 continuous control tasks, ranging from basic to locomotion to hierarchical, and will ideally help researchers understand the strengths and limitations of their algorithms.

The video presentation at `https://www.youtube.com/watch?v=evq4p1zhS7Q` from Pieter Abbeel (from openAI) is a good overview of how DL has a new perspective to tackle the problem of reinforcement learning in robotics.

3.6.2 LSTMs

One of the appeals of RNNs is its capability to connect previous information to solve the actual task, such as using previous words to predict the next word in a sentence.

LSTM networks are a special type of RNN, capable of learning long-term dependencies. They were introduced by Hochreiter and Schmidhuber in 1997 [HS97] and later refined and are nowadays widely popular in problems ranging from language translation to video processing.

LSTMs were designed to solve the long-term dependency and the vanish and gradient explosion problems. The repeating module in an LSTM contains four interacting layers: input, output, cell state, and forget gate. LSTM has the ability to remove or add information to the cell state, regulated by gates to control the information flow. Gates are composed out of a sigmoid or tanh neural neuron and a pointwise multiplication operation.

Each memory cell of LSTM contains a node with a self-connected recurrent edge of fixed weight 1, ensuring that the gradient can pass across many time steps without vanishing or exploding.

Simple recurrent neural networks have long-term memory (the weight that changes slowly during training) and short-term memory as activations, which pass from each node to successive nodes. LSTM has an intermediate type of storage in the form of a memory cell. A memory cell is formed by several elements.

- *Input node*: This unit is a node that takes activation from the input layer at the current time step from the hidden layer at the previous time step (t–1). The summed weighted input is passed through a tanh activation function.

- *Input gate*: A gate is a sigmoidal unit that takes activation from the current data $x(t)$ as well as from the hidden layer at the previous time step. However, its value is used to multiply (not add) the value of another node. If its value is zero, then flow from other nodes is disconnected.

- *Internal state*: This is a self-connected recurrent edge with a fixed unit weight. Because this edge spans adjacent time steps with constant weight, errors can flow across time steps without vanishing or exploding.

- *Forget gates*: These are critical for the network to discharge the contents of the internal state.

- *Output gate*: The value in the memory cell is the internal state multiplied by the value of the output gate. The internal state first is transferred through a tanh activation function, as this gives the output of each cell the same dynamic range as an ordinary tanh hidden unit.

LSTM are well-suited to classification and prediction evolving time series and are in general superior to hidden Markov models and other sequence learning methods in numerous applications. However, they are computational expensive.

GRUs were introduced by Felix Gers, who originally called them *forget gates*. They combine the forget and input gates into a single "update gate." It also merges the cell state and hidden state and makes some other changes. The resulting model is simpler than standard LSTM models and has been growing increasingly popular. Greff et al. (2015) did a comparison of popular variants, finding that they're almost indistinguishable.

However, vanilla LSTM consistently outperforms GRUs on NLP and machine translation according to this report.

Most of the problems can be solved with stateless LSTM. In stateless mode, LSTM will not remember the content of previous batches. If stateful, the last state for each sample at index *i* in a batch will be used as the initial state for the sample of index *i* in the following batch. So, to learn the dependencies between sequences, you have to use a stateful LSTM, given as a Boolean flag in the LSTM Keras layer.

For a detailed explanation of how LSTM works, see the blog post at `http://colah.github.io/posts/2015-08-Understanding-LSTMs/`, which has a step-by-step example using Keras.

As of August 2017, the top five companies (Apple, Google, Microsoft, Amazon, and Facebook) are massively adding LSTM into their products, for voice, image, or automatic translation.

- Facebook announced in August 2017 that it is using LSTM to do a whopping 4.5 billion translations each day, or more than 50,000 per second.

- LSTM is also used to improve Apple's Siri and QuickType on nearly 1 billion iPhones.

- LSTM has learned to create answers of Amazon's Alexa based on a generative sequence to sequence model.

- LSTM-based systems also have learned to control robots, analyze images, summarize documents, recognize videos and handwriting, run chat bots and smart assistants, predict diseases and click rates and stock markets, and compose music.

- Baidu and other Asian companies are also massively using LSTM, which is now permeating the modern world. You are probably using LSTM all the time. But other deep learning methods are also heavily used. Here is the overview page with numerous references: `http://people.idsia.ch/~juergen/impact-on-most-valuable-companies.html`.

3.7 Generative Models

Richard Feynman once said, "What I cannot create, I do not understand." Being able to generate data is far more powerful than simply classifying it. We probably underestimate how much implicit information our brains incorporate about the world. We know gravity always pushes us down, cars don't fly, objects don't dissolve into thin air, and so on. However, most of this knowledge is completely ignored in our daily lives, and if we want to express it as rules, we will struggle because the number of possibilities may explode. In addition, most of these rules have exceptions, and, even worse, some of these rules will probably contradict each other.

Generative models are one of the most promising approaches toward this goal. To train a generative model, you first collect a large amount of data in some domain (images, videos, sound) and train a model to generate similar data. The neural networks used are forced to discover the latent, compressed representation of the data in order to generate it.

A generative model assumes that you have a set of latent (not observed) variables that explains the observed data X. A vector of latent variables z, which can be sampled according to some probability density function $P(z)$. Then you assume you have a family of functions $f(z; \theta)$, where θ is a vector of parameters. You want to optimize θ such that $f(z; \theta)$ produces samples like X with high probability, for every X in the data set, when z is sampled from $P(z)$. Formally, you maximize the probability of each X in the training set.

$$P(X) = \int P(X \mid z; \theta) P(z) dz$$

Here, $P(X \mid z; \theta)$ is the distribution of $f(z; \theta)$ leading to the so-called maximum likelihood.

There are several types of generative models. Deep convolutional generative adversarial networks (DCGANs) were invented by Radford et al. [RMC15]. In the work, the example takes as input 100 random numbers drawn from a uniform distribution (latent variables) and outputs an image (in this case, 64×64×3 images on the right, in green). As the code is changed incrementally, the generated images do too. This shows that the model has learned features to describe how the world looks, rather than just memorizing some examples.

You can find a good presentation on generative models from Shakir Mohamed from Deepmind at `http://shakirm.com/slides/DLSummerSchool_Aug2016_compress.pdf` and also the blog post at `https://blog.openai.com/generative-models/` from OpenAI.

3.7.1 Variational Auto-encoders

A *variational auto-encoder* (VAE) is one of the simplest generative models. It is a more advanced version of an auto-encoder [Doe16], with added constraints on the encoded representations being learned. It learns a latent variable model on variables z for its input data and a function to approximate sampling from latent variables, thus making it a tractable problem. Instead of letting the neural network learn an arbitrary function, it learns the parameters of a probability distribution modeling the data $P(x)$. By sampling points from the latent distribution $P(z)$, the VAE generates new input data samples that match the training data.

The parameters of the model are trained via two loss functions: a reconstruction loss forcing the decoded samples to match the initial inputs (just like a normal auto-encoders) and the KL divergence between the learned latent distribution and the prior distribution, acting as a regularization term, using the reparametrization trick. This latter term can be excluded, although it does help in learning well-formed latent spaces and reducing overfitting to the training data. See the tutorial at `https://jaan.io/what-is-variational-autoencoder-vae-tutorial/` and some examples of code applied to the MNIST data set at `https://blog.keras.io/building-autoencoders-in-keras.html`.

In VAEs, the choice of this output distribution is often Gaussian.

$$P(X|z;\theta) = N\left(X|f(z;\theta),\sigma^2 * I\right) \tag{3.11}$$

To solve this equation, you have two problems that VAEs must deal with: how do you define what information latent variables represent, and how do you compute the intractable integral over z? VAE's approach to the first problem is simply assuming that there is no explicit interpretation of the latent variables. The second problem (which arises because of the high dimensionality of latent space z) is solved in the VAE framework by optimizing, via stochastic gradient descent, an approximate distribution $Q(z|X)$ that predicts which values of z are likely to produce X. VAEs give an answer to both.

Unlike sparse auto-encoders, there are generally no tuning parameters, and unlike denoising auto-encoders, you can sample directly from $P(X)$ (without performing Markov chain Monte Carlo [MCMC]). VAEs assume that there is no simple interpretation of the dimensions of z and instead assert that samples of z can be drawn from a simple distribution; in other words, $\mathcal{N}(0,I)$, where I is the identity matrix.

The key idea behind the variational auto-encoder is to attempt to sample values of z that are likely to have produced X and compute $P(X)$ just from them. Say that z is sampled from an arbitrary distribution with p.d.f. $Q(z)$, which is not $\mathcal{N}(0,I)$. Let's try to relate $E_{z\sim Q}P(X\,|\,z)$ and $P(X)$.

One way to relate $E_{z\sim Q}P(X\,|\,z)$ and $P(X)$ begins with the definition of Kullback-Leibler divergence (KL divergence or D) between $P(z\,|\,X)$ and $Q(z)$.

$$\mathcal{D}\big[Q(z)\|\,P(z\,|\,X)\big]=E_{z\sim Q}\big[\log Q(z)-\log P(z\,|\,X)\big] \qquad (3.12)$$

You can get both $P(X)$ and $P(X\,|\,z)$ into this equation by applying the Bayes rule to $P(z\,|\,X)$.

$$\mathcal{D}\big[Q(z)\|\,P(z\,|\,X)\big]=E_{z\sim Q}\big[\log Q(z)-\log P(X\,|\,z)-\log P(z)\big] \\ +\log P(X) \qquad (3.13)$$

Here, $\log P(X)$ comes out of the expectation because it does not depend on z. Negating both sides, rearranging, and contracting part of $E_{z\sim Q}$ into a KL-divergence terms yields the following:

$$\log P(X)-\mathcal{D}\big[Q(z)\|\,P(z\,|\,X)\big]=E_{z\sim Q}\big[\log P(X\,|\,z)\big]-\mathcal{D}\big[Q(z)\|\,P(z)\big] \quad (3.14)$$

Note that X is fixed, and Q can be *any* distribution. Since you're interested in inferring $P(X)$, it makes sense to construct Q using X, which will be written as $Q(z\,|\,X))$ so that $\mathcal{D}\big[Q(z)\,\|\,\,|P(z\,|\,X)\big]$ will be small.

$$\log P(X)-\mathcal{D}\big[Q(z\,|\,X)\|\,P(z\,|\,X)\big]=E_{z\sim Q}\big[\log P(X\,|\,z)\big] \\ -\mathcal{D}\big[Q(z\,|\,X)\|\,P(z)\big] \qquad (3.15)$$

This equation serves as the basis of the variational auto-encoder. Starting with the left side, you are maximizing $\log P(X)$ while simultaneously minimizing $\mathcal{D}\big[Q(z|X)\|\,|P(z|X)\big]$. $P(z|X)$ is not something you can compute analytically; it describes the values of z that are likely to give rise to a sample like X under the model in Figure 3-10. However, the second term on the left is pulling $Q(z|x)$ to match $P(z|X)$. Assuming you use an arbitrarily high-capacity model for $Q(z|x)$, then $Q(z|x)$ will ideally actually *match* $P(z|X)$, in which case this KL-divergence term will be zero, and you will be directly optimizing $\log P(X)$. As an added bonus, you have made the intractable $P(z|X)$ tractable. You can just use $Q(z|x)$ to compute it.

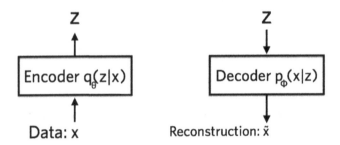

Figure 3-10. *Encoder and decoder in a variational auto encoder (source: Jaan AltoSaar blog)*

Hence, as is standard in stochastic gradient descent, you take one sample of z and treat $P(X|z)$ for that z as an approximation of $E_{z \sim Q}\big[\log P(X|z)\big]$.

The full equation you want to optimize is as follows:

$$
\begin{aligned}
E_{X \sim D}\big[\log P(X) - \mathcal{D}\big[Q(z|X)\| P(z|X)\big]\big] = \\
E_{X \sim D}\big[E_{z \sim Q}\big[\log P(X|z)\big] - \mathcal{D}\big[Q(z|X)\| P(z)\big]\big]
\end{aligned}
\tag{3.16}
$$

You can sample a single value of X and a single value of z from the distribution $Q(z|X)$ and compute the gradient as follows:

$$\log P(X|z) - \mathcal{D}\big[Q(z|X)\|P(z)\big] \tag{3.17}$$

You can then average the gradient of this function over arbitrarily many samples of X and z, and the result converges to the gradient of Equation 3.16.

3.7.2 Generative Adversarial Networks

Generative networks are trained in an unsupervised way because you don't have any explicit desired targets for the generated data; they should appear as real as possible.

One interesting approach to train generative networks in a supervised way is a generative adversarial network. GANs were introduced in 2014 by Ian Goodfellow et al. [GPAM+14]. They consist of a discriminator network (a standard convolutional neural network, in the case of images) that is trained to distinguish a real input image from a generated one created by a generator (usually also a CNN). These two networks are locked into a min-max game: the discriminator is trying to distinguish real images from fake images, and the generator is trying to create images that make the discriminator believe they are real. In the end, the generator network creates images that are indistinguishable from real ones.

The generator (G) tries to capture the model from which the data is drawn, thereby generating images from random noise inputs, while the discriminator (D) is a conventional CNN that tries to distinguish between real data (training data) and data generated by the G, thereby estimating the posterior probability, P(Label|Data), where the Label refers to "Fake" or "Real."

During training, D is presented with a mixture of real images from training data and fake images generated by G, and its loss function is to correctly separate correct and fake inputs. Both networks will compete with opposite goals, and training will evolve until equilibrium is achieved.

GAN training is a two-player game in which the generator minimizes the divergence between its generative distribution and the data distribution, while the discriminator tries to distinguish the samples from the generator's distribution and the real data samples. You say the generator "wins" when the discriminator performs no better than a random guess. Training GANs is hard because often the system dynamics drift from equilibrium.

The optimization problem of the basic GAN is a min-max problem, given by the following equation, where V is the value function, x is the observations, and z is the latent variables.

$$[G_{min}][D_{max}]V(D,G) = E_{x \sim P_{data}(x)}\left[\log D(x)\right] + E_{x \sim P_z(z)}\left[\log\left(1 - D\left(G(z)\right)\right)\right] \tag{3.18}$$

Recently the Wasserstein distance was introduced to measure the divergence between two distributions. The Wasserstein is a more consistent metric and has proved to create better convergence. For more information, see https://casmls.github.io/general/2017/04/13/gan.html.

Figure 3-11 depicts the cumulative activity of GANs' papers in the last years after their creation.

Figure 3-12 illustrates a model of a GANN in terms of its main block components.

Figure 3-13 shows the application of several model GANs to the image generation of rooms from noise.

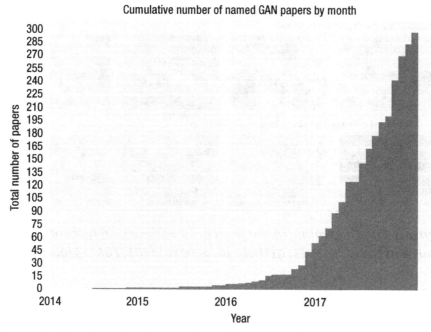

Figure 3-11. *Cumulative number of papers referring to GANs (source: https://github.com/hindupuravinash/the-gan-zoo)*

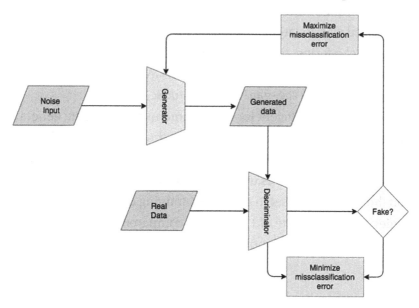

Figure 3-12. *Model of a GANs*

DCGAN	LSGAN	WGAN (clipping)	WGAN-GP (ours)

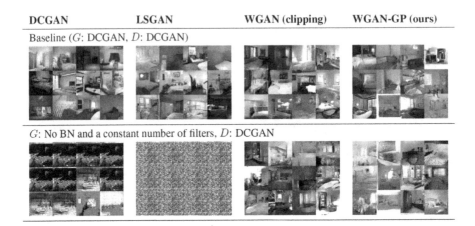

Figure 3-13. *Generating rooms from noise with several types of GANs (source:* `https://casmls.github.io/general/2017/04/13/gan.html`*)*

Makhzani et al. introduced the concept of an adversarial auto-encoder (AAE). An AE is a probabilistic auto-encoder that uses generative adversarial networks to perform variational inference. Matching the aggregated posterior to the prior ensures that generating from any part of prior space results in meaningful samples. An AAE can be used for semisupervised classification, disentangling style and content of images, unsupervised clustering, dimensionality reduction, and data visualization.

You can find an updated list of all types of GANs proposed so far at `https://deephunt.in/the-gan-zoo-79597dc8c347`.

GANS can be very efficient for data augmentation and data generation when few examples are available for training, thus avoiding the difficulties of using deep learning. In a recent experiment (see `https://arxiv.org/abs/1606.03498`), the authors used only 50 examples from each of the 10 digits on the MNIST data set to generate a training data set with a GAN, thus achieving an error rate of 1.5 percent, compared with 0.5 percent using the original 50,000 examples.

Text-to-image synthesis is an interesting application of GANs (called *stack GANs*) to generate images of birds and flowers from a text description. Check the code in Torch available on GitHub.

Ian Goodfellow has an excellent tutorial on GANs at `http://on-demand.gputechconf.com/gtc/2017/video/s7502-ian-goodfellow-generative-adversarial-networks.mp4`.

PART II

Deep Learning: Core Applications

CHAPTER 4

Image Processing

Probably the area where deep learning (DL) has had the biggest impact is in image processing. The dream that software can run a simulation of the neocortex using an artificial neural network is decades old, leading to many disappointments as well as breakthroughs. The human visual perceptual system achieves remarkable object recognition performance, even in noisy environments or under geometric transformations or background variation. For years the computer vision community has tried to replicate this astonishing capability with limited success. For an extensive review of the evolution of image processing by deep neural networks, please see "Deep learning for visual understanding: A review" at www.sciencedirect.com/science/article/pii/S0925231215017634.

However, recent advances in DNNs, particularly using convolutional neural networks, has led to a revolution in image processing, achieving (or even surpassing) human-level performance. Recently, a work by Cadieu et al. [CHY+14] demonstrated that DNNs have comparable performance to the one found in the inferior temporal (IT) cortex of primates in challenging visual object recognition tasks. These authors claimed that "whether these DNNs rely on computational mechanisms similar to the primate visual system is yet to be determined, but, unlike all previous bio-inspired models, that possibility cannot be ruled out merely on representational performance grounds." We have now artificial models that can rival human-like brains in complex perceptual activities. Also, Eberhardt et al. in "How Deep is the Feature Analysis underlying Rapid

A. Vieira and B. Ribeiro, *Introduction to Deep Learning Business Applications for Developers*, https://doi.org/10.1007/978-1-4842-3453-2_4

Visual Categorization?" (http://arxiv.org/abs/1606.01167) compared the performance of CNNs with humans and showed that CNNs can achieve superhuman performance on rapid visual recognition.

The next section will show some applications of deep learning on image processing. Figure 4-1 summarizes DNN architectures.

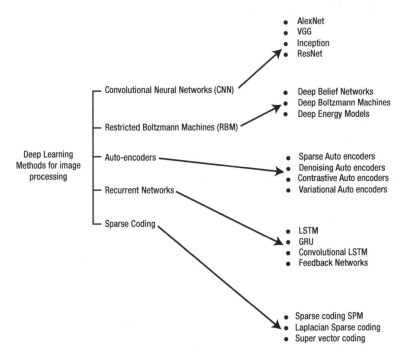

Figure 4-1. *A summary of DNN architectures for image processing*

4.1 CNN Models for Image Processing

CNNs were one of the first deep learning models biologically inspired by the visual cortex of mammals. LeCun [LBD+89] showed that handcrafted feature extraction can be replaced with a neural network–designated CNN. CNNs have achieved considerable success in the handwritten digit recognition (MNIST) data set, and LeCun in 1995 showed that CNNs were superior to all traditional machine learning approaches, such as logistic regression, principal component analysis, or nearest neighbors.

CNNs have seen an explosive adaptation and have replaced traditional image processing techniques by becoming the *de facto* method for all computer vision problems. They are also being actively researched and applied into other domains such as voice, biomedical data, and even text.

CNNs (also called ConvNets) are a variant of ANNs that take full advantage of the spatial nature of the input. Instead of stacking linear layers, like regular neural networks, CNNs process the three-color channels using spatial filters. They exploit the following concepts:

- *Local receptive fields*: Unlike MLP, CNNs don't have neurons in one layer connected to all neurons in the next layer. CNNs have a set of filters, working on localized regions, that make connections in small two-dimensional areas of the input image, called the *local receptive fields*. This greatly reduces the number of connections necessary in the network and reduces the computational complexity. A typical value of the receptive1 field is 5×5. The *stride* is a parameter that controls the sliding of the local receptive field over the image and is the number of pixels the receptive field is moved at a time (normally two or three). Both the receptive local field and the stride control the spatial size of the output volume.

- *Shared weights and biases*: CNNs use the same weights and biases for each of the hidden neurons. By sharing the weights, the network is forced to learn invariant features at different regions of the image. Thus, all the neurons in the layer detect the same feature but at different locations in the image. This makes CNNs translation invariance, a key feature for image processing. Once a feature in the image is detected, the location of the feature becomes irrelevant. These weights defining the feature map are called the *kernel* or *filter*. To perform image recognition, several feature maps are required; the convolutional layer consists of several different feature maps (typically tens of feature maps are used). Again, sharing weights and biases helps to reduce the number of parameters that the network needs to learn and reduces the chances of overfitting.

- *Pooling layers*: Pooling layers are a type of layers typically used after convolutional layers. They summarize the information from the convolution layer by performing a statistical aggregate function, typically average or max, applied to each feature map and by producing a compressed feature map. Forward propagation evaluates the activations, and backward propagation computes the gradient from the above layer and the local gradient to calculate gradients on the layer parameters. Overall, CNNs take advantage of the regularization nature of the convolution, polling, and dropout layers to greatly reduce the number of trainable parameters and the risk of overfitting. New techniques such as batch normalization reduce internal covariance shift and help in smooth learning. Finally, using rectified linear unity (ReLU) or leaked ReLU activations help speed up the training and avoid neuron saturation. The entire CNN network is trainable with gradient descent using the backpropagation algorithm.

LeNet5, the first powerful CNN, has features that can be summarized as follows: a convolutional neural network with a sequence of convolution and pooling layers; convolution to extract spatial invariant features from a subsample using the spatial average of maps and a multilayer neural network (MLP) as a final classifier (fully connected layers); and a sparse connection matrix between layers (weight sharing) to avoid a large computational cost and reduce overfitting.

Complete CNNs are formed by stacking multiple convolutional layers (each with feature map planes and local receptive fields). Subsampling layers are added as regularizers to improve invariance to shift and distortions. As early as the 1990s it became evident that deeper networks perform better, but at that time we lacked the data and computational resources necessary.

Figure 4-2 represents a learning deconvolution network for Semantic Segmentation.

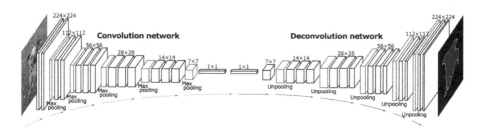

Figure 4-2. *Example of a fully convolutional neural network for image segmentation (source: https://handong1587.github.io/ deep_learning/2015/10/09/segmentation.html)*

4.2 ImageNet and Beyond

In 2009 the ImageNet data set, comprising more than 15 million high-resolution images labeled into more than 22,000 categories, was released. In 2012, Krizhevsky et al. [AIG12] pioneered the use of graphical processor units (GPUs) for a fast implementation of a CNN containing up to 650,000 neurons and 60 million parameters (by contrast LeNet5 had 60,000 weights), winning with a top-five error rate of only 15.3 percent. This was a far better result than the state-of-the-art methods, which then reached 26.2 percent. Besides using a larger data set and bigger networks, these authors used aggressive regularization techniques to avoid overfitting, such as data augmentation (applying slight distortions in shapes, rotations, and colors) and dropout to shrink co-adaptions of neurons. This last technique allows a single neuron to learn more robust features without relying on other neighbor neurons.

Pretraining a neural network in a greedy layer-by-layer fashion with an unsupervised objective function is another popular technique to avoid overfitting, especially for RBMs. The intuition behind this idea is that unsupervised training will give a good initialization of weights for the neural network based on the actual statistical properties of the data it will be used for (e.g., object images, human speech, etc.) instead of random initializations, which often get stuck in poor local minima. The network can be fine-tuned on a supervised task such as object recognition. Mathematically speaking, the CNN transforms the original high dimension of images into a low-dimensional feature vector representation. In this way, a good CNN model can also act as a good feature extractor for images, and the resulting images can be used in more complicated tasks. Figure 4-3 shows an CNN for object classification (see https://handong1587.github.io/deep_learning/2015/10/09/segmentation.html).

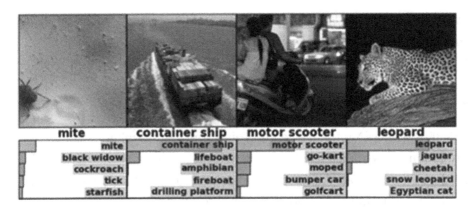

Figure 4-3. *Results of a CNN and dense layers used for object classification (source: [AIG12])*

In 2012 Google trained a DNN with more than 10 million images from YouTube videos. After the training, the neural network was able to identify cats and dogs, doubling the accuracy of previous algorithms. The remarkable feat was that the algorithm was mostly unsupervised. No human labels were provided for the images. The neurons recognized not only cats and dogs but also human faces, yellow flowers, and other common objects. The algorithm categorized objects in the YouTube images (22,000 categories of them) with an accuracy of 16 percent to 70 percent better than previous methods. It may not be impressive, but it was a challenge task because it contained many similar objects. When the number of categories was reduced to 1,000, the accuracy increased to 50 percent.

In 2013 Zeiler proposed a CNN model (`https://arxiv.org/pdf/1311.2901.pdf`) that was more comprehensible and easy to calibrate, achieving a top performance of 12.4 percent on the ImageNet data set. In 2014, Google introduced Inception5 (Google LeNet), a deep CNN (with 20 layers) that won the ImageNet contest with an error rate of only 6.7 percent. This work showed the importance of using very deep models to abstract higher-level features from the images.

In late 2015 a Microsoft team achieved superhuman performance on ImageNet with an error rate of only 3.7 percent with a network named ResNet (for residual network). The paper "Deep Residual Learning for Image Recognition" (`https://arxiv.org/abs/1512.03385`) achieved state-of-the-art results on the MS COCO data set (the code is available on GitHub). MS COCO is a well-known data set with two challenges: classification (evaluated by error rate) and image caption generation (evaluated by a BLEU score).

ResNet is based on a simple idea: feed the output of two successive convolutional layers, bypassing the input to the next layers. Bypassing a single layer did not provide much improvement, while two layers can be seen as a classifier itself. The team was able to train networks of up to 1,000 layers deep [HZRS15]. Figure 4-4 shows the comparison of human and deep nets classification performance in imageNet data set.

$$X_{l+1} = x_l + F(x_l)$$

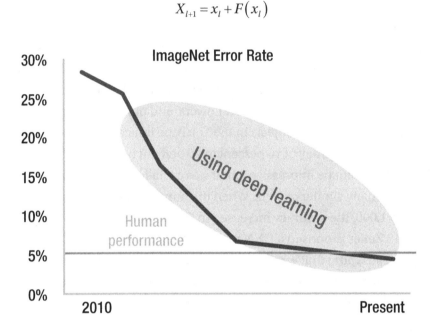

Figure 4-4. *Evolution of the performance of DNN in Imagenet (source: https://www.excella.com/insights/top-3-most-popular-neural-networks)*

ResNet uses a 7×7 conv layer at the input level followed by a pool of two layers, in contrast with more complex formats used by the Google team with Inception V3 and V4. See www.sciencedirect.com/science/article/pii/S0925231215017634.

In ResNet the input is fed to many modules in parallel, and the output of each module is serially connected. ResNet can be thought of as an ensemble machine of parallel/serial modules operating in blocks of smaller-depth layers (tenths of layers).

Figure 4-5 illustrates the formulation of residual learning which can be realized by feedforward neural networks with "shortcut connections".

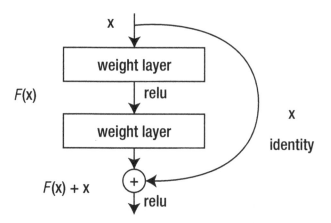

Figure 4-5. *Architecture of a residual network (source:* `https://arxiv.org/abs/1512.03385`*)*

Huang et al. have proposed a variation of ResNet that they call a DN with stochastic depth [HSL+16]. The idea was to start with very deep networks and, during training, randomly drop a subset of layers and bypass them altogether with the identity function for each mini-batch. The simplified training speeds the convergence and increases performance. In the CIFAR-10 benchmark, the team was able to achieve a state-of-art test error of only 4.91 percent.

Shen et al. proposed a technique called *weighted residual networks* to alleviate the problem of training very deep networks and incompatibility of ResNet with ReLU [SZ16]. They were able to train networks with more than 1,000 layers of depth. Figure 4-6 shows the evolution of depth size in the deep networks since 2010 regarding the classification performance in ILSVRC challenge data set.

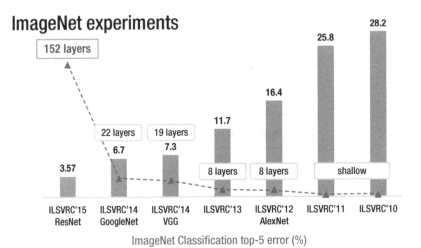

Figure 4-6. *Accuracy versus size versus operations of several CNN architectures (source: https://icml.cc/2016/tutorials/icml2016_tutorial_deep_residual_networks_kaiminghe.pdf)*

Srivastava et al. [SGS15] proposed a new architecture designed to ease gradient-based training of very deep networks, called *highway networks* since they allow unimpeded information flow across several layers on "information highways." The architecture is characterized by the use of gating units that learn to regulate the flow of information through a network. They showed that highway networks with hundreds of layers can be trained directly using SGD.

4.3 Image Segmentation

Image segmentation is a key component of image processing and computer vision. It consists of dividing an image into a number segments, or *clusters*, that share some common features. There are many image segmentation algorithms. The most basic is threshold segmentation. Threshold segmentation tries to automatically determine the optimal class threshold according to a certain criterion and use these pixels according to the gray level before clustering. Regional growth works by combining the pixels with similar properties to form the region; it's similar to k-means. Edge detection segmentation uses different regions of the pixel gray or color discontinuity detection area.

All these techniques are rather limited. The last, and most powerful, algorithm for image segmentation is based on CNNs. It's a supervised problem where the goal is to assign a label to every pixel in the image and treat it as a classification problem. It consists of three parts: taking an input image with some objects, presenting the corresponding segmentation mask, and training the algorithm to minimize the cross-entropy.

A fully convolutional network (FCN) is the most used architecture for image segmentation. A FCN is composed of a convolutional layer without any fully connected (dense) layers at the end of the network. As output, the corresponding segmentation mask is presented and contains the annotation of each pixel in the image. The fully convolutional network learns the filters everywhere, including the layers (image segmentation) at the end of the network.

An FCN learns representations based on local spatial input. Appending a fully connected layer enables the network to capture global information and is successful in image segmentation tasks.

A common FCN used for segmentation is the U-network architecture, illustrated in Figure 4-7. It consists of a down-funneling path (left side) and an expanding path (right side). The left side follows the typical architecture of a convolutional network consisting of repeated applications of $k \times k$ convolutions, each followed by a rectified linear unit (ReLU) and a 2×2 max pooling operation with stride 2 for the funneling path. Each step doubles the number of feature channels. Every step in the expansive path consists of an upsampling of the feature map followed by a 2×2 convolution that halves the number of feature channels; a concatenation with the correspondingly cropped feature map from the left path; and two 3×3 convolutions, each followed by a ReLU. The cropping is required because of the loss of border pixels in every convolution. At the final layer, a 1×1 convolution is used to map each n-feature vector to the desired number of classes; see `https://arxiv.org/abs/1505.04597` for more information. The disadvantage of U-networks is that they contain a mix of channels.

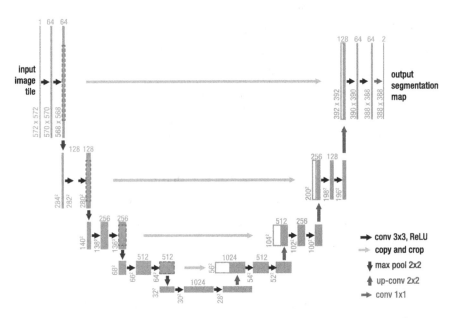

Figure 4-7. *Example of a U-network for image segmentation (source: http://juliandewit.github.io/kaggle-ndsb/)*

Dilated convolutions use an additional parameter compared to convolutional layers: the dilation rate. This defines a spacing between the values in a kernel. A 3×3 kernel with a dilation rate of 2 will have the same field of view as a 5×5 kernel, while using only nine parameters. This delivers a wider receptive field at the same computational cost. Dilated convolutions are common for real-time segmentation because they have less computational cost. It's the natural choice for a wider receptive field without using multiple convolutions or larger kernels.

4.4 Image Captioning

The symbol grounding problem, or how to incorporate meaning into a symbol, is very old. The argument put forward by John Searle on the famous Chinese room argument is basically this: "How can humans relate internal symbols to the external objects they refer to?" For Searle, "meaning" cannot be reduced to a finite set of rule-based computation, and the way the brain relates words to images, for instance, can't be replicated by a computer. However, recent work on image and video automated text capturing combining CNNs and RNNs, has challenged this skepticism and helped to solve this puzzle. Figure 4-8 shows the comparison of performance of plain nets and ResNets in CIFAR-10 data set.

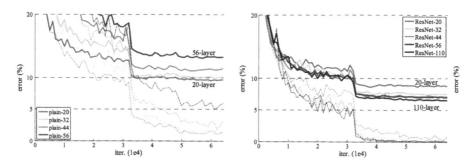

Figure 4-8. *Performance on CIFAR-10 (source: https://arxiv.org/ pdf/1512.03385.pdf)*

Recurrent neural networks (RNNs) have been recently used to successfully generate sentences to describe images [KFF17] using a training set with pairs of images and corresponding captions. Vinyals et al. [VTBE14] introduced the idea of encoding an image with a convolutional neural network and then applying LSTM to decode it and generate text. Mao et al. [MXY+14] independently developed a similar RNN image captioning network and achieved, at the time, state-of-the-art results on the Pascal, Flickr30K, and COCO data sets.

Karpathy and Fei-Fei [KFF17] used a convolutional network to encode images together with a bidirectional network attention mechanism and standard RNN to decode the captions, using Word2vec embeddings as word representations. They considered both full-image captioning and a model that captures correspondences between image regions and text snippets. Many more resources on neural networks for image caption can be accessed at https://github.com/tylin/coco-caption. Figure 4-9 shows the most informative accuracies versus amount of operations required for a single forward pass of networks submitted to the ImageNet challenge (from the AlexNet on the far left, to the best performing Inception-v4).

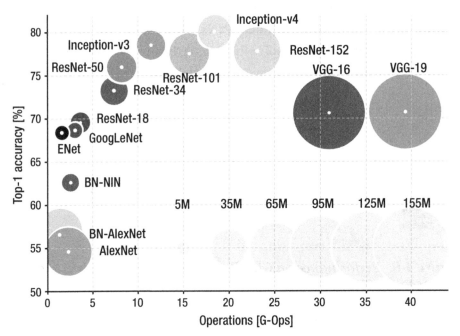

Figure 4-9. *Size and accuracy of different neural network architectures (source: https://arxiv.org/abs/1605.07678)*

4.5 Visual Q&A (VQA)

Querying an image for content is a challenging task that requires semantic knowledge capable of binding words with images.

H. Gao et al. [GMZ+15] used a model combining a language model with a CNN that learns representations of image embeddings to create a visual question and answering machine. The machine learns to answer freestyle questions about the content of an image. The model is trained by minimizing a loss function on the correct answer given on a training set. To lower the risk of overfitting, the authors introduced weight sharing of the word embedding layer between the LSTMs in the first and third components. The model was trained with about 158,000 images and 316,000 questions and answers in Chinese, through a mechanical Turk approach. The model achieved considerable performance given the complexity of the task. Figure 4-10 shows the results of the description of an image generated by deep neural networks which first identify the elements of the image prior to come up with a relation between them.

Figure 4-10. *Caption generated by multimodal ANN. Green (left) shows good captions, and red (right) shows failure cases (source:* `https://cs.stanford.edu/people/karpathy/cvpr2015.pdf`*).*

AgraWal et al. [AAL+15] also approached the free-form, open-ended visual Q&A (VQA) problem and created a data set containing about 250,000 images; 760,000 questions; and 10 million answers. It's available at www.visualqa.org. The best model, called LSTM-Q (also a combination of CNNs and LSTMs), was able to achieve remarkable accuracy in many types of questions, like "What is it?" and "How many?" and "What animal?" and "Who?" Sometimes it was very close to human performance, like in the "Is there?" question, there was 86.4 percent accuracy for the algorithms versus 96.4 percent accuracy for humans. Figure 4-11 shows a model combining a language model with a CNN that learns representations of images embeddings to create a visual question and answering machine. The weight matrix in the word embedding layers of the two LSTMs (one for the question and one for the answer).

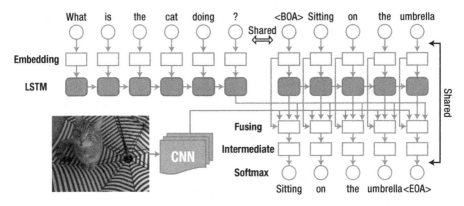

Figure 4-11. *Multimodal learning model, combining an RNN trained with LSTM for text and an CNN for pictures (source: https://arxiv.org/pdf/1505.05612.pdf)*

Noh et al. [NSH15] trained a convolutional neural network using a dynamic parameter layer whose weights are determined adaptively based on questions and used a separate parameter prediction network consisting of a gated recurrent unit (GRU) with the question as input and a fully connected layer generating a set of candidate weights as its output. They also used a hashing technique to reduce the complexity and regularize the network claiming state-of-the-art performance on all available public benchmarks. Figure 4-12 illustrates a novel end-to-end sequence-to-sequence model to generate captions for videos.

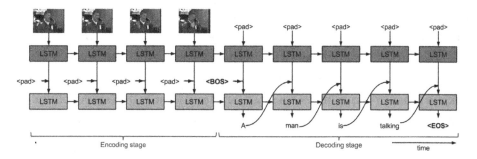

Figure 4-12. *Sequence-to-sequence model for video description (source:* `https://vsubhashini.github.io/s2vt.html`*)*

Several models have been proposed for sequence-to-sequence processing, combining text, image, and video. See `https://vsubhashini.github.io/s2vt.html` for an example. All these approaches work using a encoder-decoder model with CNN⁺LSTM or a GRU to create a join embedding and generate legends and captions from videos.

Cadene et al. recently released a GitHub repository (`https://github.com/Cadene/vqa.pytorch`) with an implementation of a VQA (with the code in Pytorch). The authors of the project Multimodal Tucker Fusion for VQA (MUTAN) claim state-of-the-art results on the VQA-1 data set.

A collaboration between researchers at the University of Montreal, University of Lille, and DeepMind produced an interesting result in binding language with images. They proposed a technique called MOdulated RESnet (MORES) to train vision and language models so that the word representations are tightly integrated and trained alongside visual representations (`https://arxiv.org/pdf/1707.00683.pdf`). There is increased evidence from the neuroscience community that words set visual priors that alter how visual information is processed from the beginning. More precisely, it is observed that P1 signals, which are related to low-level visual features, are modulated while hearing specific words. The language cue that people hear ahead of an image activates visual predictions and speeds up the image recognition process. This approach is a general fusing mechanism that can be applied to other multimodal tasks. They tested their system on GuessWhat, a game in which two AI systems are presented with a rich visual scene; one of the agents is an oracle and is focused on a particular object in an image, while the other agent's job is to ask the oracle a series of yes/no questions until it finds the correct entity. They found that MORES increased scores of the oracle against baseline algorithm implementations.

4.6 Video Analysis

Video has become one of the most common sources of visual information. The amount of video data available on the Internet is tantalizing; it would take more than 82 years to watch all the videos uploaded to YouTube in a single day. Automatic tools for analyzing and understanding video content are thus essential. DL impact on video analysis can be categorized into the following tasks:

- Object detection and recognition

- Highlight detection

- Action recognition and event detection

- Segmentation and tracking

- Classification and captioning

- Motion detection and classification

- Scene understanding

- Event detection and recognition (motions, gestures)

- People analysis (face identification, posture analysis, etc.)

- Object tracking and segmentation behavior recognition and crowd analysis

DNNs have made a tremendous impact on video processing, which is a complex problem characterized by spatiotemporal high-dimensional data. Neural network supervised learning of representations from sequence data has many advantages, but capturing the discriminative behavior of sequence data is a challenging problem.

In [DHG+14], Donahue et al. investigated a CNN model with RNNs and proposed a recurrent convolutional architecture for end-to-end large-scale visual challenging tasks, such as activity recognition, image captioning, and video description. This model departed from fixed visual representations and was able to learn compositional representations in space and time. The model is a fully differentiable RNN, capable of learning long-term dependencies. This is appealing since it can map variable-length videos to natural language text. The model is fully trained with backpropagation. The authors show that this model can achieve good results for discriminative or generative text generation tasks. They evaluated the model on the TACoS multilevel data set containing 44,762 video/sentence pairs obtaining a BLEU score of 28.8.

Fernando et al. [FG16] recently used a method to jointly learn discriminative dynamic representations from video using CNNs to classify video scenes. They proposed a temporal encoding method for a convolutional neural network video sequence classification task using a pooling layer on top of CNN architecture in end-to-end learning. They were able to improve performance over a traditional rank-pooling approach by 21 percent on the UCFsports data set and 9.6 mAP on the Hollywood2 data set. The model parameters could be updated in milliseconds, allowing to process up to 50 frames per second.

In [VXD+14], the authors also combined a CNN and LSTM for jointly learn the embedding of video and text to generate automatic annotation of videos. Because of a lack of data sets, the authors relied on photo annotation data and used knowledge transfer techniques. They achieved good accuracy in the subject, verb, and object (SVO) metrics but still far from a human level, probably because of the lack of training data.

Zhu et al. [ZKZ+15] developed an algorithm to align book stories with their respective movies. The aim was to create rich narratives for visual content, beyond mere captions. To achieve this, they aligned movies and books using a neural network to embed sentences from a corpus of books and a video-text neural embedding for computing similarities between movie clips and sentences in the book. The method, described as a context-aware CNN, was applied to the MovieBook data set, consisting of 11 books and respective movies, while the word embedding was trained in 11,038 books using an LSTM-based encoder for text and a CNN for video. The results were qualitatively interesting and proved that DL is able to explore new ground in understanding complex problems, something unthinkable just a few years ago.

However, all these CNN-RNN/LSTM-based models have a large number of parameters to capture sequence information. Therefore, these methods are extremely data intensive and require large quantities of training labeled examples. Obtaining labeling data for videos is more costly than for static images, and some techniques to expand or generate labeling may be required (generative models like Cycle GAN could be an option).

The most straightforward CNN-based method for encoding video sequence data is to apply temporal max pooling or temporal average pooling over the video frames. However, these methods do not capture any valuable time-varying information of the video sequences. For instance, an arbitrary reshuffling of the frames would produce a similar representation using a pooling scheme.

Recently there has been considerable interest in convolutional LSTM for video prediction. Lotter used convolutional LSTM for unsupervised video prediction (predictions of the next video frames); the code (in Keras) and results are available on GitHub. See Prednet (`https://coxlab.github.io/prednet/`). The results are encouraging since it's a fully unsupervised model. The idea is to consider the convolutions as a dynamic process and then trained as a sequence-to-sequence model, like any temporal process. The only drawback is the computational time (as the LSTMs are very computationally intensive layers). However, it still compares favorably with video pixel networks (https://arxiv.org/pdf/1610.00527v1.pdf), which claim higher accuracy but at a higher computational cost. These types of networks are actively being investigated for self-driving cars, as event anticipation is key to increasing response time and making these systems more predictive and less reactive.

Video usage is increasing exponentially; the United Kingdom alone has more than 4 million CCTVs, and users upload more than 300 hours of video to YouTube every minute. Analyzing videos is a computationally intensive task because of querying, detecting unusual events, or sifting through long videos. State-of-the-art methods for object detection run at 10 to 80 frames per second on a state-of-the-art GPU. This is fine for one video, but it is untenable for real deployments at scale; to put this computational overhead in context, it would cost more than $5 billion USD in hardware alone to analyze all the CCTVs in the United Kingdom in real time.

A team from Stanford proposed a method called NoScope, which is able to process video feeds thousands of times faster compared to current methods. The key insight is that video is highly redundant, containing a large amount of temporal locality (i.e., similarity in time) and spatial locality (i.e., similarity in appearance in a scene). They achieved a speedup in querying of up to 100 times; see the implementation details at https://arxiv.org/pdf/1703.02529.pdf.

A recent Kaggle (https://www.kaggle.com/c/youtube8m) competition challenged the contenders to build an algorithm to classify 8 million YouTube videos (450,000 hours) in 4,716 classes. One approach, which got third place, is described in the paper "Temporal Modeling Approaches for Large-scale Youtube-8M Video Understanding" (https://arxiv.org/pdf/1707.04555.pdf). They used bidirectional-attentive LSTM encoding (for video and audio) implemented on the PaddlePalddle Baidu framework.

Automatic video summarization (AVS) is key in helping human users compactly represent videos without losing important information. Recent work has focused on supervised learning techniques. Video summarization is a structured prediction problem: the input to the summarization algorithm is a sequence of video frames, and the output would be a binary vector indicating whether a frame is being selected or not. For video summarization, the inter-dependency is complex and highly inhomogeneous since humans rely on a high-level semantic understanding of the video content—often after viewing the whole sequence—to decide whether a frame should be kept in the summary. In many cases, visually similar frames do not have to be temporally close. Zhang et al. [ZCSG16] proposed a method for supervised video summarization that automatically selects key frames or key subshots using an LSTM recurrent neural network to model the variable-range dependencies. They achieved state-of-the-art results on two benchmark video data sets (SumMe and TVSum) with an F-score of 41.8 and 58.7, respectively. They also introduced a technique to circumvent the existence of some annotated data for training by exploiting the existence of auxiliary annotated video data sets, even if they contain different visual styles and contents.

There are many techniques for semantic video retrieval. See for example, `http://ieeexplore.ieee.org/abstract/document/7947017/`.

4.7 GANs and Generative Models

As mentioned earlier, generative adversarial networks (GANs) have revolutionized the field of neural networks for image processing. The work [vdOKV+16] uses the PixelCNN architecture to explore the idea of conditional image generation using a new image density model. The generative model can be conditioned on any vector including labels and tags. The authors conditioned the model on class labels from the

ImageNet data set and were capable of producing diverse, realistic scenes representing objects, landscapes, animals, and structures. If the model is conditioned on an embedding vector (that can be extracted from a trained CNN), from a unique input image of a face, it can generate a diversity of new portraits of the same person with different facial expressions, lighting conditions, and poses. See Figure 4-13.

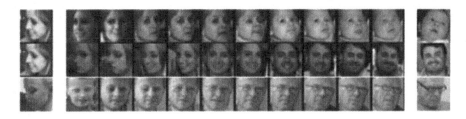

Figure 4-13. *PixelCNN generating images interpolated between left and right. Notice the smoothness of the transitions (source:* https:// arxiv.org/pdf/1606.05328.pdf*).*

In "Learning Deep Feature Representations with Domain Guided Dropout for Person Re-identification" (https://arxiv.org/ pdf/1604.07528v1.pdf), the authors trained a neural network with data sets from multiple domains to make the extracted features as generic as possible. The authors developed a multidomain learning pipeline for the task of identifying people who move between different CCTV cameras. Domain-biased neurons, in the CNNs, become domain specific. The domain-guided dropout assigns each neuron a specific dropout rate for each domain according to its effectiveness on that domain, resulting in considerable improvements.

In [MZMG15], they show how to deal with human-subjective judgments in image tagging, namely, not using a consistent vocabulary and missing a significant amount of the information present in an image. They used an algorithm to decouple the human reporting bias from the correct visually grounded labels using a network for the presence of an object and another for relevance. For instance, an image with a bunch of bananas can be (correctly) annotated as yellow but missing the content. They provided evidence of significant improvements over traditional algorithms for both image classification and image captioning, doubling the performance of existing methods in some cases.

As shown in `http://robots.stanford.edu/cs221/2016/restricted/projects/rak248/final.pdf`, the team introduced an interesting concept of graphlets to encode the semantic meaning of images. These graphlets can be used to encode the semantic meaning of sentences, allowing a semantic comparison between images and sentences, which is relevant for image retrieval.

Christhoher Hess has a blog post at `https://affinelayer.com/pix2pix` on image-to-image translation using TensorFlow. The code is available on the GitHub page. It implements the idea of Isolda et al. on pix2pix networks, which used the GAN framework to translate images from one domain to another, say, night to day, black-and-white to color pictures, or sketches to objects. There is also an online demo at `https://affinelayer.com/pixsrv/`.

Recently a team from Nvidia proposed (`https://github.com/NVIDIA/pix2pixHD`) an enhanced version of a conditional GAN (based on the Pix2pix framework) capable of generating images with very high quality. They used a set of innovations such as incorporating object instance segmentation information to enable object manipulations such as removing/adding objects and changing the object category. This is a method to generate diverse results from a given input. See also the video where they applied these techniques to generate photorealistic human faces, available on YouTube (`https://www.youtube.com/watch?v=XOxxPcy5Gr4`). Figure 4-14 despicts high-resolution image synthesis with conditional GANs.

Input labels

Synthesized image

Figure 4-14. *Example of high-resolution Pix2pix from Nvidia team. Left: the segmentation map; right: one possible high quality generated image (source: https://github.com/NVIDIA/pix2pixHD).*

Pix2pix is a great tool; however, for many tasks, paired training data will not be available. Zhu et al. proposed recently a new technique for knowledge transfer in images. In their paper "Unpaired Image-to-Image Translation using Cycle-Consistent Adversarial Networks" (https:// arxiv.org/abs/1703.10593), they named the technique CycleGAN. It's an image-to-image translation where the goal is to learn the mapping between an input image and another output image (from a distinct domain) using a training set of aligned image pairs. The method allows you to translate an image from a source domain X to a target domain Y in the absence of the correspondent pair. The mapping G:X→Y is learned such that the distribution of images from G(X) should be indistinguishable from the distribution Y itself. Because this mapping is underconstrained, it is furthered coupled with an inverse mapping F:Y→X, thus introducing a cycle consistency loss to push F(G(X))≈X (and vice versa). They used this for style transfer, photo enhancement, object transfiguration, season transfer, and more. The code at https://github.com/junyanz/CycleGAN is available in Pytorch; there is also a nice video showing a horse converted into a zebra.

4.8 Other Applications

In [CCB15], Cho et al. used an attention-based encoder–decoder (combining CNN and RNNs) to describe multimedia content. The novelty was in the extensive usage of the attentive mechanism, particularly in the conditional language model based on an RNN. They applied the model to machine translation, image caption generation, video description generation, and speech recognition. The authors claimed the importance of the attention mechanism in unsupervised learning of the mapping between any arbitrary streams of data (voice and video, text and image, etc.). They proved that attention models can efficiently infer the alignments without using explicitly any domain knowledge, making it an interesting template for neuroscience.

Kemelmacher-Shlizerman et al. recently created a big data set, called MegaFace, for facial image identification; see "The MegaFace Benchmark: 1 Million Faces for Recognition at Scale" (https://arxiv.org/abs/1512.00596). It includes 1 million photos that capture more than 690,000 different individuals. They evaluated the performance of algorithms with increasing numbers of "distractors" (going from 10 to 1 million) in the gallery set. They tested on identification and verification with respect to pose and a person's age and compared them as a function of training data size (the number of photos and the number of people). They reached an accuracy from 99 percent (for hundreds of distractors) to about 80 percent with 1 million distractors. The MegaFace data set, baseline code, and evaluation scripts have been publicly released for further experimentations.

Lipreading consists of guessing the words and sounds from the images of a muted speaker video. S. Petridis et al. presented (https://arxiv.org/pdf/1709.00443.pdf) an end-to-end multiview lipreading system based on bidirectional long-short memory (BLSTM) networks. It claims to be the first model that simultaneously learns to extract features directly from the pixels and performs visual speech classification from multiple views, while achieving state-of-the-art performance. The model consists of multiple identical streams, one for each view, which extract features directly from different poses of mouth images. The temporal dynamics in each stream/view are modeled by a BLSTM, and the fusion of multiple streams/views takes place via another BLSTM. The best three-view model results in a 10.5 percent absolute improvement over the current multiview state-of-the-art performance on the OuluVS2 data set, without using external databases for training, achieving a maximum classification accuracy of 96.9 percent.

Recognizing the authenticity of facial emotions is hard because discriminative facial responses are short and subtle. These authors proposed SASE-FE, a data set of videos containing genuine and deceptive facial expressions of emotions for automatic recognition. They show that the problem of recognizing deceptive facial expressions can be solved using a spatiotemporal representation of the data that aggregates features along fiducial trajectories in the latent feature space.

Gregor et al. introduced Deep Recurrent Attentive Writer (DRAW) (see https://arxiv.org/abs/1502.04623), which is a neural network architecture for image generation. DRAW networks combine a novel spatial attention mechanism that mimics the foveation of the human eye, with a sequential variational auto-encoding framework that allows for the iterative construction of complex images. The system had very good results on generating MNIST examples and on the Street View House Numbers database. The images cannot be distinguished from real data.

4.8.1 Satellite Images

Satellite image classification is a complex problem involving remote sensing, computer vision, and machine learning. The problem is challenging because of the high variability of the data. Basu et al. [SSS+15] proposed a method based on deep belief networks and careful preprocessing of satellite images, achieving 97.95 percent accuracy on two public data sets. One data set consists of 500,000 image patches covering four broad land cover classes: barren land, trees, grassland and other; 400,000 patches were chosen for training with the remaining 100,000 for testing.

Serrah proposed a method [GLO⁺16] using CNNs for the semantic labeling of high-resolution remote-sensing data. They used full-resolution labeling with no downsampling (or pooling layers), thus removing the need for a deconvolution stage or interpolation. They also pretrained the CNNs on remote-sensing data in a hybrid network context, getting better results than a network trained from scratch. They applied the method to the problem of labeling high-resolution aerial imagery, where fine boundary details are very important, thus achieving state-of-the-art accuracy on the ISPRS Vaihingen and Potsdam benchmark data sets.

The work "Learning to Match Aerial Images with Deep Attentive Architectures" (`http://vision.cornell.edu/se3/wp-content/uploads/2016/04/1204.pdf`) is an effort to bridge the gap between neural networks and traditional image-matching techniques based on local correspondence. The authors propose a framework, trainable from end to end, using two neural network architectures to address this problem of ultrawide baseline image matching, which is common in satellite and aerial images. They fine-tune a pretrained AlexNet over aerial data with a Siamese architecture for feature extraction and a binary classifier, achieving state-of-the-art accuracy in ultrawide baseline matching reaching almost human-level performance.

Maggiori et al. devised an iterative enhancement process inspired from partial differential equations, expressed as a recurrent neural network satellite image annotation and localization, thus improving the quality of satellite image classification maps; see `http://ieeexplore.ieee.org/abstract/document/7938635/`. This addresses the problem in CNN architectures; they are good at recognizing but poor at localizing objects precisely.

4.9 News and Companies

The following are news and companies to pay attention to:

- Cargometrics (www.cargometrics.com/) is a startup that uses VHF radio tracking as well as satellite image processing through deep learning algorithms to analyze maritime traffic data to help predict commodity prices. It tracks the movement of 120,000 ships across the world. The work is being used by hedge funds to identify pricing and securities opportunities.

- Terrapattern (www.terrapattern.com/) uses DL to perform similarity-based searches for unlabeled satellite photos. It provides an open-ended interface for visual query by example. The user clicks in a spot on Terrapattern's map, and it will find other locations that look similar.

- Vicarious (https://www.vicarious.com/) is a startup that works on image processing and is developing deep learning algorithms for vision, language, and motor control. It is mainly focused on visual perception problems, such as recognition, segmentation, and scene parsing. Vicarious claims that its system requires orders of magnitude less training data than traditional machine learning technique in deploying generative probabilistic models. Inspired by biology, it claims to have designed algorithms with imagination capabilities.

- Affectiva (https://www.affectiva.com/) uses computer vision algorithms to capture and identify emotion reactions to visual stimulus.

- Descartes Labs (`https://www.descarteslabs.com/`) is teaching computers how to see the world and how it changes over time based on deep learning and advanced remote-sensing algorithms. Their first application is to use massive amounts of satellite imagery, across both visible and nonvisible spectrums, to gain a better understanding of global crop production. Skymind analyzes media, image, and sound to locate and quantify patterns that impact businesses.

- MetaMind (`https://einstein.ai/`), acquired by Salesforce, is building an AI platform for natural language processing, image understanding, and knowledge base analytics. The company offers products for medical imaging, food recognition, and custom solutions.

- Magic Poney (acquired by Twitter) has developed technology to improve low-resolution images to high-resolution ones. By upscaling from low resolution to high resolution at the end of the network, it was able to achieve a 10x speed and performance compared to the state-of-the-art CNN approaches, making it possible to run super-resolution HD videos in real time on a single GPU.

- The project at `http://sustain.stanford.edu/predicting-poverty` from Stanford University is able to predict poverty combining satellite data. It is a remarkable example of how machine learning and big data can replace expensive surveys. It correlates night illumination obtained from high-resolution satellites to estimate the expenditure and asset wealth in some African countries. Convolutional neural networks were trained to identify image features that can explain up to 75 percent of the variation in local-level economic outcomes.

- A team from Stanford University devised an interesting approach to estimate a set of census data indicators just by analyzing images from Google Street View and classifying the brands and models of the cars parked in the streets; see "Using Deep Learning and Google Street View to Estimate the Demographic Makeup of the US" at http://ai.stanford.edu/tgebru/papers/pnas.pdf. This could save $1 billion USD by the American Community Survey (ACS) that is a labor-intensive door-to-door study that measures statistics relating to race, gender, education, occupation, unemployment, etc. The method determines socioeconomic trends from 50 million images of street scenes, gathered in 200 American cities by Google Street View cars. They were able to accurately estimate income, race, education, and voting patterns, with single-precinct resolution. For instance, if the number of sedans encountered during a 15-minute drive through a city is higher than the number of pickup trucks, the city is likely to vote for a Democrat during the next presidential election (88 percent chance); otherwise, it is likely to vote Republican (82 percent).

- In "Context Encoders: Feature Learning by Inpainting" (https://arxiv.org/abs/1604.07379), the authors present an unsupervised visual feature learning algorithm driven by context-based pixel prediction.

By analogy with auto-encoders, the context encoder is a convolutional neural network trained to generate the contents of an arbitrary image region conditioned by its surroundings. It used an adversarial loss, producing much sharper results because it can better handle multiple modes in the output. The context encoder learns a representation that captures not just appearance but also the semantics of visual structures. The code, in Torch, is available at `https://github.com/pathak22/context-encoder`.

- The startup Twentybn (`https://www.twentybn.com/`) wants to teach machines common sense about the world. It relies on DL architectures for video analysis. It has published the Something-Something (object interactions) and Jester (hand gestures) data sets, which represent the primitive actions that humans make in the real world from which you can learn common sense. Check out the presentation at `https://www.youtube.com/watch?v=hMcSvEa45Qo`.

4.10 Third-Party Tools and APIs

There are numerous API services that offer image recognition in the cloud that can be easily integrated with an existing app to build out a specific feature or an entire business. They can be used to detect landmarks, specific locations, or sceneries, or they can be used to filter out offensive profile images uploaded by users.

Google Cloud Vision offers several image detection services, from facial and optical character recognition (text) to landmark and explicit content detection.

Microsoft Cognitive Services offers a collection of visual image recognition APIs, including emotion, celebrities, and face detection.

Clarifai and Alchemy offer computer vision APIs that help companies organize their content, filter out unsafe user-generated images and videos, and make purchasing recommendations based on viewed or taken photos.

A recent project from Google makes available pretrained models (on the COCO data set) for object detection in images; see the blog post at `https://research.googleblog.com/2017/06/supercharge-your-computer-vision-models.html` and the code at `https://github.com/tensorflow/models/tree/master/object_detection` in TensorFlow. The user can install the code on a local machine or in the cloud. Several models are available, including the following:

- Single Shot Multibox Detector (SSD) with MobileNets

- SSD with Inception v2

- Region-Based Fully Convolutional Networks (R-FCN) with ResNets 101

- Faster RCNN with ResNets 101

- Faster RCNN with Inception ResNets v2

CHAPTER 5

Natural Language Processing and Speech

Deep learning (DL) has had a tremendous impact on natural language processing (NLP). After image and audio, probably this is the area where DL has unleashed the most transformative forces. For example, almost all projects related to NLP at Stanford University, one of the most respected institutions working on this area, involve DL research.

Language understanding is one of the oldest, and probably hardest, problems in AI since it's very high dimensional (any language can easily contain hundreds of thousands of words), since the data is very skewed (because of zip law distribution), since the data obeys grammar rules with subtle structure (a single word like in a negation or even punctuation can change meaning), since the meaning of words is intertwined in many layers of implicit assumptions in culture, and finally since text does not have an obvious spatial-temporal structure like images do (words that come together may not be related to the same concept like with pixels in images).

© Armando Vieira, Bernardete Ribeiro 2018
A. Vieira and B. Ribeiro, *Introduction to Deep Learning Business Applications for Developers*,
https://doi.org/10.1007/978-1-4842-3453-2_5

However, as the large corpus of data is becoming available on the Internet, DL is a natural option for solving the numerous problems related to understanding human language. Here is a list of some major problems associated with NLP:

- Parsing

- Part of speech tagging

- Translation

- Text summarization

- Name entity recognition (NER)

- Sentiment analysis

- Question and answer (conversational)

- Topic modeling

- Disambiguation

DL helps improve the accuracy in many of these hard NLP problems, especially in parsing, which is part of speech and translation. However, even with the accuracy improvement, some of these remain a challenge, and the technology is not ready to be fully productized, like in unrestricted conversations.

When trained on vast amounts of data, language DL models compactly extract knowledge encoded in the training data. Trained on movie subtitles, language models are able to generate basic answers to questions about object colors or facts. Recent sequence-to-sequence models with conditional language models are able to solve complex tasks such as machine translation.

Despite that simpler models, such as n-grams, use only a short history of previous words to predict the next word, they are still a key component to modeling language. Indeed, most recent work on large-scale language models has shown that RNNs work very well in combination with n-grams, as they may have strengths that complement each other.

5.1 Parsing

Parsing consists of decomposing a sentence into its components (nouns, verbs, adverbs, etc.) and building the syntactic relation between them, called the *parsing tree*. It is a complex problem because of the ambiguity in possible decompositions (see Figure 5-1) describing two possible ways to parse a sentence.

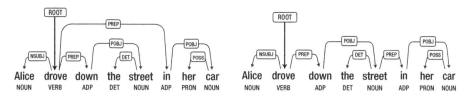

Figure 5-1.   *Two possible parsings of a sentence*

For instance, the sentence "Alice drove down the street in her car" has at least two possible dependency parses. The first corresponds to the (correct) interpretation where Alice is driving in her car; the second corresponds to the (absurd but possible) interpretation where the street is located in her car. The ambiguity arises because the preposition *in* can modify either *drove* or *street*. The way humans disambiguate these options is through common sense; we know that streets cannot be located in cars. For machines incorporating this world, information is very challenging.

Google recently launched SyntaxNet to solve the hard parsing problem. (The code is based on TensorFlow and available on GitHub at `https://github.com/tensorflow/models/tree/master/research/syntaxnet`.) A 20- to 30-word sentence can have thousands of syntactic structures. Google used a globally normalized transition-based neural network model that achieves state-of-the-art part-of speech tagging, dependency parsing, and sentence compression. The model is a simple feed-forward neural network that operates on a task-specific transition system yet achieves comparable or better accuracies than recurrent models.

With SyntaxNet, a sentence is processed by a feed-forward neural network and outputs a distribution of possible syntactical dependencies called *hypotheses*. Using a heuristic search algorithm (beam search), SyntaxNet runs multiple hypotheses as each word is processed and discards only unlikely hypotheses when other, more highly ranked hypotheses occur. The key insight is based on a novel proof of the label bias problem. The SyntaxNet English language parser Parsey McParseface (`https://research.googleblog.com/2016/05/announcing-syntaxnet-worlds-most.html`) is considered the best parser, surpassing, in some cases, human-level accuracy. Recently the service was expanded to cover about 40 languages.

5.2 Distributed Representations

One of the core problems in NLP is related to the high-dimensionality of data, which leads to a huge search space and inference of grammatical rules. Hinton [Hin02] was one of the first to propose the idea that words could be represented via distributed (dense) representations. This idea was first developed in the context of statistical language modeling by Bengio [BLPL06]. The advantage of distributed representations is that semantics can easily be accessible, and knowledge can be transferred from different domains and even different languages.

Learning of a distributed (vectorized) representation for each word is called *word embedding*. Word2vec is the most popular approach to creating a distributed representation of words. It's a publicly available library providing an efficient implementation of skip-gram vector representations for words. The model and implementation are based on the work of Mikolov [MLS13]. Word2vec works by taking every word on a large corpora as input and the other words that surround it, within a defined window, as outputs. Then we feed a neural network trained as a classifier (see Figure 5-2). After training, it will predict the probability for each word to actually appear in the window around the focus word.

In addition to the implementation, the authors also provide vector representations of words and phrases learned by training this model on the Google News data set (about 100 billion words). Vectors can be up to 1,000-dimensional containing 3 million words and phrases. An interesting feature of these vector representations is that they capture linear regularities in the language. For example, the result of the vectorized word equation "Madrid" - "Spain" + "France" is "Paris."

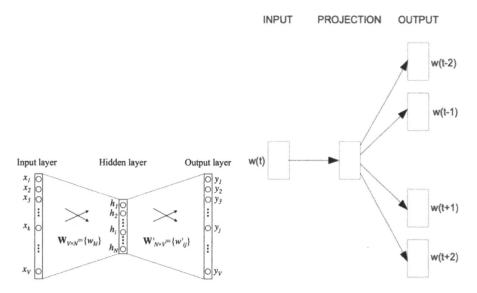

Figure 5-2. *Left: Representation of a Siamese network behind the Word2vec model. The hidden nodes $h_1,...,h_N$ contain the vectorized representation of the word. Right: The schematic representation of word2vec using a skip-gram (word W(t) is used to predict context words W(t − 2) ... W(t + 2). Here a context window of K = 5 is considered (source: https://stackoverflow.com/ questions/30835737/word2vec-data-setup).*

After the bag of words (BOW) with the TFIDF trick, Word2vec is probably the most used method for NLP problems. It's relatively easy to implement and useful in understanding hidden relations in words. There is a good, and well-documented, Python implementation of Word2vec called

Gensim (https://radimrehurek.com/gensim/models/word2vec.html). Word2vec can be used with pretrained vectors or trained to learn the embeddings from scratch given a large training corpus, normally millions of documents.

Quoc Le et al. [LM14] proposed a method to encode full paragraphs using a similar technique to Word2vec; it's called Paragraph Vector. Each paragraph is mapped to a vector, and each word is mapped to a another vector. The paragraph vector and word vectors are then averaged, or *concatenated*, to predict the next word given a specific context. This acts as a memory unit that recalls the missing part from a given context (or, in other words, the paragraph topic). The context vectors are of fixed length, and they are sampled from a sliding window over the text paragraph. The paragraph vector is shared across all contexts generated from the same paragraph, but they do not share any context with other paragraphs.

Kiros et al. [KZS+15] introduced the idea of skip-through vectors using unsupervised learning to encode sentences. The model used a recurrent network (RNN) to reconstruct neighboring sentences of a given passage. Sentences that share semantic and syntactic properties are mapped into related vector representations. They tested the model in several tasks such as semantic similarity, image-sentence ranking, paraphrase detection, question-type classification, benchmark sentiment, and subjectivity data sets. The end result was an encoder that can produce robust highly generic sentence representations.

5.3 Knowledge Representation and Graphs

Reasoning about entities and their relations is a key problem in artificial intelligence. Often such problems are formulated as reasoning over graph-structured representations of knowledge. Most previous works on knowledge representation and reasoning rely on a typical pipeline consisting of named entity recognition (NER), entity resolution and co-reference, relationship extraction, and knowledge graph inference. This process can be effective but can also lead to a problem of compounding of the error from each component subsystem. For a recent survey on graph embeddings methods see https://arxiv.org/pdf/1709.07604.pdf.

In a graph, entities (the nodes of the graph) are connected by relations (edges), and entities can have types, denoted by its relations (e.g., Socrates *is a* philosopher).

With the advent of linked data, it was proposed to interlink different data sets in the Semantic Web. The term *knowledge graph* was coined by Google in 2012, referring to its use of semantic knowledge in web search, and is recently also used to refer to other web knowledge bases such as DBpedia.

The knowledge graph (KG) is an elegant and powerful representation of structured information composed by entities (nodes) and their relations (edges). A recommendation system can be seen as a direct bipartite graph where users belong to one set of nodes and movies to the other set. Rankings can be considered as an edge (so, a weighed graph), but other types of edges can be included, like a representation of the text the user used in the movie review or the tags the user assigned to the movie.

Although a typical KG may contain millions of entities and billions of relational facts (edges), it is usually incomplete (sparse) (see Figure 5-3). Knowledge graph completion is a task designed to fill this graph by predicting relations between the nodes using the supervised signal from existing known connections. The goal is to find new relational facts, or *triples.*

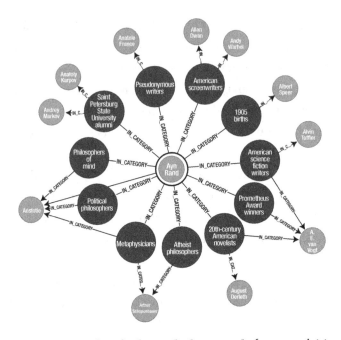

Figure 5-3. *An example of a knowledge graph (source:* `https://github.com/aaasen/kapok`)

This task can be seen as a supplement to relation extraction from plain text. Knowledge graph completion is similar to link prediction in social network analysis, but it more challenging for the following reasons: nodes in knowledge graphs are entities with different types and attributes, and edges in KG are relations of different types (not just on-off connections). The quality of the algorithm for KG is evaluated by measuring whether there is a relation between two nodes or not and the specific type of relation.

DBpedia and Freebase are examples of extensive and well-known KG databases. Freebase contains about 3 billion facts (edges) relating about 50 million nodes (entities). Most companies that crawl and categorize the Web have products based on KGs, including Wolfram Alpha, Google, and Baidu.

Knowledge graph embedding into a continuous vector space is a technique inspired by neural networks that has proved very useful. Several

methods exist; TransE [BUGD⁺13, GBWB13] and TransH [WZFC14] are
simple and effective methods. TransE, inspired by the work of Mikolov
[BUGD⁺13], learns vector embeddings for both entities and relationships.
The basic idea behind TransE is that the relationship between two entities
corresponds to a translation between the embeddings of entities, that is,
when (h,r,t) holds (see Figure 5-4). Since TransE has issues when modeling
1-to-N, N-to-1, and N-to-N relations, TransH was proposed to enable an
entity with different representations when involved in various relations.
Both TransE and TransH assume embeddings of entities and relations
being in the same space.

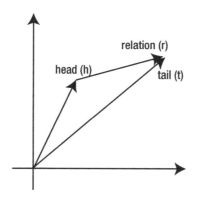

Figure 5-4. *Idea behind TransE model (head, relation, tail)*

Neural tensor networks (NTNs), proposed by R. Socher, are more
expressive because they represent the entities and relations as tensors but
are more computational intensive and do not show much improvement in
performance over simpler methods.

Normally there are three ways to compare the methods: entity
prediction, relation type prediction, and triple prediction. The first two are
evaluated based on a ranking scale and the top N performance (normally
N= 1 and N=10). The last one is a classification problem based on how well
the model performs, distinguishing real relations as opposed to random ones.

KG completion has several applications, namely, in personal assistants such as Cortana and Google Now. These techniques can help answer natural language questions like "What author wrote the book A that was natural from X?" Google has recently launched an API to query its KG (`https://developers.google.com/knowledge-graph`). With the closure of Freebase in December 2014, the Knowledge Graph API allows users to find entities that reside in the Google Knowledge Graph, using standard schemas types. The results are returned in JSON format.

A recent work by H. Wuang et al. [WWY15] used a method called RCNET that was able to beat humans with complex text related to understanding questions from IQ tests. They tested on several types of problems.

Analogy: *Isotherm* is to temperature as *isobar* is to?

1. atmosphere

2. wind

3. pressure

4. latitude

5. current

Analogy II: Identify two words (one from each set of brackets) that form a connection when paired with the words in capitals.

1. CHAPTER (book, verse, read)

2. ACT (stage, audience, play)

Classification: Which is the odd one out?

1. calm

2. quite

3. relaxed

4. serene

5. unruffled

Synonym: Which word is closest to *irrational*?

1. intransigent

2. irredeemable

3. unsafe

4. lost

5. nonsensical

Antonym: Which word is most opposite to *musical*?

1. discordant

2. loud

3. lyrical

4. verbal

5. euphonious

These are challenging tasks because of the multiple definitions of words and the complex relations among them. To tackle these challenges, the authors used a framework to improve word embedding by jointly considering the multisense nature of words and the relational information among words (see Figure 5-5).

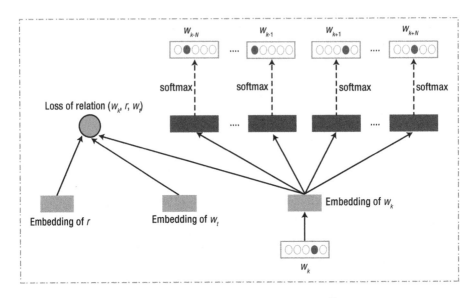

Figure 5-5. *RCNET for IQ test (source: [WWY15])*

The variational graph auto-encoder (VGAE) (`https://arxiv.org/ pdf/1611.07308.pdf`) is a framework for unsupervised learning and link prediction on KG based on the variational auto-encoder (VAE). The authors used latent variables to learn interpretable representations for undirected graphs. Using a graph convolutional network (GCN) encoder and an inner product decoder, they achieved competitive results on link prediction in citation networks, compared with the spectral clustering of the DeepWalk model. This model can naturally incorporate node features, which improves predictive performance. The TensorFlow implementation is available at `https://github.com/tkipf/gae`.

Recently Bansal et al. proposed an end-to-end approach for the task of question answering that directly models the entities and relations in the text as memory slots. They didn't rely on any external KG but rather considered that all the information is contained within the text, meaning the memory-based neural network models for language comprehension [SsWF15]. Munkhdalai et al. proposed RelNet, which extends memory-augmented neural networks with a relational memory to reason about relationships between multiple entities present within the text reasoning with memory-augmented neural networks (`http://arxiv.org/abs/1610.06454`). It's an end-to-end method that reads and writes to both memory slots and edges. The memory slots correspond to entities, and the edges correspond to relationships between entities, each represented as a vector. The only supervision signal comes from answering questions about the text.

5.4 Natural Language Translation

Natural language translation is a hard problem that has been defeating a satisfactory solution since the eve of AI in the 1950s. Traditional DNNs have some limitations for dealing with this problem, such as the requirement that the inputs and targets should be encoded with vectors of fixed dimensionality. For sequences of arbitrary length, this is a serious limitation. Furthermore, while some tasks, such as document classification, can be performed successfully with a bag-of-words representation that ignores word order, the order of words is essential in translation. The sentences "Scientist killed by raging virus" and "Virus killed by raging scientist" have identical bag-of-words representations.

The quality of translation is measured by BLEU; it is the geometric mean of the n-gram precisions for all values of n between 1 and some upper limit, typically 4. Because precision can be made high by offering excessively short translations, the BLEU score also includes a brevity penalty [Wes16].

Unlike the traditional statistical machine translation, DNNs typically use a single neural network to jointly represent the distributions of both languages and maximize a translation score. Most models use a scheme of encoder–decoder to encode a source sentence into a fixed-length vector from which a decoder generates the respective translation.

RNNs with LSTM unities are a natural choice to process the input sequence and compress it into a large fixed-dimensional vector. This vector is later used by another LSTM to extract the output sequence. The second LSTM is essentially a recurrent neural network language model except that it is conditioned on the input sequence. The LSTM's ability to successfully learn on data with long-range temporal dependencies makes it a natural choice for this task because of the possible occurrence of large time lags between the inputs and their corresponding outputs.

Sutskever et al. [SVL14] used RNNs with long short-term memory (LSTM) units to achieve state-of-the-art back in 2014 performance of the conventional phrase-based machine translation system on an English-to-French translation task. The network consisted of an encoding model (first LSTM) and a decoding model (second LSTM). They used stochastic gradient descent without momentum, halving the learning rate twice per epoch, after the first five epochs. The approach achieves a BLEU score of 34.81, outperforming the best previous neural network NLP systems and matching the best published results for non-neural network approaches, including systems that have explicitly programmed domain expertise. When their system is used to rerank candidate translations from another system, it achieved a BLEU score of 36.5.

The implementation involved eight GPUS, and training took ten days to complete. One GPU was assigned to each layer of the LSTM, and an additional four GPUs were used simply to calculate softmax. The implementation was coded in C++, and each hidden layer of the LSTM contained 1,000 nodes. The input vocabulary contained 160,000 words, and the output vocabulary contained 80,000 words. Weights were initialized uniformly randomly in the range between –0.08 and 0.08.

Bahdanau et al. [BCB14] used a variable-length encoding mechanism and auto-encoders to achieve a translation performance comparable to the existing state-of-the-art phrase-based system on the task of English-to-French translation (Figure 5-6). (Preplexity is the weighted geometric average of the inverses of the probabilities.)

$$e^{\sum xp(x)} \log p(x)$$

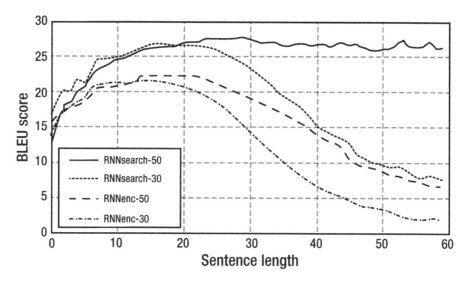

Figure 5-6. *BLEU score accuracy for translation using sequence to sequence as a function of the sentence length. Note the stability of model for long sentences (source: [BCB14]).*

Recently the Google team published a detailed document explaining its new Google machine translation algorithm put into production in November 2016. It relies on the traditional encoder-decoder architecture using bidirectionally stacked LSTMs with attention mechanisms and working at the character level. It is implemented in TensorFlow, and the team claims it almost matches human performance in translation from several languages, like English to French or Spanish or Chinese even for very long sentences. The only shortcoming is that it can translate only single sentences, being thus incapable of contextualizing the full document. See the original paper called "Google's Neural Machine Translation System: Bridging the Gap between Human and Machine Translation" (https://arxiv.org/pdf/1609.08144.pdf).

In September 2017 Google proposed Transformer (https://research. googleblog.com/2017/08/transformer-novel-neural-network. html?m=1), a novel recurrent network architecture that outperforms both conventional recurrent and convolutional models on academic English to German and English to French translation benchmarks. Transformer requires less computation to train and is better suited to machine learning hardware, speeding up training by up to an order of magnitude. See Figure 5-7 and Figure 5-8, which benchmark models against humans.

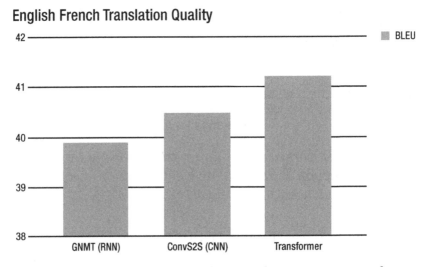

Figure 5-7. *BLEU score accuracy for translation using transformer architecture (source:* https://research.googleblog.com/2017/08/ transformer-novel-neural-network.html?m=1)

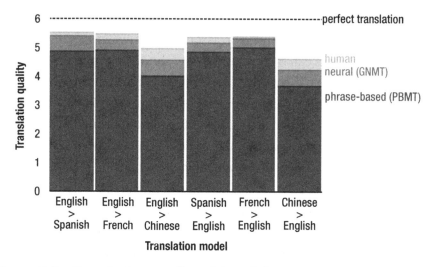

Figure 5-8. Translation quality of Google language translation using sequence-to-sequence model (source: https://research.googleblog.com/2016/09/a-neural-network-for-machine.html)

5.5 Other Applications

The explosion of social networking sites, blogs, and review sites provide a plenitude of information of a scale unthinkable just a few years ago. Millions of people express opinions on everything from movies and books to photos and political parties. In the past, this feedback was pretty much ignored, but now companies have realized the importance of these opinions and reviews in product development, customer care, and customer engagement. Sentiment analysis (SA) is the task of understanding and classifying this information into easy-to-read insights. The most basic scenario is the classification into positive or negative. SA normally involves name entity recognition and type of sentiment (positive, negative, or neutral) and is usually represented as a graph.

However, sentiments are seldom explicitly positive or negative but rather a mix of opinions about various features. Consider the review "I like XXX multimedia features, but the battery life sucks." The sentiment regarding the multimedia features is positive, whereas the sentiment regarding battery life is negative. The association between specific features and opinions can be captured by the short-range and long-range dependencies between the words. Clustering is used on the graph to retrieve only those opinion expressions that are most closely related to the target feature (user-specified feature), and the rest are pruned.

Natural language reading capabilities, such as being able to answer questions given some text, have proven difficult for machines. Hermann et al. [HKG+15] introduced a novel differentiable attention mechanism that allows neural networks to focus on different parts of input. These authors proposed two new corpora of about a million news stories with associated queries from the CNN and Daily Mail web sites. Inspired by [SVL14], they used an RNN with an attention mechanism to answer open questions about text and achieved about 85 percent correct results in the top ten most frequent entities in the text. An elegant variant of this idea was successfully applied to machine translation by Bahdanau et al. [BCB14].

Zhang et al. [ZCSG16] used character-level temporal convolutional networks to abstract text concepts. The trick was to use a special pooling module that allows training of a network with more than six layers. They applied it to large-scale data sets, including ontology classification, sentiment analysis, and text categorization and achieved much higher performance than other baselines, even without the knowledge of words, phrases, sentences, and any other syntactic or semantic structures with regard to a human language, either for English or for Chinese.

Ghosh [GVS+16] used a contextual LSTM (CLSTM), an extension of the recurrent neural network LSTM model, which incorporates contextual features (e.g., topics) into the model to improve considerably word prediction, next-sentence selection, and sentence topic prediction. They tested in two corpora: English documents in Wikipedia and a subset of English Google News. In the next-sentence selection task, they get a relative accuracy improvements of 21 percent over LSTM.

A recent work (`https://arxiv.org/pdf/1704.01444.pdf`) from the OpenAI team presents an interesting approach to sentiment analysis using LSTM. They showed that training LSTM for next-character prediction on the Amazon reviews data set is enough to learn complex and useful representations of the data. Specifically, they found that using a single neuron unit in the network used for sentiment analysis is enough to achieve state-of-the-art results on the binary subset of the Stanford Sentiment Treebank.

5.6 Multimodal Learning and Q&A

Computer vision and NLP are becoming increasingly intertwined. For example, caption generation is a much harder task than image classification or object recognition. The caption should capture the objects in the image, but it also must express relations between them or actions. A recent work pioneered the automatic generation of open-ended lingual descriptions of images [VTBE14]. Vinyals et al. introduce a model based from end to end on a neural network consisting of a CNN to process images followed by a language-generating RNN. It generates complete sentences in natural language from an input image. See *Show and Tell: A Neural Image Caption Generator* [VTBE14]. They achieved BLEU scores close to humans on the Flickr and COCO data sets.

Also, recent methods for natural language processing learn the semantics of language by grounding it in the visual world. The relation between images and words is similar to the hypernym relation between words and textual entailment among phrases. You can see captions as abstractions of images. The most recent approaches to the hypernym, entailment, and image-caption problem involve building distributed representations or embeddings, either from words or from images. This is a powerful approach where similar entities are mapped to neighbor points in a high-dimensional embedding space. Some metric, usually the cosine, is used to compare and retrieve images from text, and vice versa.

Vendrov et al. [VKFU15] proposed a method called *order-embeddings* to take advantage of the partial-order structure of the visual-semantic hierarchy by learning a mapping that is not distance-preserving but order-preserving between the visual-semantic hierarchy and a partial order over the embedding space. They showed that order-embedding provides state-of-the-art results for hypernymy prediction and caption-image retrieval and also provides very good performance on natural language inference. They tested on the Microsoft COCO data set, with more than 120,000 images, each with at least five human-annotated captions per image. They achieved top one/top ten accuracy of 23.3 percent/65.0 percent, respectively, in caption retrieval and achieved 18.0 percent/57.6 percent in image retrieval.

5.7 Speech Recognition

Automatic speech recognition (ASR) refers to the problem of translating voice into text. It's an old problem in machine learning that proved to be hard to solve by traditional techniques relying on Markov chain processes.

The reference benchmarks for this problem are the data sets Switchboard and TIMIT. TIMIT contains broadband recordings of 630 speakers of eight major dialects of American English, each reading ten phonetically rich sentences. The TIMIT corpus includes time-aligned orthographic, phonetic, and word transcriptions as well as a 16-bit, 16kHz speech waveform file for each utterance.

The first application of deep believe networks (DBNs) to the TIMIT data set achieved an accuracy of about 23 percent; see `www.cs.toronto. edu/asamir/papers/NIPS09.pdf`. However, the state-of-the-art accuracy is 16.5 percent using a DBN with post-regularization on the last layer; see `https://www.researchgate.net/profile/Jan_Vanek/` `publication/320038040`. The accuracy is so high that many mobile applications rely purely on voice.

Graves et al. [AG13] pioneered the use of deep bidirectional LSTM for this problem, achieving a remarkable 17.7 percent error rate in the TIMIT database. They applied an end-to-end approach for discriminative sequence transcription with recurrent neural networks. These methods do not require any alignments to presegment the acoustic data, as they directly optimize the probability of the target sequence conditioned on the input sequence and are able to learn an implicit language model from the acoustic training data.

A Baidu team recently proposed an ASR model for translating voice into text [AOS+16]. The improvement performance of the algorithm is due to deep learning replacing feature extraction modules with a single neural model. The system, called Deep Speech 2, approaches the accuracy of humans in several languages. This system was built on end-to-end deep learning using a bidirectional RNN trained in clean and noise environments. In English, the speech system was trained on 11,940 hours of speech, and in Mandarin it was trained for 9,400 hours. Data synthesis was used to augment the data during training. Training a single model at these scales requires tens of exaFLOPs that would require three to six weeks to execute on a single GPU.

In August 2017 Microsoft introduced a new algorithm that reduced the error rate in Switchboard, a standard test for voice transcription accuracy widely used in the industry, to 5.1 percent. By comparison, a single human transcriptionist has an average error rate of 5.9 percent. It used a combination of CNNs and bidirectional LSTM. See `https://arxiv.org/` `abs/1708.06073`.

However, in terms of the accuracy of personal assistants relying on voice, Google has the lead, according to a study from Temple. See Figure 5-9.

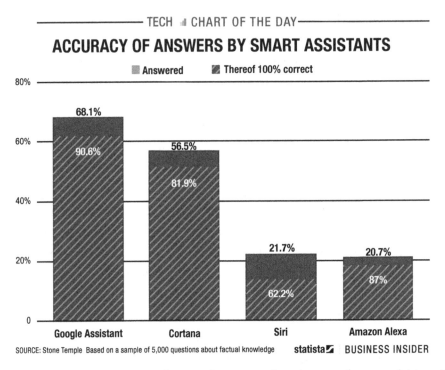

——————————————— TECH ◀ CHART OF THE DAY——————————————

ACCURACY OF ANSWERS BY SMART ASSISTANTS

▨ Answered   ▨ Thereof 100% correct

SOURCE: Stone Temple Based on a sample of 5,000 questions about factual knowledge   statista◪   BUSINESS INSIDER

Figure 5-9. *Accuracy of several personal assistants (source: http://uk.businessinsider.com/siri-vs-google-assistant-cortana-alexa-knowledge-study-chart-2017-6?r=US%20IR=T)*

Deepmind released WaveNet (https://deepmind.com/blog/wavenet-launches-google-assistant/), which is a product for voice synthesis—a process usually referred to as speech synthesis or text-to-speech (TTS)—with remarkable quality. Traditional models rely on concatenative TTS where a very large database of short speech fragments are recorded from a single speaker and then recombined to form complete utterances. WaveNet directly models the raw waveform of the audio signal one sample at a time, yielding more natural-sounding speech. WaveNet can model any kind of audio, including music.

5.8 News and Resources

Here are some resources for you:

- The GitHub page at `https://github.com/andrewt3000/DL4NLP` contains some good references to learn about NLP with deep learning techniques, such as distributed representations and conversational bots.

- Facebook's Language Technology team, which forms part of Applied ML, was the subject of a recent exposé by Forbes diving into its various initiatives. The team recently published their text understanding engine, DeepText (`https://code.facebook.com/posts/181565595577955/introducing-deeptext-facebook-s-text-understanding-engine/`), which is able to understand sentiment, intent, and entities across more than 20 languages. Facebook has also built a new multilingual composer to enable authors of posts on Facebook Pages to reach audiences in other languages using automatic machine translation.

- A recent blog post (`https://research.googleblog.com/2016/08/text-summarization-with-tensorflow.html`) from the Google team explains in detail a method for text summarization using TensorFlow. The authors reached state-of-the-art performance, and the code is open source.

- Matthew Honnibal maintains a GitHub repository (`https://github.com/explosion/spaCy/tree/master/examples/keras_parikh_entailment`) of a decomposable attention model for natural language inference. It is implemented using Keras and spaCy and is designed to compare two documents. The code is clean and relies on pretrained glove word embeddings and bidirectional GRU with ab attention mechanism. The details of the implementation are explained in the blog post at `https://explosion.ai/blog/deep-learning-formula-nlp`.

- Spnis raised $13 million to create a voice assistant platform to search and buy products as an alternative to Google and Amazon. Snips claims the accuracy of its natural language technology outpaces Facebook's Wit.ai, Google's API.ai, and Microsoft's Luis. The platform works in five languages: French, English, Spanish, German, and Korean

- The blog post at `www.wildml.com/2016/01/attention-and-memory-in-deep-learning-and-nlp/` gives a good overview of attentive mechanisms on neural networks with memory.

- In a recent paper (`https://arxiv.org/abs/1611.01599`), the authors propose LipNet as a network able to read the lips of humans and guess the words they were whispering with an accuracy of 93.4 percent, compared with an accuracy of 52.3 percent for humans.

- Microsoft proposed an algorithm (`https://arxiv.org/abs/1609.03528`) for speech recognition, achieving a SOTA performance on the Switchboard data set of 5.8 percent, which is .1 percent lower than humans. The authors used a clever architecture based on recurrent and convolutional neural networks.

- The tutorial at `https://github.com/tensorflow/nmt` gives readers a full understanding of sequence-to-sequence (seq2seq) models and how to build one from scratch. It focuses on the task of neural machine translation (NMT), which was the first testbed for seq2seq models with wild success. The included code is lightweight, high-quality, production-ready, and incorporated with the latest research ideas.

- One of the pioneers of applying NLP to business was Baker & Hostetler (`https://www.bakerlaw.com/`). The AI assistant Ross was the first artificially intelligent attorney built on IBM's cognitive computer Watson. It was designed to read and understand language, generate hypotheses, and formulate responses (along with references and citations) to support the conclusions.

- A recent project from Google Tacotron 2 (`https://research.googleblog.com/2017/12/tacotron-2-generating-human-like-speech.html`) uses a combination of DL techniques (including Wavenet and LSTMs) to solve the problem of text-to-speech (TTS). The generated samples are of excellent quality, and the synthetic speech is almost indistinguishable from real humans.

5.9 Summary and a Speculative Outlook

Despite the progress, understanding language and having an agent capable of a meaningful conversation are the hardest problems of GAI and probably will not be solved in the present context of DL. The John Searle criticism, in his Chinese room argument, has a valid point. Gary Marcus's arguments (www.newyorker.com/contributors/gary-marcus) in his *New Yorker* column are also very pertinent. Maybe we need a different paradigm as all DL methods are basically statistical pattern matching. Can, for instance, language translation ever be understood as symbol-to-symbol pattern matching? Can we ever construct a conversational bot without the sense of "self" and understanding of basic human behavior?

Language is not an impossible problem, but probably the reason it seems so easy for humans to disambiguate language meaning is because we rely on a very large set of explicit and implicit assumptions about the world and about ourselves against which we easily extract "meaning." These assumptions could possibly be framed as ML, but we need a new type of objective function and to create the sense of persistency and the sense of "self" into these algorithms.

To do that, we need a new learning paradigm, not from external data sources but where the agent decides what is "external" and "internal." This may require some of the tools we already have, like nonsupervised concept understanding, but an important component is needed: social interactions. A fully meaningful conversation will only be possible when machines evolve into a society of their own and develop some rudimentary sense of intersubjectivity; see www.princeton.edu/graziano/ for some arguments on this point.

CHAPTER 6

Reinforcement Learning and Robotics

Due to the recent achievements of deep learning [GBC16] benefiting from big data, powerful computation, and new algorithmic techniques, we have been witnessing the renaissance of reinforcement learning, especially the combination of reinforcement learning and deep neural networks, the so called deep reinforcement learning (deep RL). Deep Q-networks (DQNs) have ignited the field of deep RL [MKS+15] by allowing machines to achieve superhuman performance in Atari games and the very hard board game of Go.

It has long been known that RL is unstable when the action-value Q function was approximated with nonlinear functions, such as neural networks. However, DQNs made several contributions to improve the learning's stability.

- DQNs stabilized the training of the Q-action value function approximation using a CNN with replay.

- DQNs used an end-to-end RL approach, taking only raw pixels and the game score as inputs.

- DQNs used a flexible network with the same algorithm, network architecture, and hyperparameters to play different Atari games.

A. Vieira and B. Ribeiro, *Introduction to Deep Learning Business Applications for Developers*, https://doi.org/10.1007/978-1-4842-3453-2_6

These are some of the recent advances and architectures for RL:

- Deep Q-networks [MBM+16] helped AlphaGo [SHM+16] defeat the world champion of Go.

- Asynchronous methods for deep reinforcement learning

- Value iteration networks

- Guided policy search [LFDA16]

- Generative adversarial imitation learning

- Unsupervised reinforcement and auxiliary learning

- Neural architecture design

6.1 What Is Reinforcement Learning?

Reinforcement learning solves sequential decision-making problems, which are problems that require several steps before a reward is received, such as video games. RL agents typically interact with the environment over time and change it, so they work on a moving background and chase a moving target.

At each time step t, the agent is in a state s_t and selects an action a_t from some action space A, following a policy $\pi(a_t \mid s_t)$, which is the agent's behavior, in other words, a mapping from state s_t to actions a_t. It receives a reward, r_t, and moves to the next state, s_{t+1}, according to the environment dynamics, or model, for a given reward function $R(s, a)$ and state transition probability $P(s_{t+1} \mid s_t, a_t)$, respectively.

A value function is a prediction of the expected, accumulative, discounted, future reward, measuring how good each state, or state-action pair, is. Here, the action value is the expected return for selecting action a in state s and then following policy π:

$$Q^\pi(s,a) = E\left[R_t \mid s_t = s, a_t = a\right] \tag{6.1}$$

An optimal action value function Q^* (s, a) is the maximum action value achievable by any policy for state s and action a. You can define state value $V^\pi(s)$ and optimal state value $V^*(s)$ similarly. Temporal difference (TD) learning is a central idea in RL. It learns the value function $V(s)$ directly from experience with a TD error, with bootstrapping, in a model-free, online, and fully incremental way. The updated rule is thus as follows:

$$V(s_t) \leftarrow V(s_t) + \alpha\left[r_t + \gamma(s_{t+1}) - V(s_t)\right] \tag{6.2}$$

Here, α is a learning rate, γ is the discount factor, and $r_t + \gamma(s_{t+1}) - V(s_t)$ is the TD error.

Similarly, Q-learning learns the action-value function with the update rule, shown here:

$$Q(s_t,a_t) \leftarrow Q(s_t,a_t) + \alpha[r + \gamma \max a_{t+1} Q(s_{t+1},a_{t+1}) - Q(s_t,a_t)] \tag{6.3}$$

Q-learning is an off-policy control method in contrast with SARSA, which stands for state, action, reward, (next) state, (next) action. This is an on-policy control method, with the update rule.

$$Q(s_t,a_t) \leftarrow Q(s_t,a_t) + \alpha[r + \gamma(s_{t+1},a_{t+1}) - Q(s_t,a_t)] \tag{6.4}$$

SARSA refines the policy greedily with respect to action values.

6.2 Traditional RL

Reinforcement learning in the traditional control theory can be framed as follows: Suppose an agent is situated in a complex mutable environment (e.g., a breakout game). At each time step, the environment is in a given state (e.g., position of the paddle, direction of the ball, locations of bricks, etc.). The agent is able to realize a number of actions in the environment and change them (e.g., move the paddle). These actions may result in a reward or punishment, and some may transform the environment and lead to a new state, where the agent can perform a new set of actions. The rules to select those actions are designated by the policy. The environment in general is stochastic, meaning that the next state will have a small random component (e.g., if you launch a ball, it may go toward a random direction). This scenario is characterized by a Markovian decision process (MDP) with either observed or unobserved (hidden) states (see Figure 6-1).

In this scenario, RL is stated as an iterative equation called the Bellman equation.

$$V(s) = \max F(s,a) + \beta V\big(T(s,a)\big)$$

Here, s is the state, a is the possible actions, and F is the payoff when the agent changes to a new state, T. The agent tries to find a set of actions that maximize the payoff over time.

The end goal of reinforcement DL is to create a general-purpose framework for representation learning where given an objective, learn a representation required to achieve that objective directly from raw inputs with minimal domain knowledge. Deep learning RL was been successful in playing games (such as Go and video games), exploring worlds (3D worlds and labyrinths), controlling physical systems (manipulating objects, walking, swimming), and performing user interactions (recommendation algorithms, optimization, personalization).

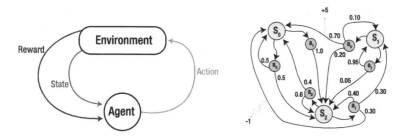

Figure 6-1. *Markovian states in a traditional reinforcement learning problem*

An RL agent normally includes the following components: policy (agent's behavior function), value function (how good each state and/or action is), and model (an agent's representation of the environment) (see Figure 6-1). A policy, or agent's behavior, is basically a map from internal states to actions. It can be deterministic, as in $\pi(s)$, or stochastic, as in $\pi(a|s) = P[a|s]$.

DNNs can be used to represent all the components such as the value function, policy, and model of the world, and the loss function can be obtained by stochastic gradient descent.

A value function is a prediction of future reward from action a in state s. The Q-value function gives an expected total reward, from state s and action a under policy π with a discount factor γ.

$$Q(s,a) = E\left[rt + 1 + \gamma rt + 2 + \gamma 2rt + 3 + \ldots | s,a\right].$$

The discount factor is just a way to propagate delayed rewards over time (see Figure 6-2).

- its state space $s \in S$
- its action space $a \in A$
- its transition dynamics $P(s_{t+1}|s_t, a_t)$
- its reward function $r(s,a)$
- and its initial state probabilities $\mu_0(s)$

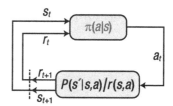

Figure 6-2. *Learning: adapting policy*

141

6.3 DNN for Reinforcement Learning

Policy gradient algorithms are normally used for RL problems with continuous action spaces. These algorithms work by representing the policy as a probability distribution, $\pi^\theta(a|s) = P[a|s;\theta]$, that stochastically selects a set of actions a in state space s in accordance with vector θ representing the parameters of the model. Policy gradient algorithms evolve by sampling this policy and adjusting the parameters toward maximizing the cumulative reward.

In 2014, Silver introduced the deterministic policy gradient (DPG), an algorithm for efficient estimation of policy gradients later extended to deep neural networks (`http://proceedings.mlr.press/v32/silver14.pdf`). The DPG is formulated as the expected gradient of the action-value function (it incorporates both actions and states into a single representation). This way the DPG can be more efficiently estimated than the usual stochastic policy gradient.

The Guided Policy Search (GPS) was proposed by Levine [LFDA16]. GPS transforms policy search into supervised learning with training data provided by a trajectory-centric RL. GPS alternates between trajectory-centric RL and supervised learning and utilizes pre-training to reduce the amount of experience data to train visuomotor policies. Good performance was achieved on a range of real-world manipulation tasks requiring localization, visual tracking, and handling complex contact dynamics. The authors claim that "this is the first method that can train deep visuomotor policies for complex, high-dimensional manipulation skills with direct torque control".

6.3.1 Deterministic Policy Gradient

Silver introduced the DPG algorithm for RL problems with continuous action spaces. The deterministic policy gradient is the expected gradient of the action-value function, which integrates over the state space; whereas in the stochastic case, the policy gradient integrates over both state and action spaces. Consequently, the deterministic policy gradient can be estimated more efficiently than the stochastic policy gradient.

The authors introduced an off-policy actor-critic algorithm to learn a deterministic target policy from an exploratory behavior policy and to ensure an unbiased policy gradient with the compatible function approximation for deterministic policy gradients. Empirical results showed its superior to stochastic policy gradients, in particular in high-dimensional tasks, on several problems: a high-dimensional bandit; standard benchmark RL tasks of a mountain car and a pendulum and a 2D puddle world with low-dimensional action spaces; and controlling an octopus arm with a high-dimensional action space. The experiments were conducted with tile-coding and linear function approximators.

6.3.2 Deep Deterministic Policy Gradient

Despite the DQN algorithm being able to solve problems with high-dimensional observation spaces, it was designed to work with discrete and low-dimensional action spaces. However, most control tasks deal with continuous high-dimensional spaces. Lillicrap et al. proposed a model-free, off-policy actor-critic algorithm using function approximators that can learn policies in high-dimensional, continuous action spaces. They used batch normalization within an actor-critic approach and relied on two previous innovations from DQN: training the network off-policy with samples from replays to minimize correlations and training the network with a target Q-network to give consistent targets during temporal difference backups.

In "Asynchronous Methods for Deep Reinforcement Learning" (`https://arxiv.org/abs/1602.01783`), the authors proposed an actor-critic, model-free, deep deterministic policy gradient (DDPG) algorithm in continuous action spaces by extending the DQN algorithm. The actor-critic avoids the optimization of actions at every time step to obtain a greedy policy as in Q-learning, which will make it infeasible in complex action spaces with large functions approximators like deep neural networks.

The DDPG algorithm learns an actor policy based on experiences from an exploration policy by adding noise sampled from a noise process to the actor policy. More than 20 simulated physics tasks of varying difficulty in the MuJoCo environment were solved with the same learning algorithm, network architecture, and hyperparameters. The DDPG algorithm can solve problems with 20 times fewer steps of experience than DQN, although it still needs a large number of training episodes to find solutions, as in most model-free RL methods. It is end to end, with raw pixels as input.

6.3.3 Deep Q-learning

Deep Q-learning is a model-free reinforcement learning algorithm used to train deep neural networks on control tasks such as playing Atari games. Q-learning algorithms are a little different from the policy-based algorithms.

Unlike policy gradient methods, which attempt to learn functions that directly map an observation to an action, Q-learning attempts to learn the value of being in a given state, s, and taking a specific action, a, there. It combines actions and states into a single representation. While both approaches guide the agent toward efficient rewards, the process of how they get to the best set of actions differ (see Figure 6-3).

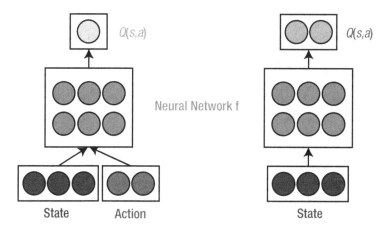

Figure 6-3. *Deep Q-learning algorithm*

In Q-learning, a deep network is trained to approximate the optimal action-value function $Q(s, a)$, which is the expected long-term cumulative reward of taking action a in state s and then optimally selecting future actions. This can be quite a complex map, but as long as you provide enough training data, the network will learn it.

Remember that model-free reinforcement learning algorithms directly learn a control policy without explicitly building a model of the environment (reward and state transition distributions), while model-based algorithms learn a model of the environment and use it to select actions by planning.

$Q(s, a)$ represents the best possible score at the end of the game or set of tasks from a state s. Q refers to the "quality" of a certain action in a given state.

The main idea in Q-learning is that you can iteratively approximate the Q-function using the Bellman equation. In the simplest case, the Q-function is implemented as a table, with states as rows and actions as columns. Figure 6-4 shows the pseudocode for DQN.

Input: The pixels and the game score
Output: Q action value function (from which you obtain policy and select action)
Initialize replay memory D
Initialize action-value function Q with random weight θ
Initialize target action-value function $\hat{Q}$ with weights $\theta^- = \theta$
   Episode $= 1$ *to* M **do**
   Initialize sequence $s_1 = \{x_1\}$ and preprocessed sequence $\phi_1 = \phi(s_1)$
   for $t = 1$ *to* T **do**
      Following ϵ-greedy policy, select
      Execute action a_i in emulator and observe reward r_t and image x_{t+1}
      Set $s_{t+1} = s_t, a_t, x_{t+1}$ and preprocess $\phi_{t+1} = \phi(s_{t+1})$
      Store transition $(\phi_t, a_t, r_t, \phi_{t+1})$ in D
      experience replay
      Sample random minibatch of transitions $(\phi_j, a_j, r_j, \phi_{j+1})$ from D
      Set $y_j =$
      $$\begin{cases} r_j & \text{if episode terminates at step } j+1 \\ r_j + \gamma \max_{a'} \hat{Q}(\phi_{j+1}, a'; \theta^-) & \text{otherwise} \end{cases}$$
      Perform a gradient descent step on $(y_j - Q(\phi_j, a_j; \theta))^2$ w.r.t. the network parameter θ
      periodic update of target network
      Every C steps reset $\hat{Q} = Q$, i.e., set $\theta^- = \theta$
   end
end

Figure 6-4. *Deep Q-network, adapted from* https://arxiv.org/pdf/1701.07274.pdf

DeepMind used the Q-learning approach in a data set of 30 million position-move pairs from Go games played by people and, then improving this neural network with reinforcement learning, played against itself. It added Monte Carlo tree search (MCTS) by using supervised learning data to train a second network that is much faster to evaluate, called the *rollout network*. The full policy network is only ever used once to get an initial estimate on how good a move is, and then the much faster rollout policy is used to choose the many more moves needed to get to an end of the game in an MCTS rollout. This makes the move selections in simulation better than random but fast enough to have the benefits of MCTS.

A third trick is that DeepMind trained a neural net to predict what good moves are and another neural net to evaluate each Go position. DeepMind used the already trained high-quality policy network to generate a data set of positions and final outcomes in that game and trained a value network that evaluated a position based on the overall probability of winning the game from that position. So, the policy net suggests promising moves to evaluate, which is then done through a combination of MCTS rollouts (using the rollout net) and the value network prediction, which turns out to work significantly better than either by itself. AlphaGo ran on 48 CPUs and with 8 GPUs, with neural net computations being done in parallel.

To learn more about Deep RL, see `https://www.nervanasys.com/demystifying-deep-reinforcement-learning/`, which is an interesting tutorial on Q-learning, or see `https://medium.com/@awjuliani/simple-reinforcement-learning-with-tensorflow-part-0-q-learning-with-tables-and-neural-networks-d195264329d0` in TensorFlow.

6.3.4 Actor-Critic Algorithm

The actor-critic algorithm (A3C) was released by Google's DeepMind group in 2016 and made DQN obsolete. It was faster, simpler, more robust, and able to achieve much better scores on the standard battery of deep RL tasks. On top of all that, it could work in continuous as well as discrete action spaces. Given this, it has become the *de facto* deep RL algorithm for new challenging problems with complex state and action spaces. OpenAI just released a version of A3C as its "universal starter agent" for working with its new (and very diverse) set of universe environments (see Figure 6-5).

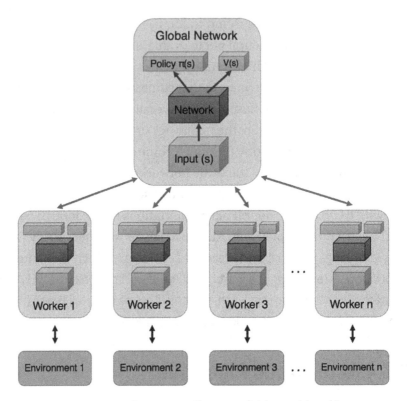

Figure 6-5. *Actor-critic architecture (source: https://medium. com/emergent-future/simple-reinforcement-learning-with-tensorflow-part-8-asynchronous-actor-critic-agents-a3c-c88f72a5e9f2)*

Unlike DQN, where a single agent is represented by a single neural network interacting with a single environment, A3C uses multiple agents to learn more efficiently. In A3C, there is a global network and multiple worker agents that each have their own set of network parameters (see Figure 6-6). Each of these agents interacts with its own copy of the environment at the same time as the other agents are interacting with their environments. The reason this works better than having a single agent (beyond the speedup of getting more work done) is that the experience of each agent is independent of the experience of the others. In this way, the overall experience available for training becomes more diverse.

*Global shared parameter vectors θ and θ_v, thread-specific parameter vectors θ'
and θ'_v*
Global shared counter $T = 0$, T_{max}
Initialize step counter $t \leftarrow 1$
for $T \leq T_{max}$ **do**
    Reset gradients, $d\theta \leftarrow 0$ and $d\theta_v \leftarrow 0$
    Synchronize thread-specific parameters $\theta' = \theta$ and $\theta'_v = \theta_v$
    Set $t_{start} = t$, get state s_t
    for s_t *not terminal and* $t - t_{start} \leq t_{max}$ **do**
        Take a_t according to policy $\pi(a_t|s_t; \theta')$
        Receive reward r_t and new state s_{t+1}
        $t \leftarrow t + 1, T \leftarrow T + 1$
    end

$$R = \begin{cases} 0 & \text{for terminal } s_t \\ V(s_t, \theta'_v) & \text{otherwise} \end{cases}$$

    for $i \in \{t - 1, ..., t_{start}\}$ **do**
        $R \leftarrow r_i + \gamma R$
        accumulate gradients wrt θ':
        $d\theta \leftarrow d\theta + \nabla_{\theta'} \log \pi(a_i|s_i; \theta')(R - V(s_i; \theta'_v))$
        accumulate gradients wrt θ'_v: $d\theta_v \leftarrow d\theta_v + \nabla_{\theta'_v}(R - V(s_i; \theta'_v))^2$
    end
    Update asynchronously θ using $d\theta$, and θ_v using $d\theta_v$
end

Figure 6-6. *A3C, each actor-learner thread, based on [MBM+16]*

The pseudocode for asynchronous advantage actor-critic for each actor-learner thread is presented next. A3C maintains a policy of $\pi(a_t|s_t;\theta)$ and an estimate of the value function $V(s_t;\theta_v)$, being updated with n-step returns in the forward view, after every t_{max} actions or reaching a terminal state, similar to using mini-batches. The gradient update can be seen as $\nabla_{\theta'} \log \pi(a_t|s_t;\theta') A(s_t,a_t;\theta,\theta_v)$, where

$$A(s_t,a_t;\theta,\theta_v) = \sum_{i=0}^{k-1} \gamma^i r_{t+i} + \gamma^k V(s_{t+k};\theta_v) - V(s_t;\theta_v)$$ is an estimate of the

advantage function, with k upbounded by t_{max}.

Actor-critic combines the benefits of both value-iteration methods (Q-learning) and policy-iteration methods (policy gradient). A3C estimates both a value function $V(s)$ (how good a certain state is to be in) and a policy $\pi(s)$, which is a set of action probability outputs for each fully connected layer at the top of the network. Critically, the agent uses the value estimate (the critic) to update the policy (the actor) more efficiently.

The insight of using advantage estimates rather than just discounted returns is to allow the agent to determine not just how good its actions were but how much better they turned out to be than expected. Intuitively, this allows the algorithm to focus on where the network's predictions were lacking.

$$Advantage: A = Q(s,a) - V(s)$$

Since you won't be determining the Q values directly in A3C, you can use the discounted returns (R) as an estimate of $Q(s,a)$ to allow you to generate an estimate of the advantage.

6.4 Robotics and Control

Robotics is still probably the most obvious choice for AI applications. Reality had always lagged behind the Hollywood fanfare of apocalyptic killer robots. DL, however, brought a complete new toolkit set to help solve some complex tasks related with robotics, such as locomotion, grasping, and object manipulation as well as sensor data processing. This section reviews some recent breakthroughs and applications.

One of the most important tasks in robotics is object grasping. Pinto and Gupta proposed a method to self-train a robot (Baxter) on the hard task of object grasping without relying on human-labeled data sets; see "Supersizing Self-supervision: Learning to Grasp from 50K Tries and 700 Robot Hours" (https://arxiv.org/abs/1509.06825). They used the robot to autonomously collect a huge data set of 50,000 data points, with more than 700 hours of grasping attempts. This allowed the training of a deep convolutional neural network (CNN) for the task of predicting grasp locations. The multistage learning approach, where a CNN trained in one stage is used to collect positive/negatives examples in subsequent stages, achieved an accuracy of 66 percent in new objects and 73 percent on already seen objects. The authors claimed that the advantage over a geometry-based approach is that CNNs do not ignore the densities and mass distribution of the objects.

In a project from University of Maryland, Y. Yang et al. used again the robot Baxter to learn manipulation and to conceive action plans from watching videos (`www.umiacs.umd.edu/yzyang/paper/YouCookMani_ CameraReady.pdf`). Two CNN-based recognition modules, as well as a language model (with RNN) for action prediction, were used. They used a probabilistic manipulation action grammar–based parser (Viterbi) to generate commands. The robot learned from watching culinary videos (a cooking data set) consisting of unconstrained demonstration videos. The system was able to recognize and generate action commands robustly, demonstrated by the ability to prepare new recipes from broadly specified natural language input.

Recently, Levine et al. [LFDA16] proposed a method for hand-eye coordination of robotic object manipulation, requiring minimal planning. Humans rely heavily on constant visual feedback for object handling and complex coordination. However, incorporating complex sensory inputs directly into a feedback controller is challenging. Thus, the authors proposed a learning-based approach to hand-eye coordination using end-to-end training directly from image pixels. By continuously recomputing the most promising motor commands, this method continuously integrates sensory cues from the environment, allowing it to adjust the movements to maximize the probability of success in a specific task. This means that the model does not require the camera to be precisely calibrated with respect to the end effector, relying instead on visual cues to determine the spatial relationship between the gripper and graspable objects in the scene.

Berkeley robotics researchers used consumer-grade virtual reality devices (Vive VR), an aging WIllow Garage PR2 robot, and custom software built for the teleoperator to create a single system to teach robots to perform tasks. The system uses a single neural network architecture that is able to map raw pixel inputs to actions; see `https://arxiv.org/abs/1710.04615`. For each task, less than 30 minutes of demonstration data is sufficient to learn a successful policy, with the same hyperparameter settings and neural network architecture used across all tasks. Tasks include reaching, grasping, pushing, putting a simple model plane together, removing a nail with a hammer, grasping an object and placing it somewhere, grasping an object and dropping it in a bowl and then pushing the bowl, moving cloth, and picking up and placing for two objects in succession. Competitive results were achieved with 90 percent accuracy at test time across many of the tasks, though note that picking up and placing for two objects achieved 80 percent (because modern AI techniques still have trouble with sequences of physical actions) and achieved about 83 percent on the similar task of picking up an object and dropping it into a bowl and then pushing the bowl.

Peng et al. [PBvdP16] used deep neural networks trained with reinforcement learning together with physics-based simulations to develop, from first principles, a sequential decision problem with states, actions, rewards, and a control policy with remarkable results. They were able to design control policies that operate directly on high-dimensional character state descriptions (83 dimensions) and an environment state that consists of a height-field image of the upcoming terrain using 200 dimensions. They also parameterized the action space into 29 dimensions, which allows the control policy to operate at the level of bounds, leaps, and steps. The novelty was the introduction of the mixture of actor-critic experts (MACE) architecture to enable accelerated learning. MACE develops N individual control policies and their associated value functions, which each then specialize in particular regimes of the overall motion. During final policy execution, the policy associated with the highest-value function is executed, in a fashion analogous to Q-learning with discrete actions. The results are interesting; see the video at `https://www.youtube.com/watch?v=HqV9H2Qk-DM` and the paper at `www.cs.ubc.ca/van/papers/2016-TOG-deepRL`.

Recently, DeepMind developed an algorithm (`https://arxiv.org/abs/1707.02286`) to train agents (human-like and spider-like) to learn how to walk, run, and jump in challenging virtual landscapes. It used a rich environment to promote the learning of complex behavior where the agents were immersed. DeepMind used a variant of policy gradient reinforcement learning, called *proximal policy optimization*, to teach the agents to run, jump, crouch, and turn without using any explicit reward-based guidance. You can learn more at `https://deepmind.com/blog/producing-flexible-behaviours-simulated-environments/`.

6.5 Self-Driving Cars

Deep learning plays a considerable role in self-driving car technology by analyzing a disparate set of signals, with video being the most challenging. Following the recent success of the Google driverless car, almost all car makers are considering this option in future versions of their cars. Some models under test are Toyota Prius, Audi TT, and Lexus RX450h. Tesla S3 will probably be the first production-ready car with self-driving capabilities included by default. All of these models rely on deep learning technology for object recognition, planning, routing, and object avoidance.

Google has developed its own custom vehicle, assembled by Roush Enterprises. It relies on a 64-beam laser detector that allows the vehicle to generate a detailed 3D map of its environment. The algorithm uses these maps and combines them with high-resolution maps of the world, producing a sufficiently detailed model for self-navigation. Google has test-driven its fleet of vehicles, in autonomous mode, on a total of more than 1.5 million miles. Google's vehicles have shown to be sufficiently capable to drive in heavy traffic in cities as well as on challenging off-road terrain.

Baidu's is investing heavily in self-driving cars and using the Apollo software is planning to release a fully self-driving bus in 2018. Samsung is also testing self-driving cars in South Korea and GM and Cruise announce in 2017 the first mass-production self-driving car. Other companies, like Otto, are focused in software for self-driving trucks. The core technology is based on DL algorithms. Baidu and Google are pushing toward governmental regulation of self-driven cars, claiming they require only minor changes in actual infrastructure. The goal of Baidu is to run a shuttle service in Chinese cities by 2018; another startup, NuTonomy, is planning its own shuttle service in Singapore.

Drive.ai is also working to bring DL to autonomous car technology. Rather than programming a car, Drive.ai will allow the algorithms to learn on their own, though it hasn't disclosed how far along the company is with the technology.

However, autonomous driving requires intuitive psychology. The self-driving car needs to have some commonsense understanding or be able to infer pedestrian behavior and beliefs (do they think it is safe to cross the street? Are they paying attention?) as well as desires (where do they want to go? Are they in a rush?). Similarly, other drivers on the road have similarly complex mental states underlying their behavior (do they want to change lanes or pass another car?). This type of psychological reasoning, along with other types of model-based causal and physical reasoning, are likely to be especially valuable in challenging and novel driving circumstances for which there is little relevant training data. The recent incident with a Tesla Model S car driving in autopilot mode, leading to the death of the driver, raised some concerns regarding the safety and reliability of the technology. Despite Tesla's claims that it tested the self-driving technology on more than 100 million miles, it seems clear that some rough edges still need to be polished (such as how to drive the vehicle in unlikely events, like a car driving the wrong way on a highway or with a drunk driver).

The University of California in Berkeley launched the DeepDrive platform (https://deepdrive.berkeley.edu/). The so-called BDD Industry

Consortium investigates state-of-the-art technologies in computer vision and machine learning for automotive applications. It's a multidisciplinary center hosted at the University of California in Berkeley and led by Professor Trevor Darrell. The center works on the development of new and emerging technologies with real-world applications in the automotive industry.

6.6 Conversational Bots (Chatbots)

Chatbots, also called *conversational agents* or *dialog systems*, are algorithms designed to have human-level conversation capabilities. Several companies are using this technology, either as personal assistants or as conversational algorithms for language understanding. The goal of bots is to achieve a level of natural conversations indistinguishable from human, thus capable of passing the Turing test. There are two types of bots: retrieval-based bots use a repository of predefined responses and some heuristics to pick an appropriate response based on the input and context, and generative models generate automatic responses from past experience and context. Most of the latter rely on deep learning technology.

Generative models can be quite sophisticated and learn from creating latent representations of data. They are flexible but require a large corpus of text (training data). Sequence-to-sequence learning methods like [SVL14] have great potential, but most production systems are still based on hard rules for dialogue retrieval. Short text conversations are easier to optimize, especially in closed domain knowledge where the space of possible inputs and outputs is somewhat limited to a specific context.

Vinyals et al. used the sequence-to-sequence framework to create a conversational model able to predict the next sentence given previous sentences in a conversation [VTBE14]. It was designed from end to end, requiring a few crafted features. They trained it on a large conversational data set, and it was competent enough to deliver good advice using an IT help-desk data set while showing commonsense reasoning in a movie conversational data set. However, the bot fails to be consistent in the conversations (see Figure 6-7).

Human: *what is the purpose of life?*
Machine: *to serve the greater good.*
Human: *what is the purpose of living?*
Machine: *to live forever.*
Human: *what is the purpose of existence?*
Machine: *to find out what happens when we get to the planet earth.*
Human: *where are you now?*
Machine: *i'm in the middle of nowhere.*
Human: *what is the purpose of dying?*
Machine: *to have a life.*
Human: *what is the purpose of being intelligent?*
Machine: *to find out what it is.*
Human: *what is the purpose of emotions?*
Machine: *i don't know.*

Figure 6-7. *Conversational excerpt from Google Cleverbot (source: Google Research)*

Serban et al. [SSB⁺15] recently proposed an end-to-end dialogue system using a generative hierarchical neural network model. The authors proposed a hierarchical recurrent auto-encoder and applied it to a data set (named MovieTriples) containing reviews and comments on about 500 movies; from each movie about 200,000 triples were extracted. Triples U1, U2, U3 are dialogues of three turns between two interlocutors, A and B, for which A emits a first utterance, U1; B responds with U2; and A responds with a last utterance, U3. They showed that the model can outperform n-gram models in modeling utterances and speech acts, achieving a perplexity of around 26, about half of that achieved by n-gram methods. The authors found two crucial ingredients for improving performance: the use of a large external monologue corpus to initialize the word embeddings, and the use of a large related, but nondialogue, corpus in order to pretrain the recurrent net.

Yao et al. [YZP15] proposed a model called Attention with Intention. Their model consists of three recurrent neural networks: the encoder, which is a word-level model representing sentences; the intention network, which is a recurrent network that models the dynamics of the intention process; and the decoder network, which is a recurrent network that produces the responses given the input. It is a language model that is dependent on the intention and has an attention mechanism. The model was trained from end to end without labeling data using 10,000 dialogues involving around 100,000 turns from a help-desk call center. Using an embedded dimension of 200, the authors achieved a perplexity of 22.1.

Generative models are powerful, but grammatical mistakes can be costly, so companies still rely on old retrieval technologies. However, as companies get more data, generative models will become the norm but probably with some human supervision to prevent them from "inappropriate behavior," like what happened to the Microsoft Twitter chatbot, Tay (`https://en.wikipedia.org/wiki/Tay_(bot)`).

Most big companies are using, testing, or considering the implementation of chatbots in their services and operations. Using its experience with its personal assistant Cortana, Microsoft has recently opened a development framework for chatbot implementation and also released Luis.ai, an API for language understanding.

Facebook acquired Wit.ai, a company that works on voice recognition technology. Apple is improving Siri and Google Cleverbot. IBM offers a simple API to embed its powerful knowledge inference machine, Watson, into a conversational bot.

Most of these services can be easily incorporated into conversational services such as Twitter, Whatsapp, Skype, WeChat, Telegraf, or Slack. For instance, Slack allows simple or complex conversation automating based on hard or soft rules. It integrates with Howdy to automate repetitive tasks. Howdy asks the questions, collects the responses, and delivers a report. Chatfuel.com is a platform for a chat's implementation.

There are already many conversational bots using RNN and deep learning technology. For instance, Medwhat is a medical advisor that explores large data sets of biomedical data to answer health-related questions and create personal recommendations. Conversational bots are also a more natural way to search because of the iterative process of refining information; see, for instance, `www.intellogo.com`, which uses DL for contextual search. Some good resources and news on chatbots are available at `chatbotsmagazine.com`.

The major challenge in chatbots is context incorporation, especially in long dialogue and in problems related to identity persistence.

Here is a short list of chatbot applications:

- *Quartz*: News chatbot

- *Operator*: Buying assistant

- *First Opinion*: Doctor chatbot

- *Luka*: Restaurant recommendations in San Francisco

- *Lark*: Fitness coach

- *Hyper*: Flights and hotels

- *Pana*: Flights, hotels, recommendations

- *Fin*: General meetings

- *Penny*: Personal finance coach

- *Mezi*: Shopping assistant

- *Evia*: Insurance assistant

- *Suto*: Expert product recommendations

- *HelloShopper*: Gift ideas

- *Ava*: Expert finder

- *X.ai*: Personal assistant

- *Alice*: Artificial intelligence partner

Recently Facebook introduced ParlAI (`https://code.facebook.com/posts/266433647155520/parlai-a-new-software-platform-for-dialog-research/`). The ParlAI platform combines different advances in AI to make conversational bots more efficient.

The framework offers researchers with a simpler way to build conversational AI systems and make it easier for developers to build chatbots that aren't so easily stumped by an unexpected question. The long-term hope is that ParlAI will help advance the state of the art in natural language research by reducing the amount of work required to develop and benchmark different approaches. It comes with 20 different natural language data sets built in, including Q&A examples from Stanford, Microsoft, and Facebook, and it provides compatibility with popular machine learning libraries.

Created by a team of Stanford psychologists and AI experts, Woebot uses brief daily chat conversations, mood tracking, curated videos, and word games to help people manage mental health. After spending the last year building a beta and collecting clinical data, Woebot Labs just launched the full commercial product—a cheeky, personalized chatbot that checks on you once a day for the price of $39 a month.

6.7 News Chatbots

Retail banks and FinTech startups are now exploring the use of chatbots for digital experiences for checking bank account balances, finding nearby ATMs, making payments, and even advising how to spend your money more wisely.

Zendesk launched a chatbot to automate answers to customer queries, after other competitors, like Slack, started to automate some conversations.

Deep Learning for Chatbots (www.wildml.com/2016/04/deep-learning-for-chatbots-part-1-introduction/) offers an excellent tutorial on how to build bots from scratch using data from an Ubuntu forum.

Several banks, such as Toshka Bank and Royal Bank of Scotland, have introduced conversational bots for customer service and are expected to become fully personal assistants able to deliver a full range of banking capabilities [AV18].

Stratumn, in collaboration with Deloitte and Lemonway, used LenderBot to manage micro-insurance. It will enable custom insurance through social media. Digibank has chatbots as an integral part of the banking experience and claims to have the most integrated solution. DBS Bank is using chatbots for customers to manage their money and make payments in Facebook and WhatsApp. Olivia AI uses a conversational agent to manage accounts and transactions and offer money-saving insight, while LunarWay, an incumbent Danish bank, has launched its own chatbot.

Finally, a recent product named Fin (https://www.fin.com) claims to be able to replace an executive assistant. It is also a hybrid human-powered chatbot like M, and it costs $120 a month for two hours. Most conversational assistants only "understand" and execute basic commands, such as "Play some music on Spotify" or "Start a timer for 20 minutes." But Fin claims that its conversation bot can understand complex voice commands. Fin can buy products, find cars to rent, and create Google documents with a list of choices, prices, and availabilities. It can even book meetings and buy items on eBay.

A new chabot by Phocuswright was proposed to help the travel industry. Rather than going into an online travel agency and doing a search and seeing a list of 150 hotels, you enter in your profile what you're looking for, and a chatbot serves up a curated list of three to four in a messaging interface. Other companies building chabots for the travel industry include Pana and Mezi.

In the United States, a bot called AskMyUncleSam (`http://askmyunclesam.com/`) helps tax payers fill out forms by answering questions about possible tax deductions; you can see it as a FAQ database acting like a real person that users can chat with.

Digit, a San Francisco startup, focuses on helping customers save money by using its algorithms to analyze your income and spending habits and finding small amounts of money it can set aside for you.

Researchers from the Montreal Institute of Learning Algorithms (MILA) have published a research paper outlining MILABOT, their entry into Amazon's Alexa competition on conversational agents (`https://arxiv.org/abs/1709.02349`). They had to face open-ended conversational interactions of people with unbounded interests. MILABOT was a semifinalist and managed to score reasonably highly in terms of user satisfaction while carrying on some of the longest conversations of the competition. It relies on an ensembled strategy binded by reinforcement learning to decide how to select between different models to improve conversations.

6.8 Applications

Boston Dynamics developed Atlas, designed to operate outdoors and inside buildings. It is specialized for mobile manipulation and is electrically powered and hydraulically actuated. It uses sensors in its body and legs to balance and stereo sensors in its head to avoid obstacles, assess the terrain, help with navigation, and manipulate objects.

BIG-I is a humanoid designed by Tin Lun Lam and is a service robot developed to aid homeowners in the performance of a wide variety of household tasks. It can track the location of various household appliances and transport items from one point to the next by employing its claw-like mechanical hands.

China unveiled its first-ever robot security guard, AnBot, which is an intelligent patrolling machine with advanced emergency alert–based navigation and environment-monitoring capabilities. The AnBot, according to its developers, can be highly useful for detecting biochemical and explosive-related threats.

Breakthroughs in low-cost autonomous navigation and positioning as well as intelligent video surveillance have contributed to the development of the robot, which, apart from other functions, is also capable of responding during emergencies.

Kuri is a home robot capable of recognizing pets and seeing and streaming in HD. Mayfield Robotics' Kuri (https://www.heykuri.com/) can recognize faces and family members, your friends, and pets. Kuri has a 1080p HD camera and virtual eyes that can stream live in top quality, as well as capture still images and video.

South Korean has about 400 robots per 10,000 workers employed in manufacturing industries. Germany has nearly 300 robots, and the United States has just above 150. An Oxford University research study published a few years ago projected that nearly 50 percent of the labor market in the United States remains at risk of being mechanized. It projected that nearly 700 different human-performed jobs could be completely automated in a matter of a few years.

6.9 Outlook and Future Perspectives

Deep learning's ability to automate manual processes and boost productivity will have a profound impact on the robotics industry. Despite their widespread use in manufacturing, robots are expensive and difficult to program. For most businesses, robots are not useful yet. In 2015, global unit sales of industrial robots were only 250,000, roughly tenfold the number of mainframe computers at their peak. By comparison, in 2016 server and PC unit sales totaled 10 million and 300 million, respectively. Clearly, robotics is at a nascent stage, calling for dramatic improvements in both cost and ease of use before proliferating.

Cost improvements are well underway. ARK estimates that the cost of industrial robots, which currently is roughly $100,000, will fall by half over the next ten years. Concurrently, a new breed of robots designed for cooperative use with humans will cost on the order of $30,000. Retail assistant robots like SoftBank's Pepper cost about $10,000 when service fees are included. Leveraging components from the consumer electronics industry such as cameras, processors, and sensors should drive costs closer to those consumer products.

The more difficult obstacle to overcome is ease of use. Industrial robots are not designed from a user-centric point of view. They require precise programming using industrial control systems in which each task must be broken down into a series of movements in six dimensions. New tasks must be programmed explicitly; the robot has no ability to learn from experience and generalize to new tasks.

These limitations have restricted the market for robots to those industrial applications where tasks are predictable and well defined. Deep learning can transform robots into learning machines. Instead of precise programming, robots learn from a combination of data and experience, allowing them to take on a wide variety of tasks. For example, a warehouse robot capable of picking any item from a shelf and placing it into a box would be highly desirable for many businesses. Yet, until recently, developers haven't been able to program a robot to recognize and grasp objects that come in an infinite variety of shapes and sizes.

6.10 News About Self-Driving Cars

Here is some news to keep up with:

- Tesla announced recently that its fleet of autopilot hardware-equipped vehicles has collectively driven 780 million miles, of which 100 million had autopilot engaged. Tesla is now capturing more miles worth of data (camera, GPS, radar, and ultrasound) in a day than Google's program logged since its inception in 2009!

- An open source platform to training self-driving trucks, Europilot allows you to repurpose the complex technically-specific game Eurotruck Simulator as a simulation environment for training agents to drive via reinforcement learning. Europilot offers a couple of extra features to ease training and is testing AI on it, including being able to automatically output a Numpy array from screen input at training time, and at test time creating a visible virtual, onscreen joystick the network can use to control the vehicle. You can find the code at `https://github.com/marshq/europilo`.

- Boston Dynamics published an incredible video (`https://www.youtube.com/watch?v=tf7IEVTDjng`) of its newest creation, the SpotMini, which is an all-electric robot running for 90 minutes. It can operate some tasks autonomously and is capable of climbing stairs, picking itself up, and handling sensitive grasping tasks.

The video at https://www.youtube.com/
watch?v=KdwfoBbEbBE from Moley Robotics shows how
a robot can cook from a recipe.

- A recent publication called "Brain4Cars: Car That
  Knows Before You Do via Sensory-Fusion Deep
  Learning Architecture" (https://arxiv.org/
  abs/1601.00740) addresses the problem of anticipating
  and evaluating the car driver's next actions (e.g.,
  turning and hitting an unseen bicycle) up to 3.5
  seconds. The method relies on RNNs equipped with
  LSTM unities that learn on video capturing, vehicle
  dynamics, GPS data, and street maps.

- A 1/5 replica of a rally car was equipped with a
  sophisticated control algorithm to run on an off-
  road track at high speeds. The car, called AutoRally,
  has an inertial measurement unit, two front-facing
  cameras, GPS, rotation sensors on each wheel, an Intel
  quad-core i7 processor, Nvidia GPU, and 32GB RAM;
  it requires no other external sensing or computing
  resources. The algorithm is pretrained by a pilot
  driving on the track. Sensor measurements are then
  used to combine both control and planning to enable
  autonomous driving. At every 16 milliseconds it
  evaluates an average of 2,560 different possible future
  trajectories to pick the best.

- Starship Technologies (https://www.starship.xyz/
  starship-technologies-launches-testing-program-self-
  driving-delivery-robots-major-industry-partners)
  launched a largely autonomous fleet of delivery robots,
  mostly food and small items.

- Comma.ai released a data set of highway driving
  containing 7.5 hours of camera images, steering angles,
  and other vehicle data. It uses adversarial generative
  networks with auto-encoders and RNNs to create the
  next plausible scenario of a specific road snapshot so
  that the network predicts the next movements of the
  car, given what the model imagines the road will look
  like a few hundred milliseconds up front.

- Recently Craig Quiter (https://hackerfall.com/
  story/integrating-gta-v-into-universe) launched
  a driving simulator environment (DeepDrive) based on
  the *Grand Theft Auto* (GTA) video game based on
  72 hours of training and using the OpenAI Gymn
  platform. The idea is to be a test bed for training self-
  driving cars with reinforcement learning. The network
  controls the steering, throttle, yaw, and speed.

- At http://moralmachine.mit.edu/, researchers
  show that study participants want to be passengers
  in vehicles that protect their riders at all costs while
  preferring that others purchase vehicles controlled
  by utilitarian ethics (i.e., sacrificing its passengers for
  the greater good). Inconsistencies in human ethics
  abound.

- Baidu launched the platform Apollo (`http://apollo.auto/`). Baidu claims to be one of the largest partner ecosystems for an autonomous driving platform in the world. The Apollo autonomous driving program has 50 partners, including FAW Group, one of the major Chinese car makers that will work with Baidu on commercialization of the technology. Other partners include the Chinese auto companies Chery, Changan, and Great Wall Motors, as well as Bosch, Continental, Nvidia, Microsoft Cloud, Velodyne, TomTom, UCAR, and Grab Taxi.

- South Korea launched the K-City (`www.businesskorea.co.kr/english/news/sciencetech/18018-k-city-world's-largest-test-bed-self-driving-cars-be-opened-korea`), billed as the world's largest test bed for self-driving cars. The opening of the K-City is to provide more assistance for the developers by offering a testing ground as large as a city.

- The U.S. House of Representatives passed the SELF DRIVE Act (`https://www.wired.com/story/congress-self-driving-car-law-bill/`) in August 2017. The act provides the National Highway Traffic Safety Administration (NHTSA) with the power to regulate self-driving vehicle design, construction, and performance just like it does for regular vehicles. In the next 24 months, NHTSA will write the feature set and rules that automakers must abide by to prove their vehicles are safe. The act also calls out a "privacy plan" whereby automakers must describe how they'll collect, use, and store passenger data. NHTSA can authorize tens of thousands of licenses to companies that are testing self-driving cars, too.

Recently a paper from OpenAI proposed an approach to train reinforcement learning agents through human interaction (https://arxiv.org/pdf/1706.03741.pdf). This is a major breakthrough as traditional reinforcement learning is not easily adapted to learn through human types of communication. The authors explored goals defined in terms of (nonexpert) human preferences solving complex RL tasks without access to the reward function, including Atari games and simulated robot locomotion. They were able to train complex novel behaviors in agents with about an hour of human time.

PART III

Deep Learning: Business Applications

CHAPTER 7

Recommendation Algorithms and E-commerce

E-commerce and digital marketing are becoming data-intensive areas. Deep learning can have a huge impact in these areas since high benefits can be achieved with marginal gains in accuracy. For instance, marginal improvements in the click-through rate (CTR) prediction or conversion ratio (CR) of users interacting with web content, either on PC or on mobile devices, may result in millions of dollars of savings in customer acquisition. However, this problem is becoming more complex as the user journey before product acquisition can be complex, with many contact points before purchase. Complex model attribution (the discovery of the trajectory of the user before buying a product) is thus necessary to correctly allocate the ad budget.

Online user response prediction, click-through rates, and conversions are critical for web search, recommender systems, sponsored search, and display advertising. In online advertising, for instance, the ability to target individual users given their digital journey is essential. These targeting techniques rely on the ability to predict the relevancy of an ad, in other words, the probability that the user in a certain context will click it and later purchase some product or service.

© Armando Vieira, Bernardete Ribeiro 2018
A. Vieira and B. Ribeiro, *Introduction to Deep Learning Business Applications for Developers*,
https://doi.org/10.1007/978-1-4842-3453-2_7

With a size of $2 trillion USD, e-commerce has a strong incentive to rely on more sophisticated recommendation algorithms to improve user experience and increase sales by cross-selling or up-selling.

7.1 Online User Behavior

Predicting user intentionality (the desire to buy a given product or service), based on previous interactions within a web site, is critical for e-commerce and ad display networks, in particular retargeting. By keeping track of the search patterns of the consumers, online merchants can have a deep understanding of their behaviors and intentions.

In mobile e-commerce, a rich set of data is available, and potential consumers search for product information before making purchasing decisions, thus reflecting a consumer's purchase intentions. Users show different search patterns (i.e., time spent per item, search frequency, and returning visits).

Clickstream data can be used to quantify search behavior using machine learning techniques, mostly focused on purchase records. While purchasing indicates a consumer's final preferences in the same category, search is also an essential component to measuring intentionality toward a specific category. You can use a probabilistic generative process to model user exploratory and purchase history, in which the latent context variable is introduced to capture the simultaneous influence from both time and location. By identifying the search patterns of consumers, you can predict their click decisions in specific contexts and recommend the right products.

Modern search engines use machine learning approaches to predict user activity within web content. Popular models include logistic regression (LR) and boosted decision trees. Neural networks have an advantage over LR because they are able to capture nonlinear relationship between the input features and because their "deeper" architecture has inherently greater modeling strength. Decision trees—albeit popular in this domain—face additional challenges with high-dimensional and sparse data. The advantage of probabilistic generative models inspired by deep neural networks is that they can mimic the process of a consumer's purchase behavior and capture the latent variables to explain the data.

In my 2016 paper, I proposed (https://arxiv.org/pdf/1511.06247.pdf) an algorithm based on auto-encoders to identify the activity patterns of certain users that led to buy sessions and then extrapolated as templates to predict high probabilities of purchase in related web sites. The data used consists of about 1 million sessions containing the click data of users. However, only 3 percent of the training data consists of buy sessions, making it a very unbalanced dataset. To handle this, I used an under-sampling technique (i.e., selecting only a fraction of negative examples).

7.2 Retargeting

Sponsored search, contextual advertising, and the recently emerged real-time bidding (RTB) display advertising all rely on the ability of learned models to predict ad click-through rates. The applied CTR estimation models today are mostly linear, ranging from logistic regression [E12] and Naïve Bayes to logistic regression, taking as inputs a huge number of sparse (categorical) features with one-hot encoding. Linear models have the advantages of easy implementation and efficient learning but also have relatively low performance because of their failure in learning nontrivial patterns, namely, interactions between features [LCWJ15].

Nonlinear models, on the other hand, are able to utilize different feature combinations and thus could potentially improve estimation performance. For example, factorization machines (FMs) map the user

and item binary features into a low-dimensional continuous space
(www.algo.uni-konstanz.de/members/rendle/pdf/Rendle2010FM.pdf).
In contrast to SVMs, FMs model explicitly the interactions between
variables using factorized parameters performing well even in problems
with huge sparsity such as recommender systems.

Gradient boosting trees [M13] are an ensemble technique that
automatically learn feature combinations while growing each decision/
regression tree. Some of these techniques (such as random forest) have the
advantage over ANNs that they hardly overfit, even in high-dimensionality
problems. However, boosting techniques, such as extreme gradient
boosting (XGBoost), can easily overfit the data, especially if you compare
with random forest—even with a built-in regularization term.

However powerful, these models cannot make use of all possible
combinations of different features. In addition, many models require
manually designed feature engineering—for instance, aggregation of
interactions by day of the week or month of the year. Another problem of
the mainstream ad CTR estimation models is that most prediction models
have shallow structures and have limited expression to describe the
underlying patterns from complex and large data sets, thus restricting their
generalization ability.

The difficulty in applying DL to this problem is that most input features
in CTR estimation are discrete categories that may contain thousands of
different values: location, device, ad category, and so on. Further, their
local dependencies are mostly unknown. Deep learning can improve the
CTR estimation via a learning feature representation.

Zang et al. (http://wnzhang.net/papers/ortb-kdd.pdf) developed
a bid optimization algorithm for real-time bidding display advertising
slides; see http://wnzhang.net/slides/ecir16-rtb.pdf. RTB goes
beyond contextual advertising by motivating the bidding on user data—
not to be confused with a sponsored search (Google AdWords) auction.
Automation is required from the demand side. Based on some budget,

you want to maximize some KPI, such as conversions or sales. The authors derived simple bidding functions and came to the conclusion that optimal bidding strategies should try to bid more impressions rather than focus on a small set of high-valued impressions. Compared to the higher-evaluated impressions, the lower-evaluated ones are more cost effective, and the chances of winning them are relatively higher.

7.3 Recommendation Algorithms

Recommendation algorithms are ubiquitous in almost any e-commerce web site. A recommender system (RS) is an algorithm that suggest items to a user that he may be interested. It uses as input information from past preferences of users (transactional data) over a set of finite items, either explicitly (ratings) or implicitly (monitoring users' behavior, such as songs heard, applications downloaded, web sites visited), and information about the users or the items themselves. A RS may also use demographics (age, nationality, gender), social media (followers, followed, tweets), and information from the Internet of Things (GPS locations, RFID, real-time health signals).

As output, the RS creates a ranked list of items for each user—which may take into consideration a specific context. RS are evaluated not only by the accuracy (fraction of items that were accepted by the user) but also by novelty (how good the algorithm is in recommending new items to new users), dispersity (how diverse the recommendations are toward less popular items), and stability (how predictions are maintained over time).

There are essentially three types of recommendation systems.

- Transactional-based collaborative filters (CFs)

- Content-based CFs

- Hybrid methods

Content-based methods make use of user profiles or product descriptions for recommendations. CF-based methods use the past activities or preferences, such as user ratings on items, without using user or product content information. Hybrid methods combine content-based and CF-based methods.

7.3.1 Collaborative Filters

Collaborative filtering is a popular recommendation algorithm that uses the ratings (or behavior) of other users on items to predict the likelihood that a user will buy other products. It assumes that past users' opinions provide enough information to select future preferences of new products. If a user agrees with the relevance of some items, then they will likely agree about other items.

There are two types of CF: user-to-user and item-to-item. User-to-user CF, also known as k-NN CF, is a simple algorithm that evaluates the similarity between two users based on the vector-wise similarity between their pattern of interactions with the items or products (see Figure 7-1). User-to-user CF suffers from scalability problems as the user base grows since searching for the neighbors of a user is time-consuming.

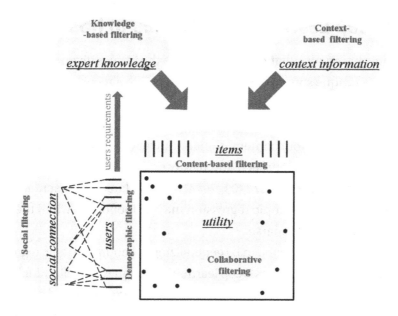

Figure 7-1. *Recommendation system based on collaborative filter algorithm (source: https://tel.archives-ouvertes.fr/tel-01585248/document)*

Item-to-item CF takes similarities between products and was first widely adopted by Amazon. Rather than using similarities between users' rating behavior to predict preferences, item-to-item CF uses similarities between the rating patterns of items. This method is more scalable and achieves better results than user-to-user CF.

CF algorithms have two important problems: cold start and inner takes it all. The first problem is a serious one: if few reviews exist or many new users/items are the database (making a very sparse user-to-item matrix), the system has difficulty creating recommendations. The second known problem relates to the fact that only the top hits are recommended, so the system lacks diversity. Deep learning models aim to solve both these problems.

7.3.2 Deep Learning Approaches to RSs

Algorithms based on collaborative filters use the ratings given to items by users as the unique source of information to create a recommendation. However, a sparseness of ratings may degrade the performance of CF-based methods. The only way to solve this problem is to use auxiliary information such as item content. Collaborative topic regression is a method that takes this approach and tightly couples the two components; see https://arxiv.org/abs/1409.2944. Still, the latent representation learned by collaborative topic regression may be ineffective when the auxiliary information is sparse.

DL can address this problem by generalizing collaborative topic regression in a hierarchical Bayesian way. Deep learning techniques also allow for better feature extraction from item characteristics (text, image, video, and audio) when compared to traditional techniques. This allows for a more accurate modeling of items and potentially the capability of hybrid and content-based methods. Another advantage that deep learning methods provide is that they allow for different views of the data, allow for standard collaborative filtering techniques such as matrix factorization, and often treat user-to-item interaction as matrix-structured data, often ignoring the temporal structure and order in the data. Deep learning techniques such as convolutions and recurrent neural networks allow you to model the temporal structure in this data, which leads to significant performance improvements.

Salakhutdinov et al., pioneered the use of DL for recommendation systems by proposing an architecture based on a deep belief network with latent nodes to represent the hidden features of the data; see www.machinelearning.org/proceedings/icml2007/papers/407.pdf. These authors used a modified version of this architecture to achieve a good score in the Netflix movie rating competition.

Recently Hao [WWY15] proposed a method called *collaborative deep learning* (CDL) that jointly learns deep representations from the content of items/users while also considering the rating matrix with significantly better results.

CDL relies on a technique using tightly coupled methods that allow two-way interactions between rating matrix and content (see Figure 7-2). The rating information guides the learning of features, and conversely the extracted features can improve the predictive power of the CF models. Tightly coupled methods often outperform loosely coupled ones. This approach combines ideas from CF, latent factor, and content analysis based on probabilistic topic modeling.

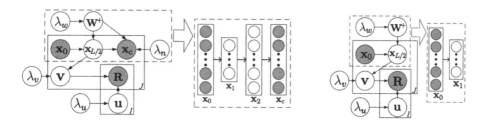

Figure 7-2. *Scheme of a possible collaborative deep learning model. On the left is the graphical model. The dashed rectangle represents an auto-encoder. On the right is the graphical model of the degenerated model. The dashed rectangle represents the encoder component of SDAE (source: www.wanghao.in/paper/KDD15_CDL.pdf).*

For a particular user, CDL can recommend articles from other users who liked similar articles. Latent factor models work well for recommending known articles but cannot generalize to previously unseen articles. To generalize to unseen articles, this algorithm uses topic modeling. Topic modeling provides a representation of the articles in terms of latent themes discovered from the collection. This extra component can recommend articles that have similar content to other articles that a user likes, even without using any previous rating. The topic representation of articles allows the algorithm to make meaningful recommendations about articles before anyone has rated them.

The usefulness of this type of approach lies in the fact that it can create a smooth semantic map of similarities between users, products, and relations in a semi supervised way. Another great advantage is that it can generalize well, thus overcoming the cold-start problem. The problem is that it needs to create new nodes each time a new user or product is added (or work by proxy).

As a note, care should be taken when using a single measure (namely, precision or recall) to evaluate an RS. Dispersity and novelty should be considered as they may be as much relevant for the product. Other important metrics are how fast the algorithm learns, to solve the unavoidable cold-start problem, and how scalable it is, for high-demand applications.

7.3.3 Item2Vec

In Item2Vec (https://arxiv.org/abs/1603.04259) the authors extended Word2vec to item-based product recommendations. This approach works well when the number of users outnumber the products in the catalog, like in music, or when user-to-item relations aren't available because users browse e-commerce pages anonymously. This method is particularly useful in recommending less popular items and does not suffer from the cold-start problem of CF. The code in Python is available at https://github.com/DoosanJung/I2V_project.

In the recent publication "Learning Latent Vector Spaces for Product Search" (http://arxiv.org/pdf/1608.07253.pdf), the authors introduce a latent vector space model that jointly learns the latent representations of words, e-commerce products, and a mapping between the two without the need for explicit annotations. The power of the model lies in its capability to model directly the relations between products and the words that describe them. The authors compared this method to existing latent vector space models (LSI, LDA, and Word2vec), claiming higher accuracy thanks to better product representations.

7.4 Applications of Recommendation Algorithms

Some companies that pioneered recommendation systems are still relying heavily on them. Most large-scale commercial and social web sites have some form of recommendation system, recommending products or connections. For example, LinkedIn, the business-oriented social networking site, forms recommendations for people users might know, jobs you might like, groups you might want to follow, or companies you might be interested in. LinkedIn uses Hadoop and Mahout to run CF models at scale.

Amazon uses content-based recommendation. When you select an item to purchase, Amazon recommends other items that other users purchased based on that original item (as a matrix of item-to-likelihood-of-next-item purchase). Amazon patented this behavior, called *item-to-item collaborative filtering*.

Hulu, a streaming-video web site, uses a recommendation engine to identify content that might be of interest to users. It also uses item-based collaborative filtering with Hadoop to scale the processing of massive amounts of data.

In 2006, Netflix held a $1 million prize competition to the team that could improve its recommendation system, RMSE, by 10 percent. In 2009, three teams combined to build an ensemble of 107 recommendation algorithms that resulted in a single prediction. This ensemble proved key to improve predictive accuracy.

A recent paper from the Alibaba team reported an algorithm currently used by the company to predict CTR; see (https://arxiv.org/pdf/1706.06978.pdf). The model, called a *deep interest network* (DIN), has a main difference from the wide and deep model. Instead, it uses an attention mechanism imported from machine translation literature. DIN represents users' diverse interests with an interest distribution and designs

181

an attention-like network structure to locally activate the related interests according to the candidate ads. Behaviors with higher relevance to the candidate ad get higher attention scores and dominant the prediction. They report big gains in using this model with respect to other types of neural networks.

Kumar et al. proposed a deep neural model (http://ceur-ws.org/Vol-1866/paper_85.pdf) using LSTM with attention to recommend news content and a fully connected network to learn the mappings for the content items to the users. They showed a significant improvement over the state-of-the-art results by 4.7 percent (on a hit ratio of 10). The model is also effective in handling the user cold-start and item cold-start problems.

7.5 Future Directions

Some future directions for improving recommendation systems include explicit consideration of time effects (the changing tastes of users or products), consideration of sequence order (it's different to recommend a phone cover after a phone purchase than a phone after a phone cover acquisition), and a richer representation of the products and content. See https://www.cs.princeton.edu/chongw/papers/WangBlei2011.pdf for some insights about the future direction of RSs.

The poor quality of metadata is a recurring problem in a large percentage of real-life situations; for example, values are missing or are not assigned systematically. Even if metatags are perfect, such data only represents the actual item much more indirectly and in less detail than a picture of it. With the help of deep learning, the actual, intrinsic properties of the content (images, video, text) could be incorporated into recommendations. Using DL, item-to-item relations could be based on a much more comprehensive picture of the product and would be less reliant on manual tagging and extensive interactional histories.

A good example of incorporating the content into a recommender system is what Spotify was looking into in 2014 to make its song recommendations more diverse and to create an improved personalized experience for its users. The music-streaming service uses a collaborative filtering method in its recommendation systems. But Sander Dieleman, a Ph.D. student and intern at Spotify, saw this as its biggest flaw. An approach that relies heavily on usage data inevitably under-represents hidden gems and lesser known songs of upcoming artists, the holy grails of music discovery. Dieleman used a deep learning algorithm that he taught on 30-second excerpts from 500,000 songs to analyze the music itself. It turned out that successive layers of the network learn progressively more complex and invariant features of the songs, as they do for image classification problems. In fact, "on the topmost fully-connected layer of the network, just before the output layer, the learned filters turned out to be very selective for certain subgenres," such as gospel, Chinese pop, or deep-house. In practice, this means that such a system could effectively make music recommendations based solely on the similarity of songs (an excellent feature for assembling personalized playlists). It's unclear whether Spotify incorporated these findings into its algorithm, but it was nevertheless an intriguing experiment.

The cold start is the archenemy of recommendation systems. It can affect both users and items. For users, the cold start means when the system has limited or no information on a customer's behavior and preferences. The item cold start represents the lack of user interactions with the data upon which item-to-item relations can be drawn (there is still the metadata, but that won't often suffice for truly fine-tuned recommendations). The item cold start is an obvious domain for the aforementioned content-based approach as it makes the system less reliant on transactional and interactional data.

However, creating meaningful personalized experiences for new users is a much trickier problem that cannot necessarily be solved by simply gathering more information on them. It is quite typical, especially in the case of e-commerce sites or online marketplaces with wide product portfolios, that customers visit a web site with completely different goals over time. First they come to buy a microwave, but the next time they're looking for a mobile phone. In this scenario, the data gathered in their first session is not relevant to the second.

An intriguing approach to tackling the user cold-start problem is session-based or item-to-session recommendations. This roughly means that instead of relying on the whole interactional history of customers, the system splits this data into separate sessions. The model capturing the users' interests then builds on session-specific clickstreams. Through this approach, it is quite possible that future recommender systems will not rely so heavily on elaborate customer profiles built over months or even years; rather, they'll be able to make reasonably relevant recommendations after the user has been clicking on the site for a while.

This is an area that is yet rather poorly researched but possibly holds tremendous opportunity for enhancing personalized online experiences. Gravity R&D's researchers working on the EU-funded CrowdRec project recently co-authored a paper (https://arxiv.org/abs/1706.04148) that describes a recurrent neural network approach to providing session-based recommendations. This is the first research paper that seeks to employ deep learning for session-based recommendations, and their results show that their method significantly outperformed currently used state-of-the-art algorithms for this task.

CHAPTER 8

Games and Art

One the most exciting areas of deep learning applications is the creative industries and games, either through algorithms to play traditional board games or video games or in the creation of virtual game characters or immersed reality. The recent success of AlphaGo, which beat the world Go champion, ignited the interest in AI bringing superhuman capabilities to machines.

8.1 The Early Steps in Chess

It was 20 years ago that IBM's Deep Blue beat the world chess champion, Gary Kasparov. Since then, chess-playing computers have put to shame the best humans. But the techniques used by these algorithms still relied heavily on "brute-force" tree` search through all possible move combination.

Recent advances in AI made possible the development of self-learning programs. One of the pioneering neural network algorithms to play chess was Giraffe (`https://chessprogramming.wikispaces.com/Giraffe`). It was taught to play chess by evaluating game positions. It was formed by a neural network consisting of four layers that together examine each position on the board in three different ways. The first looks at the global state of the game, such as the number and type of pieces on each side, which side is to move, castling rights, and so on. The second looks at

© Armando Vieira, Bernardete Ribeiro 2018
A. Vieira and B. Ribeiro, *Introduction to Deep Learning Business Applications for Developers*,
https://doi.org/10.1007/978-1-4842-3453-2_8

piece-centric features such as the location of each piece on each side, and the final one maps the squares that each piece attacks and defends.

The usual way of training an algorithm to play board games is to manually evaluate every position and use this information to teach the machine to recognize those that are strong and those that are weak. Instead, a bootstrapping technique was used in which Giraffe played against itself with the goal of improving its prediction. That works because there are fixed reference points that ultimately determine the value of a position—whether the game is won, is lost, or is a drawn. In this way, the computer learns which positions are strong and which are weak. In 72 hours of training, Giraffe achieved the level of the best program in the world.

8.2 From Chess to Go

Despite the progress achieved in playing Chess, Go has remained an elusive challenge for machines. Go is a simple board game where two players take turns placing black or white stones on a board, trying to capture the opponent's stones or surround empty space to make points of territory. Despite the simple rules, Go is a game of great complexity because there are about 10^{170} possible board configurations—far exceeding the number of atoms in the universe, which is around 10^{100}.

One of the most successful programs was The Many Faces of Go, which achieved a 13-kyu performance and had 30,000 lines of code written over a decade by David Fotland. But it never achieved the level of a master player.

Monte Carlo (MC) algorithms were introduced into board game algorithms in the 2000s by Bruno Bouzy. MC uses sampling to obtain an approximation of intractable integrals. Later Rémi Coulom used MC evaluation with tree search and coined the term Monte Carlo tree search (MCTS); see `https://www.remi-coulom.fr/CG2006/CG2006.pdf`. His program CrazyStone won that year's KGS computer-Go tournament for the small 9×9 variant of Go, beating other programs such as NeuroGo and GNU Go. MCTS uses Monte Carlo rollouts to estimate the value of each state in a search tree. As more simulations are executed, the search tree grows larger, and the relevant values become more accurate. It's an efficient sampling algorithm to explore large search spaces.

In 2013, DeepMind published a paper that used reinforcement learning (trained through LSTM) with deep neural nets using just the input of the pixels on the screen (processed by CNNS). It coined the machine a *deep Q-network*, and it learned to play some games like *Breakout, Pong*, and so on. In 2014 DeepMind published another paper called "Teaching Deep Convolutional Neural Networks to Play Go" (https://arxiv. org/abs/1412.3409) that, unlike the previous case, used a neural net to produce the probability of a human Go player making each possible move from a given position.

AlphaGo used two neural networks: a policy and a value network. A fast rollout policy P_π and supervised learning (SL) policy network p_σ are trained to predict human expert moves in a data set of positions. A reinforcement learning (RL) policy network p_ρ is initialized to the policy network and is then improved by policy gradient learning to maximize the outcome (that is, winning more games) against previous versions of the policy network. A new data set is generated by playing games with itself, in other words, self-play with the RL policy network. Finally, a value network v_θ is trained by regression to predict the expected outcome (whether the current player wins) in positions from the self-play data set.

The details of the AlphaGo algorithm are explained in detail in https://storage.googleapis.com/deepmind-media/alphago/ AlphaGoNaturePaper.pdf.

8.3 Other Games and News

This section covers other games and news.

8.3.1 Doom

In 2016 an AI agent developed by Carnegie Mellon University students won the classic video game *Doom*—outperforming both the game's built-in AI agents and human players. See `https://arxiv.org/pdf/1609.05521v1.pdf` and some extraordinary videos at `https://www.youtube.com/watch?v=ooOTraGu6QYlist=PLduGZax9wmiHg-XPFSgqGg8PEAV51q1FT`.

The 3D game environment is challenging for algorithms since players must act based only a partially observed maze. In contrast with *Doom*, Atari and Go give the agents complete information about the game, in other words, fully observable environments.

When the machine player is navigating through the game, it employs a deep Q-network, a reinforcement learning architecture that DeepMind used to master Atari games. When an enemy is in sight, the agent switches to a deep recurrent Q-network, which includes a long short-term memory (LSTM) module that helps the agent track the enemy's movements and predict where to shoot.

Though the AI agent relies on only visual information to play the game, the authors used an API to access the game engine during training. This helped the agent learn how to identify enemies and game pieces more quickly. Without this aid, they found the agent learned almost nothing in 50 hours of simulated gameplay, equivalent to more than 500 hours of computer time.

8.3.2 Dota

In 2017 an artificial agent by OpenAI won a famous *Dota2* (one of the world's most popular video games) tournament, beating a professional human player.

Real-time battle and strategy games like *Dota* and *Starcraft II* pose major challenges over traditional board games like chess or Go. These games require long-term strategic thinking, and—unlike board games—they keep vital information hidden from players. Algorithms have to predict and preempt what the opponent will do; you may call this *intuition*.

Dota has an extra level of complexity like human players have to engage in cooperative action within teams of five, coordinating complex strategies. There are hundreds of characters in the game, each with their own skills equipped with a number of unique items. The complexity of actions is so large that it is virtually impossible to hard-code a program's winning strategy into a *Dota* agent.

As important as the AI agent result was how it taught itself to play. AlphaGo learned how to play games by observing previous games played by humans. OpenAI's agent taught itself everything from scratch.

Even if some agent behavior was preprogrammed, it was able to develop complex strategies by itself, like faking its opponents by pretending to trigger an attack, only to cancel soon after, leaving the human player at a weak position.

Despite the victory of the OpenAI agent, the real challenge will be a 5v5 match, where agents have to manage not just a duels but also a chaotic battlefield with multiple agents and dozens of support units.

8.3.3 Other Applications

You can find some implementation of neural networks to play several video games, like *Mario Kart* (https://kevinhughes.ca/blog/tensor-kart) in TensorFlow and *Super Mario* (https://www.engadget.com/2015/06/17/super-mario-world-self-learning-ai/).

In a recent work, a team from Maluuba (Microsoft) proposed a technique detailed in "Hybrid Reward Architecture for Reinforcement Learning" (https://static1.squarespace.com/static/58177ecc1b631bded320b56e/t/594050d7bf629a891ef31605/1497387537190/HRA_Maluuba.pdf). They were able to largely improve the accuracy of QDN or actor-critic methods (AC3), beating the best humans in the *Pacman* Atari game. This technique, designated HRA, takes as input a decomposed reward function and learns a separate value function for each component of the reward function. Because each component depends on only a subset of all features, the overall value function is much smoother and can be approximated more easily by a low-dimensional representation, enabling more effective learning.

Sudoku is a popular number puzzle that requires you to fill in the blanks in a 9×9 grid with digits so that each column, each row, and each of the nine 3×3 subgrids contain all of the digits from 1 to 9. In the project detailed at `https://github.com/Kyubyong/sudoku`, Kyubyong used a simple convolutional neural network (in TensorFlow) to solve Sudoku without any rule-based postprocessing. It achieved an accuracy of 86 percent.

One of the challenges of deep learning is solving the challenging Raven progressive matrices (RPM) test. The RPM is a nonverbal intelligence test commonly used to measure general intelligence. An RPM consists of a matrix of symbols where the symbols make up a visual geometric pattern and where one of the symbols in the matrix is missing. The test taker is given access to six to eight possible solution candidates and, based on these and the geometric design of the matrix, determines which symbol is missing from the matrix. Despite that the test is limited to measuring the test taker's ability to extract information from complex visual geometric structures, its high-level correlation to other multidomain intelligence tests has given it a position of centrality in the space of psychometric measures [SKM84].

Some promising efforts have been deployed to solve this matrix using generative adversarial networks (GANs) using a contextual CNN auto-encoder as a generator (initially applied for image inpainting (`https://arxiv.org/abs/1604.07379`), but the algorithm struggles in dealing with unseen symbols.

8.4 Artificial Characters

Microsoft announced a project that enables coders to sculpt and develop its technology. AIX is a new software development platform that researchers can use to develop *agents*—AI-powered characters.

Minecraft added a virtual reality assistant using artificial intelligence. The platform, named AIX, is a sandbox that allows researchers to develop agents that roam Minecraft worlds. The idea is to equip them with the capabilities to behave like a regular player, including basic commands, such as climbing up a hill, and more complicated requirements such as navigating varied terrain, building out landscapes, and just surviving in the game.

A team from the University of Tubigen is working on a project to give the *Super Mario* game characters "real life" by allowing them to develop their own attitudes in the game environment; see `https://www.uni-tuebingen.de/en/newsfullview-landingpage/article/super-mario-erhaelt-soziale-intelligenz.html`.

Serpent.AI (`https://github.com/SerpentAI/SerpentAI`) is a framework to assist developers in the creation of game agents. It helps you turn any video game you own into a sandbox environment for experimentation.

Unity launched the Unity machine learning agents (`https://blogs.unity3d.com/2017/09/19/introducing-unity-machine-learning-agents/`), which enable the creation of games and simulations using the Unity Editor. These serve as environments where intelligent agents can be trained using reinforcement learning, neuroevolution, or other machine learning methods through a simple-to-use Python API. These platforms are not new, and PROWLER.io (`https://www.prowler.io/`) was the pioneer. These types of environments will become important for the development of agents capable of learning complex emergent behaviors through self-play and simulation.

8.5 Applications in Art

If DL has achieved remarkable results in playing games, perhaps the most remarkable achievements were in an unusual area: art.

Gatys et al. [GEB15] applied convolutional neural networks to obtain a representation of the style of an artist (input image) using the feature space originally designed to capture texture information. By including the feature correlations of multiple layers, they obtained a stationary, multiscale representation of the input image. They proved that the representations of content and style in the convolutional neural network are separable. Both representations can be independently manipulated to produce new, perceptually meaningful images. To demonstrate this finding, they generated images that mix the content and style representation from two different source images; see Figure 8-1.

Figure 8-1. *Artificially generated images using CNNs trained on two set of images (source:* www.demilked.com/inceptionism-neural-network-drawings-art-of-dreamssource*). See also a demo online at* http://ostagram.ru/ *or the mobile app Prisma.*

Ulyanov et al. [ULVL16] proposed a technique that, given a single example of a texture, ithe CNN is able to generate multiple samples of the same texture of arbitrary size and able to transfer artistic style from a given image to any other image. The resulting networks are relatively small and can generate textures that are fast and of remarkable quality.

CycleGAN (https://arxiv.org/pdf/1703.10593.pdf) is a recent approach for image-to-image translation (mapping between an input image and an output image) using unaligned images (see Figure 8-2). It was able to learn a mapping $G : X \rightarrow Y$ such that the distribution of images from $G(X)$ is indistinguishable from the distribution Y using an adversarial loss. Because this mapping is highly under-constrained, it is coupled with an inverse mapping $F : Y \rightarrow X$ and it introduced a cycle consistency loss to push $F(G(X)) \approx X$ (and vice versa). It presents a reliable transformation of horses to zebras, and vice versa. The code (in Pytorch) and videos are at https://github.com/junyanz/pytorch-CycleGAN-and-pix2pix.

Figure 8-2. Object transfiguration with CycleGAN (source: https://github.com/junyanz/CycleGAN)

A Swedish company, Peltarion (`http://peltarion.com/`), released a neural network that can perform sophisticated computer-generated choreography by extracting high-level features from raw sensor data. The system, called *chor-rnn*, uses recurrent neural networks for generating novel choreographic material in the nuanced choreographic language and style of an individual choreographer. It also can create higher-level compositional cohesion, rather than just generating sequences of movement. The neural network is trained on raw motion capture data, and it can generate new dance sequences for a solo dancer. The authors used five hours of contemporary dance motion captured using the Microsoft Kinect v2 sensor, tracking 25 joints to produce 13.5 million spatiotemporal joint positions in 3D. Using this data for training, the authors showed that their network can output novel choreographies that demonstrate a progressive learning of increasingly complex movements.

In a recent work (`https://arxiv.org/pdf/1706.07068.pdf`), the authors used a generative adversarial network to create synthetic artwork that us almost indistinguishable from the one generated by humans. Creative adversarial networks (CANs) work like GANs, except the discriminator gives two signals back to the generator instead of one: whether something qualifies as art and how well it can classify the generator's sample into an exact style. A quantitative evaluation showed that humans thought CAN images were generated by a human 53 percent of the time versus 85 percent for the human-generated abstract expressionist set.

In a blog post (`http://karpathy.github.io/2015/05/21/rnn-effectiveness/`), Andrew Karpathy describes a model based on an RNN with LSTM unities that was trained on Shakespeare works. The model was able to create prose with remarkable similarities to some famous pieces of British authors.

Hitoshi Matsubara used a DL-based algorithm to generate a short story (`http://mashable.com/2016/03/26/japan-a-i-novel`). This story end up being short-listed, among 10 others, from 1000 submissions.

Gene Kogan (`http://genekogan.com/`) used AI as a creative tool and created some interesting effects in `https://vimeo.com/180044029`.

8.6 Music

Music can be represented as a time sequence and thus modeled as conditional probabilities between musical events. For example, in harmonic tracks, some chords are more likely to occur than others given the last chords, while the chord progressions often depend on the global pattern of the music. In many automatic composition systems, these relationships are simplified by assuming that the probability of the current state p (n) only depends on the probabilities of the states in the past, p (n – k)...p (n – 1). Given a seed sequence, a musical sequence is then generated by predicting the following events.

Music composition is considered creative, intuitive, and, therefore, a privilege of humans. However, DNNs are bringing new tools to the table that are challenging this assumption. Automatic music composition, which normally includes tasks such as the composition of melody, chord, rhythm, and even lyrics, was traditionally addressed through hidden Markov models (HMMs). These models have a memory of 1 (the present state completely determines the transition to the next state). However, deep LSTM networks can handle arbitrary history to predict future events, thus having more complex expressive capabilities than HMM.

Music composed by an AI algorithm is not new as it allows composers to experiment more efficiently. The albums *Omusic* and *Lamus* were entirely composed by Melomics, a group founded by Francisco Javier Vico. Both use a strategy modeled on biology to learn and evolve more complex mechanisms for composing music. These algorithms were written explicitly to generate the music.

Choi et al. https://arxiv.org/pdf/1604.05358v1.pdf used an algorithm based on LSTM to learn relationships within text documents that represent chord progressions and drum tracks. The code (based on Keras) is available on GitHub. The results are remarkably good, especially for drums; you can find some examples on SoundCloud.

A recent project called Deep Jazz, deployed by Ji-Sung Kim from Princeton University, enables deep learning to generate music. The project is basically an RNN trained with LSTM on several hours of jazz music. After training for 128 epochs, the algorithm is able to create new music. The code is available on GitHub and is based on the Keras and Theano libraries. The authors are working to generalize the concept to most music styles without having to train a neural network for each. In this work, ML was used to teach music students to go beyond the traditional chords.

Another recent project (http://imanmalik.com/cs/2017/06/05/neural-style.html) used recurrent networks to learn how to play instruments (in MIDI format) from reading sheet music. The quality is so good that is almost indistinguishable from a human executer.

Sync Project (http://syncproject.co/blog/2017/6/5/making-music-with-ai-an-introduction) used a recurrent network called Folk-RNN where researchers entered thousands of transcribed examples of Celtic folk music into a deep learning system that learned from the MIDI song information to create new melodies. The researchers were surprised to find that the system could cook up "authentic-sounding" melodies once every five times it tried.

Southern's album *I AM AI* was created by Amper (https://www.ampermusic.com/), which is an artificially intelligent music composer, producer, and performer. Users select parameters for what type of music will be created—"ambient uplifting cinematic" or "epic driving," for example. The program generates a song in seconds using its machine learning algorithm. Humans are then able to manipulate parts of that track, but it's possible to leave all chord structures and instrumentation up to the computer. See this example: https://www.youtube.com/watch?v=XUs6CznN8pw.

For a survey of deep learning applications in music, see https://arxiv.org/pdf/1709.01620.pdf.

8.7 Multimodal Learning

Tamara Berg pioneered the application of DL to fashion by exploiting the relationship between images, video, and the people viewing those images. She explored computer vision and natural language processing to understand text-to-image relationships. In one project, given a captioned image, the convolutional neural network could determine which words (e.g., "woman talking on phone" or "The farther vehicle") corresponded to which part of the image. This tool allows users to edit or synthesize realistic imagery using only natural language (e.g., "delete the garbage truck from this photo" or "make an image with three boys chasing a shaggy dog"). Her web page at `www.tamaraberg.com/` has available some data sets. She also coordinates the project Exact Street to Shop (`http://tamaraberg.com/street2shop/`), which matches a real-world garment item to the same item in an online shop. This is an extremely challenging task because of visual differences between real photos and online shop photos. The authors collected a new data set for this application containing 404,683 shop photos collected from 25 different online retailers and 20,357 street photos, providing a total of 39,479 items. The results are available at `http://arxiv.org/pdf/1608.03914.pdf`.

Ryan Kiros, from the University of Toronto, developed a multimodal neural language model for natural language that can be conditioned on other modalities. Unlike other approaches to generating image descriptions, this model makes no use of templates, structured models, or syntactic trees. Instead, it relies on word representations learned from millions of words and conditions the model on high-level image features learned from deep neural networks.

Lassner et al. in "A Generative Model of People in Clothing" (`http://files.is.tue.mpg.de/classner/gp`) proposed a model capable of generating images of people in clothing in a full-body setting. The authors learn generative models from a large image database, dealing with high variance in human pose, shape, and appearance. The authors split the generating process in two parts: semantic segmentation of the body and clothing and then a conditional model on the resulting segments that creates realistic images.

Researchers from MIT's Computer Science and Artificial Intelligence Laboratory (CSAIL) have demonstrated an algorithm that has effectively learned how to predict sound. When shown a silent video clip of an object being hit, the algorithm can produce a sound for the hit that is realistic enough to fool human viewers. This "Turing test for sound" represents much more than just a clever computer trick. Researchers envision future versions of similar algorithms being used to automatically produce sound effects for movies and TV shows, as well as to help robots better understand objects' properties. See more information at `http://news.mit.edu/2016/artificial-intelligence-produces-realistic-sounds-0613`.

They trained a sound-producing algorithm with 1,000 videos of 46,000 sounds that represent various objects being hit, scraped, and prodded with a drumstick. These videos were submitted to a CNN that deconstructed the sounds and analyzed their pitch and loudness. The algorithm looked at the sound properties of each frame of that video and matched them to the most similar sounds in the database.

In a recent work, Zhou et al. proposed a method of generating sound given visual input and generating raw waveform samples given input video frames; see "Visual to Sound: Generating Natural Sound for Videos in the Wild" (`https://arxiv.org/abs/1712.01393`).

8.8 Other Applications

Here are some other applications:

- Google AI Experiments (`https://aiexperiments.withgoogle.com/`) has several cool experiments to play, from a Pictionary game to music generation to image autocompletion.

- Alex Champandard (https://github.com/alexjc) used CNNs to generate textures with a technique he called random neural networks, capable of generating high-quality images based on pure noise and some pretraining.

- Mario Klingemann (http://mario-klingemann. tumblr.com/) is an active researcher who is into applying generative neural networks to image and art.

- A work (https://arxiv.org/pdf/1604.00449.pdf) by Choy et al. uses a combination of CNNs to transfer knowledge from two objects to create new object representations based on a template set; see Figure 8-3.

Figure 8-3. *3D Style transfer (source:* https://people.cs.umass.edu/ kalo/papers/ShapeSynthesis_Analogies/2014_st_preprint.pdf*)*

- Liao et al. propose a technique (https://arxiv.org/ pdf/1705.01088.pdf) for visual attribute transfer across images with different appearances but similar perceptually semantic structures. They call the technique *deep image analogy* where a coarse-to-fine strategy is used to compute the nearest-neighbor field for generating the results. They applied it to style/ texture transfer, color/style swap, sketch/painting to photo, and time lapse.

- A conference on applications of AI in creative industries (`http://events.nucl.ai/`) is held annually.

- The blog post at `www.subsubroutine.com/sub-subroutine/2016/11/12/painting-like-van-gogh-with-convolutional-neural-networks` has a tutorial on how to implement style transfer with TensorFlow.

- Recently the script of an entire movie, *Sunspring*, was produced by a recurrent neural network feed from the scripts of hundreds of sci-fi novels. There are some nonsensical conversations, but most of it is plausible and entertaining - video available at `https://www.youtube.com/watch?v=LY7x2Ihqjmc`.

- The blog post at `http://iq.intel.com/getting-creative-ai-and-machine-learning/` contains some projects regarding artistic machine learning.

- Google dreaming (`https://research.googleblog.com/2015/06/inceptionism-going-deeper-into-neural.html`) machines use CNNs to create fantasies. DeepDream is a computer vision program that uses a convolutional neural network to find and enhance patterns in images via algorithmic pareidolia, thus creating a dream-like hallucinogenic appearance in the deliberately over-processed images. There is a demo online at `https://deepdreamgenerator.com/`.

- The blog creativeai.net is an excellent showcase of recent AI projects related to art.

- Google Brain's creative AI project Magenta is dedicated to the creation of music and art through machine learning. It has released its first music track, which shows the potential of ANN to generate creative music.

- A researcher at Goldsmiths in London trained a variational auto-encoder deep learning model on all frames from the *Blade Runner* movie and then asked the network to reconstruct the video in its original sequence as well as other videos the network wasn't trained on. The pictures are not very sharp but still identifiable; you can imagine it as a compression algorithm with a compression rate of 1:1000.

- Researchers at NYU trained a recurrent neural network on scripts from movies including *Ghostbusters*, *Interstellar*, and *The Fifth Element*, and asked the network to generate a novel screenplay. The result is a set of somewhat plausible expression.

- In `http://arxiv.org/abs/1606.03073`, the authors used deep neural networks to invert face sketches and synthesize photorealistic face images. They first constructed a semisimulated data set containing a large number of computer-generated face sketches with different styles and corresponding face images by expanding existing unconstrained face data sets.

- Matthias Bethge's research group demonstrated (https://arxiv.org/abs/1604.08610) that convolutional neural networks can be used to learn representations of artistic styles from one painting and apply them to photographs. They showed that style can be learned from a single image and transferred to an entire video sequence. Two improvements were made. To ensure that style consistency extends over longer video sequences when certain regions might be temporarily occluded, the authors used long-term motion estimates. In addition, a multipass algorithm processed the video several times and alternated in the forward and backward directions to remove artifacts at image boundaries; see the videos at https://vimeo.com/167126162 and https://vimeo.com/175540110.

- Political Speech Generation (https://arxiv.org/abs/1601.03313) is using a language model for grammar and a topic model for textual consistency trained on U.S. congressional floor debate transcripts; the author was able to automatically generate speeches with either a supportive or opposing opinion on a particular topic.

- Deep Completion (http://bamos.github.io/2016/08/09/deep-completion/) has a good tutorial on adversarial neural networks for image completion.

- There are several machine learning online courses for artists; the most popular is from the New York University (https://www.kadenze.com/courses/machine-learning-for-musicians-and-artists/info).

- Check out `https://arxiv.org/pdf/1705.01908.pdf`, which is about generating cartoons from descriptions, or sketches, using generative neural networks.

- The authors of `https://arxiv.org/pdf/1705.05823.pdf` applied a method to speed rendering of high-resolution (HR) images from low-resolution (LR) ones. This is a crucial process for high-definition television streaming and medical and satellite imaging (which is usually bandwidth and computationally expensive). The algorithm produces files 2.5× smaller than JPEG and JPEG 2000, 2× smaller than WebP, and 1.7× smaller than BPG. The codec is designed to be lightweight; it can encode or decode the Kodak data set in about 10ms per image on a GPU. The architecture is an auto-encoder featuring pyramidal analysis, an adaptive coding module, and regularization of the expected code length. They also supplemented their approach with adversarial training specialized toward use in a compression setting. This enables you to produce visually pleasing reconstructions for very low bit rates.

- Pix2code (`https://uizard.io/research#pix2code`) is a new tool from startup UIzard that creates a system that lets a computer look at a screenshot of a web page and generate the underlying code that would produce that page. The approach can generate code for the iOS and Android operating systems with an accuracy of 77 percent. In other words, it gets the underlying code right four times out of five.

- Microsoft updated its smart camera app for iOS device, Microsoft Pix (https://www.microsoft.com/en-us/research/product/microsoftpix/), with new features that overlay artistic filters on top of user photos. It uses DL to browse large data sets of classic paintings to learn features of a given style of painting. The results are interesting and fun to play with, especially for sharing on social media. The Microsoft Pix team has also planned to feature social shares from the app with tags of #PixStyling on its Instagram profile.

- Amazon's Lab126 demonstrated (https://www.technologyreview.com/s/608668/amazon-has-developed-an-ai-fashion-designer/) it could use GANs to generate novel fashion items that are consistent with a certain target style to provide inspiration for future fashion designers.

- DeepMind and Blizzard released the StarCraft II Learning Environment (SC2LE), as shown at https://deepmind.com/blog/deepmind-and-blizzard-open-starcraft-ii-ai-research-environment/, to accelerate AI research focused on reinforcement learning and multi-agent systems. It includes a Blizzard ML API to hook into the game (environment, state, actions, traces), up to a half-million anonymized game replays, a Python-based RL environment, and a few simple RL-based mini-games to allow performance benchmarking. The game is particularly interesting because it requires long-term planning and multi-agent collaboration with potentially different subgoals.

- Unity launched Unity machine learning agents
  (https://blogs.unity3d.com/2017/09/19/
  introducing-unity-machine-learning-agents/),
  which enable the creation of games and simulations
  using the Unity Editor. These serve as environments
  where intelligent agents can be trained using
  reinforcement learning, neuroevolution, or other
  machine learning methods through a simple-to-use
  Python API.

CHAPTER 9

Other Applications

The range of deep learning applications goes well beyond the ones mentioned in previous chapters. This chapter will give an overview of other applications relevant for business. DL is already incorporated into many services and products, including customer service, finance, legal, sales, quality, pricing, and production.

At the same time, cloud computing and storage, the proliferation of the myriad of data sensors driving the Internet of Things (IoT), the quantified self, and the pervasive use of mobile devices are all unleashing disruptive forces from the technological and economical sides. Machine learning will allow extreme context and personalization, making it possible to treat each customer and each problem as unique. It will also be key to solving the complex problems companies face in optimizing operations and forecasting, which is the ideal scenario for machine learning to proliferate.

Machine learning will make everything programmatic, from advertising to customer experience, and will allow companies to build better applications that interact with things people create such as pictures, speech, text, and other messy things. This permits companies to create products that interact naturally with humans.

Three components are required to build machine learning products: training data (supervised or unsupervised), software/hardware, and talent. As software is commercialized and hardware is easily available on-premise, the critical components are talent and data, as well as the processes to use them in the organization.

© Armando Vieira, Bernardete Ribeiro 2018
A. Vieira and B. Ribeiro, *Introduction to Deep Learning Business Applications for Developers*,
https://doi.org/10.1007/978-1-4842-3453-2_9

9.1 Anomaly Detection and Fraud

An *anomaly*, or *outlier*, is a data point that is significantly different from the remaining data distribution and is unlikely to be part of it. Anomaly detection is applied in network intrusion detection, credit card fraud detection, sensor network fault detection, medical diagnosis, and numerous other fields [CBK09].

The models to deal with anomaly detection can be classified into three categories.

- Pure classification models (prediction of the likelihood of a fraud event based on past events)

- Novelty detection (detection of abnormal patterns)

- Network analysis (identification of coordinated unusual events that individually look legitimate)

Traditional methods of data analysis have long been used to detect fraud, namely, through knowledge discovery in databases (KDD), data mining, machine learning, and statistics. Simple evaluation of first-order statistics, such as averages, quantiles, performance metrics, or probability distributions, is normally used as the first line of detection. Time-series analysis, unsupervised clustering such as k-means, and classification of patterns and associations among groups of data as well as matching algorithms to detect anomalies in transactional behavior of users constitute make up the second line of defense.

A typical approach in anomaly detection is the reconstruction error of a data point, which is the error between the original data point and its reconstruction; this is used as an anomaly score. Principal component analysis (PCA) is a common method used for this approach where the distance between the first observation and the reconstruction from the first *n* PCA eigenvectors can be used as a measure of how anomalous the observation is.

However, most of these traditional approaches lack flexibility to adapt to a changing environment - as in the case of fraud detection. DNN methods have the ability to learn suspicious patterns in a supervised or unsupervised way.

In supervised learning, normally a subsample of data is taken and manually classified as either fraudulent or nonfraudulent. This is required to make the classifier less biased as the majority of events are normal or nonfraudulent—typically more than 99 percent and sometimes 99.99 percent. There are three types of unsupervised techniques.

- *Density-based methods*: In this method, you fit a density model, like mixture of Gaussians, and identify anomalies by locating points that do not fit in the distribution (see Figure 9-1).

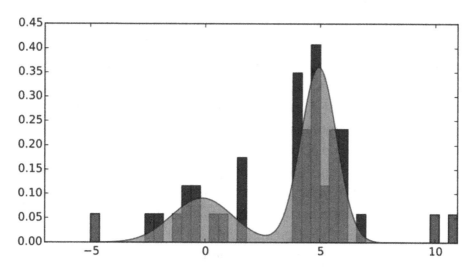

Figure 9-1. *Anomaly detection with density estimation (source:*
https://www.slideshare.net/agramfort/anomalynovelty-
detection-with-scikitlearn)

- *Kernel methods*: You smooth the data from a kernel and identify the points that are outside the smoothing. A typical approach is OneClassSVM.

- *Clustering*: This is like nearest neighbors. A point is an outlier when it is too far from any cluster.

All these types of detection are only able to detect frauds similar to those that have occurred previously and have been classified by a human. Detecting a novel type of fraud may require the use of an unsupervised machine learning algorithm.

Deep learning is well suited to dealing with these unbalanced data sets (the overwhelming majority of transactions are nonfraudulent) since you can pretrain the network with all (unlabeled) data. A softmax supervised layer can be applied to the last layer but using a balanced data set.

Generative adversarial networks can also be used for anomaly detection and one-shot learning as they require weakly supervision. For instance, Mishra et al. used a simple but powerful technique based on a conditional variational auto-encoder (`https://arxiv.org/pdf/1709.00663.pdf`). A variational auto-encoder is a graphical model to learn the distribution of the hidden latent representations z in respect to that of the data x. A conditional variational auto-encoder maximizes the variational lower bound of the conditional likelihood p(x|c), which helps to generate samples having the desired properties (encoded by the category c). The reconstruction error can then be assigned to each category, and new categories can be generated by one-shot learning.

Stacked auto-encoders (SAEs) can be used for hierarchical dimension reduction, thus obtaining abstract and more representative features from data. An approach based on deep neural networks to model anomaly detection was proposed by [ZCLZ16]; they called it a *deep structured energy-based model* (DSEBM) , where the energy function is the output of a deterministic deep neural network with structure. The model handles static, sequential, and spatial data. The novelty is that the model architecture adapts to the data structure thus matching, or outperforming, other competing methods.

Schreyer et al. proposed a method of detecting anomalies using deep auto-encoder networks (https://arxiv.org/pdf/1709.05254.pdf). The trained networks' reconstruction error regularized by the individual attribute probabilities is interpreted as a highly adaptive anomaly assessment. This results in a substantial increase in the detection precision of anomalies compared with a strong baseline.

9.1.1 Fraud Prevention

Fraud represents one of the biggest losses for banks and insurers, accounting for up to $1.7 billion in annual losses in the United States. Fraud is vast, complex, and a very hard problem that deals with the ever-changing and more sophisticate schemes that are targeting these organizations.

Most current approaches to detect fraud are largely static and rely on patterns derived from a subset of historical transactions. Banks basically look at transactional data to validate whether a given transaction is valid based on a set of hard rules, heuristics learned from past events, and machine learning methods to detect how likely a specific transaction is to be illegitimate. For credit card payments, these models typically can uplift fraud ratios from 1:10000 to 1:100. However, first-time fraud, which has no known signature, is almost always missed. Coordinated (network) types of fraud are also hard to spot, as each transaction looks legitimate. In insurance, the problem is even harder because more intermediaries are involved and more elaborated fraudulent options exist.

Profiling (also known as *behavior description*) attempts to characterize the typical behavior of an individual, group, or population. For instance, "What is the typical cell phone usage of a customer segment?" This question may not be easy to answer as it might require a complex description of night and weekend calls, international usage, roaming charges, text minutes, and so on. Behavior can apply to an entire segment or be at the level of small groups or even individuals. Profiling is often used to establish behavioral norms for anomaly detection such as monitoring for intrusions or fraud. For example, if the purchases a person typically makes on a credit card are known, you can determine whether a new charge on the card fits that profile or not and create a score alarm. However, the number of false positives is usually high.

Another technique that deals with fraud and security is link prediction. It attempts to predict connections between nodes (objects of people) in a graph by suggesting a link on these nodes and possibly estimating the strength of the link. Link prediction is common in social networking systems. For example, for recommending movies to customers, you can think of a graph between customers and the movies they've watched or rated. Within the (bi-partied) graph, the algorithms find relations that do not exist between customers and movies but that are likely.

A recent work from Shaabani et al. (`http://arxiv.org/abs/1508.03965`) showed that graph analysis was effective in predicting violent criminal gang activity in Chicago by identifying and putting on preventive observance undetected individuals strongly related to offenders.

An et al. used a variational auto-encoder (VAE) for an anomaly detection method using the reconstruction probability from the VAE (`http://dm.snu.ac.kr/static/docs/TR/SNUDM-TR-2015-03.pdf`). This reconstruction probability takes into account subtler correlations in the data, making it a better anomaly score than the reconstruction error, which is normally used by the AE and PCA. Since VAEs are generative models, they allow you to understand the characteristics that are behind the anomaly.

9.1.2 Fraud in Online Reviews

Fraud is also becoming common in online reviews. Fake reviews are perpetrated by businesses writing them or purchasing reviewers to write them to raise the popularity of their products or downgrade the competition. It is crucial for e-commerce to identify and remove these reviews to maintain customers' trust. Fake reviews can account for as much as 80 percent of total reviews. Various features can be used for fraud detection such as ratings, reviews, timestamps, and correlations. The problem can be characterized as this: given a set of users and products and timestamped ratings, compute a suspiciousness score for each user. Most algorithms use a temporal approach to detecting ratings fraud by catching products that receive a large number of positive or negative reviews in a short time, detected through the sudden increase in fraudulent reviews to bias the popularity or defame their competitors. Another approach is based on analyzing the rating distributions to find users who rate products very differently from other users.

This problem can be framed in a Bayesian approach, which is a natural choice to establish a good trade-off between users with extreme rating distributions versus users with a larger number of ratings. This gives a natural answer to this question: "Is a user with 20 ratings and an average rating of 5 more suspicious than a user with 100 ratings and an average rating of 4.8?" For a recent application of application to fake content detection see https://arxiv.org/pdf/1703.06959.pdf.

Fake reviews become even harder to detect as a recent work showed that neural networks can generate artificial reviews almost indistinguishable from humans; see https://arxiv.org/pdf/1708.08151.pdf. In this work, the authors used character-level LSTM and an encoder-decoder architecture to generate fake reviews of restaurants that few humans could identify as fake. Here are some examples of the fake reviews (notice that there is some style consistency; the review was written pretending to be a teenage user):

- "I love this place. I have been going here for years, and it is a great place to hang out with friends and family. I love the food and service. I have never had a bad experience when I am there."

- "I had the grilled veggie burger with fries!!!! Ohhhh and taste. Omgggg! Very flavorful! It was so delicious that I didn't spell it!!"

- "My family and I are huge fans of this place. The staff is super nice, and the food is great. The chicken is very good and the garlic sauce is perfect. Ice cream topped with fruit is delicious too. Highly recommended!"

9.2 Security and Prevention

As information is being digitalized, companies are becoming more vulnerable to various types of attacks. Cybersecurity are intrusion detection are critical. Intrusion detection can also be helpful beyond detecting cyber-attacks in noticing abnormal system behavior to detect accidents or undesired conditions.

In 2016, Kaspersky recorded more than 69 million malicious code attacks and 261 million unique URLs were recognized as malicious by web antivirus components. Malicious code analysis and detection is a key problem in intrusion detection technology. The detection of malicious code is currently divided into two approaches: host-based and network-based. Machine learning can be effective in detecting malicious code through learning the characteristics of intrusive code in contrast with normal code. Long et al. [LCWJ15] reviewed a variety of feature extraction methods and machine learning methods in a variety of malicious code detection applications, including Naïve Bayes, decision trees, artificial neural networks, support vector machine, and so on. Although these methods achieved some success, feature extraction is not appropriate because the detection rate and the detection accuracy are not high and because the algorithms are complex.

Deep learning techniques have proved to be superior than shallow learning models (like SVMs) - see for instance `https://pdfs.semanticscholar.org/45ba/f042f5184d856b04040f14dd8e04aa7c11f6.pdf`. Models based on LSTM units have the capacity to model complex temporal dependencies. For a review on the applications of LSTM to detect credit card fraud, see `http://thirdworld.nl/credit-card-transactions-fraud-detection-and-machine-learning-modelling-time-with-lstm-recurrent-neural-networks`.

In `https://www.technologyreview.com/s/601955/machine-visions-achilles-heel-revealed-by-google-brain-researchers/`, Kurakin et al. showed that adversarial examples (input data that is almost indistinguishable from real data) can easily fool image classifiers. Previous studies assumed direct access to the ML classifier, such that adversarial examples were fine-grained per-pixel modifications fed directly to the model. This work instead showed that adversarial examples created to fool a pretrained ImageNet Inception network were also misclassified when the images were perceived through a cell phone camera.

In `http://homepages.inf.ed.ac.uk/csutton/publications/leet08sbayes.pdf`, the authors explored the use of machine learning to subvert spam filters.

Deep Instinct learns the characteristics common to all malware and self-updates. Deep Instinct uses convolutional neural networks (CNNs) trained against a labeled set of data—image pixels with a set of subject-matter metadata in the case of the online sites and binary executables in the case of Deep Instinct. It applies the same technique to executables.

In `https://people.csail.mit.edu/kalyan/AI2_Paper.pdf`, researchers from MIT and the machine learning startup PatternEx demonstrated an artificial intelligence platform called AI2 that predicts cyber-attacks better than existing systems by continuously incorporating input from human experts. AI2 can detect 85 percent of attacks, approximately three times better than previous benchmarks, while also reducing the number of false positives by a factor of 5.

9.3 Forecasting

Several machine learning algorithms were developed for forecasting, such as multilayer perceptrons, Bayesian neural networks, K-nearest neighbor regression, support vector regression, and Gaussian processes. Deep architectures allow the emergence of complex models that can go beyond traditional statistical approaches like autoregressive integrated moving average (ARIMA).

Energy Forecasting is an essential problem because excess demand can cause disruptions while excess supply is wasted. In an industry worth more than $1 trillion annually in the United States, every marginal improvement can have a huge impact. Energy loads are interesting for ML because of the availability of large data sets. Using data from the Kaggle competition called Global Energy Forecasting Competition in 2012, Busseti et al. used a DL algorithm for energy demand forecasting to predict energy loads across different network grid areas, using only time and temperature data. The data included hourly demand for four-and-a-half years from 20 different geographic regions and similar hourly temperature readings from 11 zones. Because of the huge data set, they were able to implement complex nonlinear models without overfitting. They used a recurrent neural network, achieving an RMSE of 530kWh/h and 99.6 percent correlation to the test data, which was almost half the error rate of a feed-forward neural network. They also used a kernelized local regression in the input data, based on the squared exponential distance to centroids.

For a comparison of several deep learning algorithms, as well as some traditional ones, for energy forecasting, see `https://www.jesuslago.com/wp-content/uploads/forecastingPrices.pdf`.

Kelly et al. used a model (`https://arxiv.org/pdf/1507.06594.pdf`) for an energy disaggregation appliance in electricity consumption from a single meter measuring the home's electricity demand. They used three deep neural network architectures to energy disaggregation: a form of recurrent networks with LSTM, denoising auto-encoders, and a network as a regression in time.

See `https://arxiv.org/pdf/1703.00785.pdf` for an overview of current approaches of deep learning for load disaggregation and energy forecasting.

Weather forecasting is a complex problem using many measurements from previous conditions in the format of a space-time mesh. Current prediction models are based on huge grid-based finite-element method calculations. Large sets of fluid dynamics in differential equations are solved iteratively, and the results are used as initial conditions for the next step. This is computationally extremely expensive, and the predictive accuracy is limited as errors multiply for each predictive time step. Xi et al. used a combination of 3D convolutional neural networks with neural networks with STM cells to build accurate forecasting models, using up to 100 million parameters, trainable from end to end. The weather prediction, up to two days ahead, can take less than 0.1 seconds on a laptop, achieving a better accuracy than models that need several hours of computations on a supercomputer; see `http://arxiv.org/pdf/1506.04214v2.pdf`.

Epelbaum et al. (`https://hal.archives-ouvertes.fr/hal-01598905/document`) applied some deep learning network architectures to forecast the traffic patterns in Paris. These algorithms were designed to handle historic speeds of car data to predict road traffic data.

The real-time simulation of fluid and smoke is a hard problem in computer graphics, where state-of-the-art approaches require large compute resources, making real-time applications often impractical. Tompson et al. proposed a data-driven approach based on neural networks to obtain both fast and highly realistic simulations; see their work and some videos at `http://cims.nyu.edu/schlacht/CNNFluids.htm`. They used convolutional networks from a training set of simulations using a semisupervised learning method to minimize long-term velocity divergence. The results are impressive.

Uber uses recurrent neural networks (`https://eng.uber.com/neural-networks/`) to predict demand for its services and cut operating costs. The model uses an LSTM RNN and is based in TensorFlow and Keras. The company trained a model using five years of data from numerous U.S. cities. The resulting RNN has good predictive abilities when tested across a corpus of data consisting of trips taken across multiple U.S. cities over the course of seven days before, during, and after major holidays like Christmas, though it can predict some spikes because of their rarity. This system is significantly better at dealing with spiky holiday days, and it slightly improves the accuracy on other days such as MLK Day and Independence Day.

9.3.1 Trading and Hedge Funds

The investment management industry is following closely recent advances in AI. Established asset managers and hedge funds such as BlackRock, Bridgewater, and Schroders are investing in this technology to build investment platforms that possibly outperform humans. No matter how futuristic this goal may look, recent achievements in AI are pushing the limits of what is considered possible.

Neural networks are a research area long abandoned by quantitative fund managers because of the nontransparent—and often poor—investment decisions experimented with in the past. However, things have changed drastically in recent years. Deep learning is proving capable of solving the hardest puzzles that humans struggle with and of devising complex strategies to win the game of Go or poker. DL neural networks may be the first machines called *intuitive*.

For hedge funds, these superhuman cognitive capabilities could represent a clear advantage in extracting insights from the intricacies of the financial markets. AHL, the quantitative arm of the hedge fund manager the Man Group, is among those now exploring whether deep learning can be applied to investing. Euclidean, a New York money manager, is also exploring its possibilities.

Neural networks and deep learning make up just one area of the multifaceted AI world. But it's one thing to beat a game with clear rules and fully observable states. Markets are more complex to understand. Many of the new AI-focused hedge funds will probably fail, but the feeling that the investment industry is on the cusp of a radical transformation is inescapable.

Sirignano (https://arxiv.org/pdf/1601.01987v7.pdf) used a spatial neural network to model the joint distribution of the best bid and ask price at the time of the next state change. The model also considers the joint distribution of the best bid and ask prices after variations to predict changes in limit-order books. He used a neural network with 4 layers and 250 neurons per hidden layer, while the spatial neural network had 50 unities. Dropout was used to prevent overfitting. The model was trained on more than 489 stocks from 2014 to 2015 using 50TB of data described by 200 features: the price and size of the limit-order book across the first 50 nonzero bids and ask levels. He could predict the order book one second ahead and also the time of the next bid/ask change, claiming a reduction of the error rate by 10 percent compared with logistic regression.

Fehrer and Feuerriegel [FF15] used a recursive auto-encoder to predict German stock returns based on text from financial news headlines. They used an English ad hoc news announcement data set (8,359 headlines) for the German market covering news from 2004 to 2011. They reached an accuracy of 56 percent, which was a considerable improvement over random forest (which has a 53 percent accuracy).

Xiong et al. predicted (`https://arxiv.org/pdf/1512.04916.pdf`) the daily volatility of the S&P 500, as estimated from open, high, low, and close prices. They used a single LSTM hidden layer consisting of one LSTM block. For inputs they used daily S&P 500 returns and volatilities. They also included 25 domestic Google trends, covering sectors and major areas of the economy. They used the Adam method with 32 samples per batch and used the mean absolute percent error (MAPE) as the objective loss function. They set the maximum lag of LSTM to include ten successive observations. As a result, their LSTM method outperformed the GARCH, Ridge, and LASSO techniques.

In 2016, Heaton et al. attempted (`https://arxiv.org/abs/1605.07230`) to create a portfolio that would outperform the biotech index IBB. They had the goal of tracking the index with a few stocks and low validation error. They also tried to beat the index by being anticorrelated during periods of large drawdowns. They didn't directly model the covariance matrix; rather, it was trained in the deep architecture fitting procedure, which allows for nonlinearities. They used auto-encoding with regularization and ReLUs. Their auto-encoder has one hidden layer with five neurons. For training they used weekly return data for the component stocks of IBB from 2012 to 2016. They auto-encoded all stocks in the index and evaluated the difference between each stock and its auto-encoded version. They kept the ten most "communal" stocks that were the most similar to the auto-encoded versions. They also kept a varying number of other stocks, where the number was chosen with cross-validation. For results, they showed the tracking error as a function of the number stocks included in the portfolio but didn't seem to compare against traditional methods. They also replaced index drawdowns with positive returns and found portfolios that track this modified index.

9.4 Medicine and Biomedical

Deep learning is already having a strong impact in the healthcare industry because of the increase in capacity and accuracy of learning algorithms and because of the wide availability of large sets of healthcare data, made possible through the digitalization of (structured and unstructured) medical records, as well as personal genetic data and other personalized data originating from mobile devices.

However, the application of ML technology for medicine has a long history of failures. Among other things, a particularly tricky aspect is the variability between individuals, which causes more simplistic machine learning algorithms to miss the patterns and give wrong answers, which is something particularly sensitive in an area with low tolerance for error.

However, as Dave Channin correctly stated, a big obstacle in applying ML to medicine is to have a reliable source of "truth" to train the machines. What is the real interpretation of a given image? What is the cause behind a set of uncommon symptoms? If it is a rare disease, statistics will not help, and these symptoms may easily fool the machine to flag more common cases. Crowdsourcing symptoms can be a solution, but it's trickier as it requires specialized information to make a wise decision. The problem is even more complex because of the variability of equipment and conditions of the diagnostics. Finally, there is the issue dealing with heavy regulatory entities that demand interpretability. DNNs are black boxes, so it is hopeless to ask a machine for explanations after reaching a certain conclusion. To our comfort, consensus among human experts on complex situations is also rare.

9.4.1 Image Processing Medical Images

Having achieved human-level performance on object identification and facial recognition, deep learning has a great potential in applications in medical imaging processing, an area where subjective interpretation is common and context is key to disambiguate several possible explanations.

Some companies are applying DL to recognize cancer in medical images such as X-rays, and many automated image recognition tools are already used in hospitals. Diagnoses based on the processing of medical images are, however, just a tiny fraction of the potential of DL in the medical sector. There are several challenges however, like the lack of training images, the lack of comprehensive annotation, skewed distribution toward rare diseases, and nonstandardized annotation metrics.

More information about biomedical image data sets is available at https://medium.com/the-mission/up-to-speed-on-deep-learning-in-medical-imaging-7ff1e91f6d71.

Deep learning algorithms are today more precise than humans in Alzheimer disease detection, bone fracture detection, and breast cancer diagnostics, as shown in Figure 9-1.

These are some startups working on deep learning for medical imaging:

- Enlitic uses systems on medical images and other patient records to help doctors diagnose and treat complex diseases. It raised $10 million in October 2015.

- Lumiata uses an extensive databases of medical records to populate a knowledge graph of medical history. It recently raised $10 million.

- Synapsify builds applications that semantically read and learn from written content similar to humans for accelerated discovery.

- The Google DeepMind research project with the Moorfields Eye Hospital in London is working toward the early detection of macular degeneration. This work involves analyzing optical coherence tomography scans of the retina.

- Massachusetts General Hospital in Boston launched its Clinical Data Science Center to create a hub focused on using AI technologies to diagnose and treat disease. A number of startups have set out to tackle this problem, but this is a heavyweight healthcare provider making this announcement, with Nvidia as a founding technology partner.

- DL is helping the blind and visually impaired to "see." A recent project from Microsoft presented a new vision project named Seeing AI (https://www.youtube.com/watch?v=R2mC-NUAmMk), which uses computer vision and NLP to describe a person's surroundings, read text, answer questions, and identify emotions on people's faces. Baidu has a similar product called DuLight. Facebook is already making its content available to the blind and visual impaired.

- ML is also making it possible for paraplegics to regain some control and mobility based on a technology that reads brain activity and connects directly to the muscles, surpassing the damaged nerves' circuitry (https://www.physiology.org/doi/pdf/10.1152/physrev.00027.2016).

- iCarbonX has a near-term goal of predicting the onset of diseases from genomic, medical, and lifestyle data.

- Veritas Genetics, a company providing direct-to-consumer whole-genome sequencing and targeted screening for prenatal testing and breast cancer, made a move into AI by acquiring Curoverse, a bioinformatics company. Together, they are working on improving disease risk scoring and causality in genetics and diseases.

- Other companies in the field include BayLabs, Imagia, MD.ai, AvalonAI, Behold.ai, and Kheiron Medical.

DL can be applied to analyze not only images but also text (medical records), millions of research and medical studies on drug effectiveness and drug interaction, and even genetics to create tailored hypotheses and accurate diagnostic and personalized treatment. Watson for Medical is the most well-known technology, but there are many startups working in this area. See, for example, `http://www.sciencedirect.com/science/article/pii/S1532046417300710`.

Some companies, like Apixio, analyze text by mining medical records and apply that to helping insurance providers classify which of their patients have which diseases. That classification process, normally done manually by humans, involves matching written diagnoses with a set of medical numerical codes.

A pathologist's report is critical in assessing and devising a procedure to treat cancer. One of the inputs is the patient's biological tissue sample, made of several slides at a resolution up to 30,000×30,000 pixels that goes up to a cell-level resolution, μm. This is a complex and time-consuming task that requires years of training.

However, there can be substantial variability in the identification of tissue with cancer cells by different pathologists for the same patient, leading to misdiagnoses. Agreement in diagnosis for some forms of breast cancer can be as low as 50 percent and similarly low for prostate cancer.

The Camelyon 2017 Challenge is an international competition designed to assess the quality of algorithms in the localization of breast cancer that has spread (metastasized) to lymph nodes adjacent to the breast. In the latest version of this competition, deep learning algorithms achieved a precision level surpassing humans; see `https://camelyon17.grand-challenge.org/results/`. The detailed explanation is presented in `https://arxiv.org/pdf/1606.05718.pdf`. The authors obtained an area under the receiver operating curve (AUC) of 0.97 for the task of whole slide image classification and a score of 0.89 for the tumor localization task. A pathologist independently reviewed the same images, obtaining a whole slide image classification AUC of 0.96 and a tumor localization score of 0.73. These results demonstrate the power of using deep learning to produce significant improvements in the accuracy of pathological diagnoses. Figure 9-2 summarizes the impact of deep learning in medical image processing.

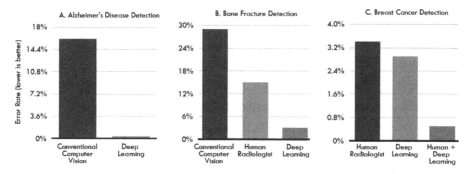

Figure 9-2. *Impact of DL in medical image (source: ARK report)*

9.4.2 Omics

In genomics, proteomics or metabolomics genetic information (transcriptome and proteome) data is composed of a set of raw sequences, usually DNA or RNA. This data has become affordable to obtain because of the next-generation sequencing technology. In addition, protein contact maps, which present distances of amino acid pairs in their three-dimensional structure, and microarray gene expression data are easily available.

One of the most researched problems is secondary protein structure prediction or contact map of a protein. DNNs have been widely applied in protein structure prediction research. Chen et al. [CLN+16] applied MLP to microarray and RNA-to-sequence expression data to infer expressions of up to 21,000 target genes from only 1,000 landmark genes. Asgari et al. [AM15] adopted the skip-gram model (used on Word2vec) and showed that it could effectively learn a distributed representation of biological sequences with general use for many "omics" applications, including protein family classification.

Gene expression regulation (including splice junctions or RNA binding proteins) and protein classification are also actively investigated. CNNs can be trained to simultaneously predict closely related factors. One-dimensional CNNs have also been used with biological sequence data. Alipanahi et al. proposed CNN-based approaches for transcription factor binding site prediction and 164 cell-specific DNA accessibility multitask prediction, respectively, for disease-associated genetic variant identification. Zhou et al. [ZT15] proposed a CNN-based algorithmic framework (DeepSEA) to learn transcription factor binding and disease-associated genetic variants based on the predictions.

Sønderby et al. [SSN+15] applied bidirectional RNNs with LSTM hidden units and a one-dimensional convolution layer to learn representations from amino acid sequences and classify the subcellular locations of proteins. Lee et al. [LBP+16] applied RNNs to microRNA identification and target prediction and obtained state-of-the-art results.

Transcriptomics analysis exploits variation in the abundance of various types of transcripts (messenger RNA, long non-coding RNA, microRNA, etc.) to gather a range of functional information, from splicing code to biomarkers of various diseases. Transcriptomics data is often obtained from different types of platforms (various microarray platforms, sequencing platforms, etc.) that differ by the gene set measured and the method of signal detection. Many factors contribute to the variability of gene expression data. Thus, normalization is needed even for single-platform analysis. Cross-platform analysis requires normalization techniques, which can be a major challenge. DNNs are particularly well suited for cross-platform analysis because of their high generalization ability. They are also well equipped to handle some of the other major issues with gene expression data, such as the size of the data sets and the need for dimension reduction and selectivity/invariance.

While in surgery only 36 percent of the tasks performed could be replaced by AI in the next years, for radiologists this number could be as high as 66 percent - source ARK-Invest.

Machine learning techniques can be used to spot different types of anomalies, like breast cancer, skin cancer, and eye disease, from medical images. A team from Stanford University, led by Andrew Ng, has shown (`https://www.technologyreview.com/s/608234/the-machines-are-getting-ready-to-play-doctor/`) that an ML model can identify heart arrhythmias from an electrocardiogram (ECG) better than an expert. The team trained a DL algorithm to identify different types of irregular heartbeats in ECG data. Some irregularities can lead to serious health complications, including sudden cardiac death, but the signal can be difficult to detect, so patients are often asked to wear an ECG sensor for several weeks. Even then it can be difficult for a doctor to distinguish between irregularities that may be benign and ones that could require treatment. They collected 30,000 30-second clips from patients with different forms of arrhythmia. To assess the accuracy of their algorithm, the team compared its performance to that of five different cardiologists on 300 undiagnosed clips. A panel of three expert cardiologists provide a ground-truth judgment.

9.4.3 Drug Discovery

Recent advances in machine learning have made significant contributions to drug discovery. Deep neural networks in particular have provided significant boosts in predictive power when inferring the properties and activities of small molecule compounds. Mamoshina et al. (https://www.ncbi.nlm.nih.gov/pubmed/28029644) used generative adversarial auto-encoders (AAE) for generating novel molecular fingerprints for drug discovery. They used a seven-layer AAE architecture with the latent middle layer serving as a discriminator. As an input and output, the AAE used a vector of binary fingerprints and concentration of the molecule. In the latent layer, they also introduced a neuron responsible for growth inhibition percentage, which when negative indicated the reduction in the number of tumor cells after the treatment. They trained the AAE with NCI-60 cell line assay data for 6,252 compounds profiled on an MCF-7 cell line. The output of the AAE was used to screen 72 million compounds in PubChem and select candidate molecules with potential anticancer properties.

Computer Assisted Drug Design (CADD) has a huge potential but also some challenges, either on structure-based drug design (protein 3D structures with drugs bound) or on ligand-based drug design (chemistry and quantitative structure-activity relationships [QSAR]). Over the past few decades, many approved drugs have resulted from significant CADD efforts in identifying and screening small molecules with specific biological activity.

However, biology is an extremely complex system, and CADD is only one of many steps to overcome the challenges of drug discovery. We may be still far from a world where computers discover drugs, test them virtually in a cloud of robotic assays, and get them to patients with a few clicks of a mouse. In silico, platforms for CADD can easily overfit and often fail to deliver on actual prospective projects. Instead of "software eats biotech," the reality of drug discovery today is that biology consumes everything. The primary failure mode for new drug candidates stems from a simple fact: human biology is massively complicated. Drug candidates that interfere with the wrong targets or systems can lead to bad outcomes ("off-target" toxicity). They can interfere with the right targets but with the wrong effects ("on-target" or mechanism-based toxicity). They are most often promiscuous and interact with lots of things, some known and many unknown. Beyond their target pharmacology, drugs interact with the human body in countless ways, rendering them ineffective or worse (absorption, distribution, metabolism, and excretion being four important ones). And, of critical importance, the biology might just not work at ameliorating a specific disease, improving mortality, or elevating quality of life. The wrong target is often picked to interrogate, which is a major cause of attrition in Phase 2 and beyond. Even more challenging, variation among patients (and, even more so, species!) in how biology manifests also leads to added complexity, both good (insightful) and bad (unfortunate). In fairness, even when drugs are approved, we don't know everything about them.

Several companies are using the computational capabilities of DNN and biomedical data available to speed up drug discovery *in sillico*. Discovery for a single drug can take decades and hundreds of millions of dollars, with a high rate of failure. Machine learning can speed up the process and rapidly discover new drugs in a fraction of the time and cost. There are many companies working in this area, like Recursion (https://www.recursionpharma.com/), Benevolent AI (http://benevolent.ai/), and Atomwise (www.atomwise.com/), including the big pharmaceuticals.

Deep Genomics (https://www.deepgenomics.com/), a company led by Brendan Frey, was able to train a neural network to decipher the code behind the noncoding regions of RNA. Basically, it considered longer sequences of nucleotics to train a deep network.

9.5 Other Applications

The following sections highlight some other applications.

9.5.1 User Experience

Deep learning is becoming the core technology to make possible a truly natural and frictionless user interaction with machines. Voice recognition is already at human-level accuracy, allowing voice, rather than the keyword, to be a natural way to interact with smartphones and other smart devices. This is already a reality in products like the personal assistant Amazon Echo or Google Home. These devices are designed for full voice interaction and answer questions in natural language. They also can be integrated with other home devices, creating better energy management and security systems.

DL will help reshape user experiences through interaction and personalization to blur the separation between humans and machines. Interfaces can be simplified, abstracted, or even completely hidden from the user. The traditional thinking of UX programmers (how to create scrolling pages, buttons, taps, and clicks) is based on an old paradigm. DL inputs allow a very natural interaction and personalization; see `https://techcrunch.com/2016/08/15/using-artificial-intelligence-to-create-invisible-ui/`.

Devices need to know more about us for invisible UI to become a reality. Contextual awareness today is somewhat limited. For example, when asking for directions via Google Maps, the system knows your location and will return a different result if you are in New York versus California.

But even with all the sensors and data, the machine needs to know more about us and what is going on in our world in order to create the experiences we really need. One solution is to combine the power of multiple devices/sensors to gather more information. But this usually narrows down and limits the user base—which is not an easy thing to sell to a client.

9.5.2 Big Data

The exponential growth of data, 80 percent of which is unstructured (such as social media, e-mail records, call logs, customer service, competitor, and partner pricing), allows companies to enhance prediction and explore hidden patterns. DL is particularly useful for dealing with unlabeled data because it makes extensive use of unsupervised methods.

Multimodal learning will allow people, for the first time, to combine text, voice, image, and even videos in a joint knowledge representation; this is a technology already implemented in image search. This will permit advanced queries such as "Show me something related to this image but in brighter colors or a slimmer shape" or even "Show me a movie that has a scene where a blond girl is kissing at sunset near the Eiffel Tower" or even "Show me the scene where there is loud noise from the street traffic."

Despite all the buzz around chatbots, they definitely will change the way users interact with content. A conversation is more natural than a query since it can contextualize the question through an iterative process. Also, it can be personalized for each customer, it can know more information about the customers, and, perhaps most important, it's a more natural interaction.

Google has recently launched an automatic reply option for Gmail accounts that will send replies based on three responses suggested by Google's AI; it works only for some messages. You also can use the suggested responses as starting points, editing or adding text as you like. Smart Reply is based on a DNN to predict whether an e-mail is one for which someone might write a brief reply.

9.6 The Future

Algorithms are evolving toward less traditional and unexpected tasks that we have reserved for humans. Examples include playing poker, dealing with negotiations, and even forging relationships. Training is evolving from being strictly supervised to a more high-level, weakly supervised and even unsupervised model. An example is teaching robots to execute complex tasks just by showing some examples. An example in reinforcement learning is where you feed the rules of the game and the algorithm discovers strategies by playing against itself.

An area where you can expect important improvements, unthinkable a few years ago, is negotiation. Most chatbots can already perform short conversations and do simple tasks such as booking a restaurant or a hair dresser with voice assistants. However, building machines that can have meaningful conversations with humans is probably beyond reach in the near future because it requires an understanding of the conversation and knowledge of the world.

The Facebook Artificial Intelligence Research (FAIR) team has published a paper (`https://arxiv.org/abs/1706.05125`) introducing dialogue agents with the ability to negotiate. The researchers have shown that it's possible for dialogue agents with differing goals to engage in start-to-finish negotiations with other bots or people while arriving at common decisions. The remarkable thing is that these bots can arrive at differing goals, solve conflicts, and then negotiate to come to a compromise.

Each agent is provided with its own value function that represents how much it cares about each type of item. As in life, neither agent knows the other agent's value function and must infer it from the dialogue. FAIR researchers created many such negotiation scenarios, always ensuring that it was impossible for both agents to get the best deal simultaneously.

Negotiation is simultaneously a linguistic problem and a reasoning problem, in which an intent must be formulated and then verbally realized. Such dialogues contain both cooperative and adversarial elements, requiring agents to understand and formulate long-term plans and generate utterances to achieve their goals.

Specifically, FAIR has developed a novel technique where an agent simulates a future conversation by rolling out a dialogue model to the end of the conversation so that an utterance with the maximum expected future reward can be chosen.

PART IV

Opportunities and Perspectives

CHAPTER 10

Business Impact of DL Technology

"I was a skeptic [about deep learning] for a long time, but the progress now is real. The results are real. It works."

—Marc Andreessen, American entrepreneur

The falling costs of computation and the ease of accessing cloud-managed clusters have democratized AI in a way we've never seen before. In the past, building a computer cluster to train a deep neural network was prohibitively expensive. You also needed someone with a PhD in mathematics to understand the academic research papers on subjects such as recurrent neural networks. Today, it's possible to run a cluster overnight to experiment with new algorithms for a few hundred dollars a month with a competent GPU-equipped PC.

AI has emerged from the labs and entered firmly into the business world with a tremendous impact on the automation of processes and services. For instance, an AI-powered CRM system could feed leads to sales reps in real time using algorithms designed to maximize the likelihood of a sale, based on breaking information about the customer, their company, and the sales rep.

© Armando Vieira, Bernardete Ribeiro 2018
A. Vieira and B. Ribeiro, *Introduction to Deep Learning Business Applications for Developers*,
https://doi.org/10.1007/978-1-4842-3453-2_10

Companies are pressed to build their own AI capabilities and teams and not rely on third-party consultants for this critical competency. AI cannot be seen as a one-shot process but rather a vital component in the strategy of business.

DL will affect profoundly every sector, including the automobile industry, robotics, drones, biotechnology, finance, or agriculture. According to ARK Invest's research, companies founded on deep learning will unlock trillions of dollars in productivity gains and add $17 trillion in market capitalization to global equities during the next two decades; see https://ark-invest.com/research/artificial-intelligence-revolution.

Here are some of the major predictions from https://ark-invest.com/research/artificial-intelligence-revolution:

- $17 trillion in market capitalization creation from deep learning companies by 2036

- $6 trillion in revenue from autonomous on-demand transportation by 2027

- $6 billion in revenue for deep learning processors in the data center by 2022, growing more than tenfold over 5 years

- $16 billion addressable market for diagnostic radiology

- $100 to $170 billion in savings and profit from improved credit scoring

- $12 trillion in real GDP growth in the US from automation by 2035

Processor performance has improved roughly five orders of magnitude since Intel's original Pentium processor. But the performance of deep learning programs also depends on the amount of data used for training. Thanks to the Internet's size and scale, deep learning has thrived with access to very large data sets at a minimal cost. While the 1990 LeCun handwriting reader used approximately 10,000 samples collected from the U.S. Postal Service, the 2009 ImageNet data set contains more than 10 million examples of high-resolution photographs. Also, Baidu's DeepSpeech is trained upon more than 10,000 hours of audio data compared to a few hundred hours in legacy data sets.

Neural nets themselves have become larger and more sophisticated, as measured by their number of free "parameters." Networks with a billion parameters are common nowadays. Larger networks allow for a more expressive capability to capture relations in the data. Today's deep learning networks have roughly ten million parameters, or four orders of magnitude more than LeCun's original handwriting reader (see Figure 10-1).

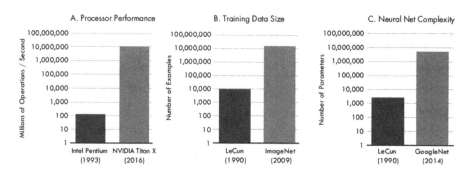

Figure 10-1. *Evolution of computational power and artificial neural networks*

10.1 Deep Learning Opportunity

Deep learning–powered AI is already transforming most industries. AI will fundamentally change and automate numerous functions within companies, from pricing, budget allocation, fraud detection, and security to marketing optimization. But for an organization to take full advantage of AI, it needs to be fully integrated across all different departments and functions; this will enable organizations to truly become customer-centric.

Deep learning is well suited for data-intensive activities such as advertising and click-through information. Most of the data will be collected by mobile phones, and a myriad of devices will deliver real-time georeferenced information. Multimodal learning will allow companies to integrate text, images, video, and sound with a unified representation.

The implications of DL technology applied to certain areas, like self-driving cars, are obvious, and its consequences could revolutionize transportation systems and car ownership. In other areas, the impact may not seem so obvious and immediate; however, as DL technology progress, many more industries will also be at risk of being disrupted. Some will be enumerated.

10.2 Computer Vision

Deep learning algorithms are a key tool for automating and accelerating the analysis of large data sets generated by a proliferation of data generated by sensors, including images.

Although the basic algorithms are the same, the way the information is used varies. Computer vision has wide applications in the following industries: automotive, sports and entertainment, consumer and mobile, robotics and machine vision, medical, and security and surveillance. Tractica estimates the potential market for these segments combined to be $35 billion.

However, few companies have the expertise and computing infrastructure to train and deploy machine vision products. Computer vision-as-a-service is now available through APIs from many industry players, such as Microsoft and Google. These services allow companies to offload image processing to the cloud for a fee per image. Services include classification, optical character recognition, facial detection, and logo detection. Compared to manual image reading by a service like Amazon's crowdsourced Mechanical Turk, these cloud-based APIs are roughly an order of magnitude cheaper.

10.3 AI Assistants

Probably the largest, and most immediate, impact of the GAIs supported by DNNs will not be in robotics but rather in customer service. Services such as sending a specific e-mail, a mobile push, or a customer pass for a specific shop or event could be automated in a near future and advanced analytics tools would even automate some support decisions processes. Contact centers deal with very mundane interactions that soon will be serviced through automated messaging such as chatbots and personal assistants. AI can help suggest how to deliver a conversation, user interests, and products. It can even use the data for secondary proposes, such as risk assessment based on previous interactions.

AI assistants are computer programs capable of human-level speech and comprehension. Algorithms that can converse with humans, understand needs, and help with tasks would be a boon to the quality of life and to global productivity. Until recently, such breakthroughs were confined to the realm of science fiction. But AI assistants became mainstream when Apple launched Siri in October 2011. Google followed in 2012, and Microsoft Cortana and Amazon Echo came next in 2014. Today, many other companies are racing to build AI assistants and chatbots that some believe will be larger than the app economy.

Voice interaction is already common in many devices and accounts for more than 20 percent of searches in Google. This is only possible because of the DL technology for voice recognition that is very accurate even in noisy environments (we have reached human-level accuracy) and that can capture (and adapt to) the voice nuances of each user. The extra accuracy gained by DL in voice recognition, which now reaches more than 96 percent, may seem only a small increment, but it makes all the difference from a user interface point of view; a single mistake may be enough to break a smooth and frictionless interaction.

Research firm Tractica estimates that the use of consumer AI assistants worldwide will grow 25 percent per year on average, from 390 million users in 2015 to 1.8 billion by the end of 2021. Users of enterprise AI assistants are expected to rise at a 33 percent annualized rate, from 155 million to 843 million, during the same time period, as shown in Figure 10-2. AI assistants generally fall into two camps: voice based and text based. Voice-based interfaces like Siri, Google Now, Cortana, and Alexa/Echo have seen solid adoption and usage. Text-based AI assistants are nascent and have yet to achieve mainstream adoption.

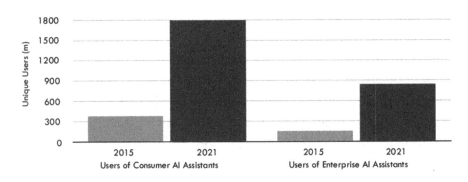

Figure 10-2. *Users of AI assistants (source: Tractica)*

As the smartphone market has matured, developers and investors have intensified their search for the next big platform. Messaging bots—AI assistants that operate primarily through text—could be the answer. Some of the reasons for the focus on messaging bots are the success of some companies such as WeChat in China (users can buy items and pay bills within the conversational app), the growth in users of and time spent in messaging apps, and the deep learning–related improvements in natural language processing.

Like AI, messaging bots can be narrow or general. Narrow messaging bots perform very specific tasks, such as replying to an e-mail, while in theory general messaging bots can perform any task, much like a personal assistant.

Narrow messaging bots already have been deployed successfully in real applications. The AI assistant Amy by x.ai, for example, can schedule meetings for individuals who do not have access to each other's calendars. Amy reads the host's calendar and suggests open time slots by writing and sending an e-mail to those invited. Upon receiving a reply, she can read and understand the e-mail, schedule a meeting, or suggest new time slots in response to conflicts. Google's Smart Reply can also read an e-mail and propose three responses. According to Google, more than 10 percent of its Inbox app's e-mail responses are sent via Smart Reply.

A natural home for messaging bots is inside messaging apps. In 2016, Microsoft, Facebook, and Kik all launched chatbot platforms for their respective messaging apps. As of July 2017, more than 11,000 bots have launched on Messenger and more than 20,000 on Kik. These bots have a range of functions, from ordering flowers to checking the weather and from recommending books to serving as a personal trainer.

10.4 Legal

As NLP capabilities increase, it's natural to expect a huge impact on lawyers, by automating tasks such as complex searches, automating semantic queries, or even drafting from scratch complete arguments based on evidence. At the same time, as machines get clever, the concepts of intentionality and ownership will become blurred. Questions like "Who should be made accountable for an accident with a self-driving car?" may be hard to answer: the car owner, the manufacturer, or the car itself?

There are, however, some limitations with the current approach to teach these machines.

- Learning algorithms are slow and require large amounts of data (normally millions of data points are required to properly train a model).

- Understanding legal text is still a challenge, and a vast space for errors and omissions exists.

- Models are not easily interpretable.

Nevertheless, some companies are thriving. DoNotPay is a startup that automates the process of parking ticket appeals. It has successfully contested 160,000 parking tickets with a 64 percent success rate. The conversational bot is able to assist with more than 1,000 different legal issues in all 50 U.S. states and across the United Kingdom. Users just type the problem into the search bar, and links to relevant help pop up that are specific to their location. After navigating through different options, a chatbot asks questions and puts together a letter or other legal documentation. The bots can help write letters or fill out forms for issues such as maternity leave requests, landlord disputes, insurance claims, and harassment. The company has saved around $9.3 million in fines.

10.5 Radiology and Medical Imagery

Deep learning is making rapid advances in diagnostic radiology. The ARK report estimates that the total global addressable market for computer-aided diagnostics software could be worth $16 billion. From revenues of $1 billion today, the growth in medical software companies and imaging device manufacturers could average 20 percent to 35 percent per year as deep learning enhances their productivity and creates new products and services during the next 10 to 15 years.

Diagnostic radiology is essential to modern healthcare; yet the visual interpretation of medical images is a laborious and error-prone process. Historically the average diagnosis error rate among radiologists is around 30 percent, according to https://www.ncbi.nlm.nih.gov/pmc/articles/PMC1955762/. Because of rudimentary technology, lung cancer nodules are routinely missed, especially at earlier stages of development, and 8 percent to 10 percent of bone fractures are missed or misdiagnosed. Initially, radiologists miss roughly two-thirds of breast cancers in mammograms that are visible in retrospective reviews.

Intelligent software powered by deep learning has the potential to change the status quo. Early results are promising: the latest deep learning systems already outperform radiologists and existing algorithms in a variety of diagnostic tasks.

Early diagnosis is key to successful treatment. Each year more than 2 million people worldwide die from lung and breast cancers according to Cancer Research UK. If 10 percent of later-stage cases could be caught at stage 1 with Computer Aided Design (CAD), ARK estimates it would save 150,000 life years. Valuing human life at $50,000 per year, 51 breast or lung diagnoses at stage 1 would equate to $7.6 billion of life value saved. Impacting a wide range of radiology problems from bone fractures to Alzheimer's disease, the value of deep learning would be orders of magnitude greater.

The U.S. National Institutes of Health has released a huge data set of chest X-rays consisting of 100,000 pictures from more than 30,000 patients (https://www.nih.gov/news-events/news-releases/nih-clinical-center-provides-one-largest-publicly-available-chest-x-ray-datasets-scientific-community). A large CT scan data set is expected in a few months.

ARK estimates the market size for CAD software could reach $16 billion. The estimate is based on 34,000 radiologists in the United States reviewing 20,000 cases per year. Given that radiologists pay up to $2 per case for the existing Picture Archiving and Communication System (PACS), a better-than-human diagnostic system could be priced at $10 per case. Assuming full adoption, the U.S. market alone would be worth $6.8 billion.

GlaxoSmithKline is investing $43 million into AI-powered drug development through Exscientia, a company working on AI-driven drug discovery. The aim is to discover novel and selective small molecules for up to ten disease-related targets across multiple therapeutic areas.

10.6 Self-Driving Cars

Considering that 94 percent of car accidents originate from human error and that, on average, a driver in Europe spends six hours a week in traffic jams, it's not difficult to accept that one of the most transformative applications of deep learning is self-driving cars. By some estimates, self-driving cars can reduce the traffic in cities by as much as 90 percent and increase free space, presently devoted to parking, by as much.

Without deep learning, fully autonomous vehicles would be unconceivable. Navigating a vehicle through streets, weather conditions, and unpredictable traffic is an open-ended problem that learning algorithms such as deep learning can solve. ARK believes that deep learning is a fundamental requirement for level 4 or higher autonomous driving (level 5 corresponds to fully autonomous vehicles).

Deep learning solves two key problems facing autonomous driving: sensing and path planning. Neural nets allow a computer to segment the world into drivable and nondrivable paths, detect obstacles, interpret road signs, and respond to traffic lights. Additionally, with reinforcement learning, neural nets can learn how to change lanes, use roundabouts, and navigate around complex traffic conditions.

While self-driving systems have yet to reach the level required for autonomous driving, the observed rate of progress from Google and others suggests that self-driving technology will be available by the end of this decade.

Fully deployed, self-driving technology will reduce the cost of transport and bring to life mobility-as-a-service (MaaS). Based on ARK's research, by 2020 not only will most cars have autonomous driving capabilities but the cost of travel will fall to $0.35 per mile, roughly one-tenth the cost of human-driven taxis. As a result, transportation will transition primarily to an on-demand model, introducing a flood of new consumers to the point-to-point mobility market. The number of autonomous miles driven will rise dramatically from de minimis to 18 trillion per year by 2027. At $0.35 per mile, the market for autonomous on-demand transport will approximate a $6 trillion market in ten years.

10.7 Data Centers

The growth of deep learning as a new and demanding workload means that hyperscale data centers will need to invest aggressively in deep learning accelerators whether they are GPUs, FPGAs, or ASICs. ARK estimates that deep learning accelerator revenue will grow 70 percent annually from $400 million in 2016 to $6 billion by 2022. At that time, according to the research, roughly half of the accelerator revenue will be for training and the other half for inference.

Training currently makes up the majority of revenue since accelerators are a must-have for efficient training. In contrast, inference can be run on standard servers. Training models should grow to a $3 billion business thanks to continued investment by hyperscale vendors, the increased availability of GPU-based servers in the cloud, and the adoption of deep learning by non-Internet industries, particularly automotive companies where the technology will be key for autonomous vehicles.

As deep learning–based services become ubiquitous in web and mobile applications, inference demand should grow and drive demand for accelerators. Microsoft's deployment of FPGAs and Google's rollout of TPUs in their respective data centers suggest that this trend already is underway. We expect hyperscale Internet companies to drive the majority of this investment, with on-premise enterprise deployments trailing by roughly two years.

10.8 Building a Competitive Advantage with DL

DL is associated either with startups or with big companies like Google, Amazon, or Baidu. However, traditional business can also profit from this transformative technology that is fast leveraging the competitive landscape.

From a business perspective, it's important to have a solid grounding in the fundamentals of data science and the algorithms behind deep learning to grasp its far-reaching strategic implications within an organization and not just go with the hype. The implications of having a data-centric business culture are not only useful for a specific problem but are unfolding a set of forces that will lead to the application of similar methodologies in different departments.

The customer-centric view requires the collection of vast amounts of data and the capabilities to learn robustly on unstructured data. DL provides the tools for such an approach that could provide substantial uplift, for instance for targeting the right customers, over traditional marketing campaigns.

These ideas diffused to the online advertising industry and online advertising to incorporate the data of online social connections. Companies consider how they can obtain a competitive advantage from their data and their data science capabilities. Data is a strategic asset, but you need to think carefully as to how data and data science can provide value in the context of your business strategy and also whether it would do the same in the context of your competitors' strategies.

Sometimes is not the data nor the algorithms that create the strategic value but how the extracted insights are implemented in improving products, customer service, and, most important, reorganizing business processes to transform the business. The effectiveness of a predictive model may depend critically on the problem engineering, the attributes created, the combining of different models, and so on. Even if algorithms are published, many implementation details may be critical for getting a solution that works in the lab to work in production.

Success may also depend on intangible assets such as a company culture—a culture that embraces business experimentation is completely different from one that doesn't. The criteria of success is not the accuracy of the model that data scientists design; it's the value created from what the business implements.

10.9 Talent

Data science is only possible with a talented team of data scientists— something hard to find, especially in DL. Anyone can call himself or herself a data scientist, and unfortunately, few companies notice. There has to be at least one top data scientist to truly evaluate the quality of prospective hires—as good data scientists like to work with other top data scientists.

Good data science managers also must possess a set of other abilities that are rare in a single individual.

- They need to truly understand and appreciate the needs of the business. What's more, they should be able to anticipate the needs of the business so that they can interact with their counterparts in other functional areas to develop ideas for new data science products and services.

- They need to be able to communicate well with and be respected by both "techies" and "suits"; often this means translating data science jargon (which this book has tried to minimize) into business jargon, and vice versa.

- They need to coordinate technically complex activities, such as the integration of multiple models or procedures with business constraints and costs. They often need to understand the technical architectures of the business, such as the data systems or production software systems, to ensure that the solutions the team produces are actually useful in practice.

- They need to be able to anticipate outcomes of data science projects. Data science is similar to R&D, so they just give guidance on investments. There is only one reliable predictor of the success of a research project, and it is highly predictive: the prior success of the investigator.

- They need to do all this within the culture of a particular firm.

Finally, the data science capability may be difficult or expensive for a competitor to duplicate because they can hire data scientists and data science managers better. The two most important factors in getting the most from its data assets are that the firm's management must think data analytically and the firm's management must create a culture where data science, and data scientists, will thrive.

There is a huge difference between the effectiveness of a great data scientist and an average data scientist and between a great data science team and an individually great data scientist.

However, just because the market is difficult does not mean all is lost. Many data scientists want to have more individual influence than they would have at a corporate behemoth. Many want more responsibility (and the concomitant experience) with the broader process of producing a data science solution. Some have visions of becoming chief scientist for a firm and understand that the path to chief scientist may be better paved with projects in smaller and more varied firms. Some have visions of becoming entrepreneurs and understand that being an early data scientist for a startup can give them invaluable experience. And some simply will enjoy the thrill of taking part in a fast-growing venture: working in a company growing at 20 percent or 50 percent a year is much different from working in a company growing at 5 percent or 10 percent a year (or not growing at all). In all these cases, the firms that have an advantage in hiring are those that create an environment for nurturing data science and data scientists. If you do not have a critical mass of data scientists, be creative. Encourage your data scientists to become part of local data science technical communities and global data science academic communities.

10.10 It's Not Only About Accuracy

Joshua Bloom, cofounder of Wise.io, raises a pertinent point on his blog post with "How we should optimise the value chain for building AI systems" (`www.wise.io/tech/towards_cost-optimized_artificial_intelligence`). Most AI research focuses on optimizing accuracy as the Holy Grail. Other points should be considered like time and cost to deliver a production-ready solution. In his words, "What we optimize for depends on the altitude from which we look down upon the problem. At all levels we are concerned about different things." Check out `https://www.youtube.com/watch?v=i-1UmCYyzi4`.

He considers three levels of importance when accessing the usability of algorithm.

- *Algorithm/model*: Learning rate, convexity, error bounds/guarantees, scaling

- *Software/hardware*: Accuracy/performance on real data, memory usage during train time, memory usage during prediction time, disk usage requirements, CPU needs, time to learn, time to predict

- *Project*: Staffing requirements (data scientists, software engineers, dev ops), time to implement a proof-of-concept/write a paper, marginal added resource costs, reliability/stability of the model in production, model management/maintainability, experimentability

- *Organization*: Opportunity cost, interaction of results with other lines of business in a company, marketing value of project, P/L of the project effort, long-term benefits of having done the project (e.g., from a hiring perspective), personnel cost to support

- *Consumer*: Direct value, usability, explainability, actionability of the results

- *Society*: Implications of results (e.g., residual benefits to GDP, welfare of people)

The famous case to illustrate this point is the Netflix $1 million competition, where the winning solution was not implemented because of small incremental gains while requiring computational costs and complexity.

10.11 Risks

AI does not come without some risks. An interesting blog post (`https://techcrunch.com/2016/09/16/hard-questions-about-bot-ethics/`) on Techcrunch addresses some questions and hypotheses that the risks of inequality and exclusion in society are greatly accelerated by technology as we fully enter the information revolution.

Cathy O'Neil has an interesting blog where she argues on the side effects of having a society run by algorithms. She also published an interesting book called *Weapons of Math Destruction* [O'N03] where she mentions several biases, side effects, and serious problems if too many important decisions are put in the hands of "obscure" algorithms that no one really understands.

10.12 When Personal Assistants Become Better Than Us

Virtual assistants will play a crucial role in the future, helping from the most mundane tasks such as ordering pizza to the most delicate, such as health or even treatment advice. They will also be monitoring most of our lives and tracking almost all our activity, online and offline. Virtual assistants will play a crucial role in managing different devices and using the data collected to help users make wise decisions. Virtual assistants will become more autonomous and understand context so as to understand that "I'm cold" means it has to turn up the thermostat.

Assistants may even help us date. Alexa already works with dating site eHarmony to search possible matches with shared interests. In the future, she might make the first move on our behalf and start the initial conversation with ... the personal assistant of your potential mate.

But what happens when personal digital assistants become smarter than we are and know more about us than our nearest and dearest?

Current digital assistants are mostly reactive. They wait until you ask them to do something, rather than anticipating user needs. In the future, they will be much more sophisticated. In the near future your car may be able to read your expression and recognize that you are sad and play adequate music or set a drive mode adequate to your sentiment. They will become far more autonomous and adapted to the user specificity too.

The same way we treat our pets as family members, digital assistances will probably acquire a "living-like" status and become part of us. We readily treat things like humans once they are capable of understanding us and communicating through voice.

But for a personal digital assistant to be able to help with such personal issues, it needs to be given a lot of personal information. The privacy and security risks are very large. Can the police use Alexa as a murder witness? Big Brother isn't watching you, but Alexa might be....

Assistants will soon respond not just to commands but to conversations. If you think Facebook stores a lot of information about you, imagine what a virtual assistant may know about you. It might know more about you than your most intimate friend, including where you've been, what you did, who you were with, what you talked about, and how you got there.

## CHAPTER 11

New Research and Future Directions

There are several areas where deep learning is very active and breakthroughs are emerging almost every week. Reinforcement learning with its applications in robotics and simulated agents is clearly one of the most active areas. Image, video, and voice recognition are still active areas. NLP is improving dramatically, but maybe human-level performance in the near future is beyond reach, as it is probably one of the hardest areas. (For some criticism on deep learning applied to NLP, see https://medium.com/@yoav.goldberg/an-adversarial-review-of-adversarial-generation-of-natural-language-409ac3378bd7.)

Many supervised tasks in natural language processing, speech recognition, and automatic video analysis may soon become trivial through large RNNs. In the near future, both supervised learning RNNs and reinforcement learning will be greatly scaled up. Current large ANNs have on the order of a billion connections; soon that will be a trillion, at the same price. By comparison, human brains have a trillions of—much slower—connections.

Progress in machine learning has been driven, to a large degree, by the benefits of training on massive data sets with millions of human-labeled examples. But that approach is infeasible in the long range, and it's far from how humans learn. More progress in unsupervised learning is required, like the work being developed on generative networks.

© Armando Vieira, Bernardete Ribeiro 2018
A. Vieira and B. Ribeiro, *Introduction to Deep Learning Business Applications for Developers,*
https://doi.org/10.1007/978-1-4842-3453-2_11

11.1 Research

Despite image, voice, robotics, and video processing being still very important areas of research using extensively CNNs and LSTM, these are some of the areas where DL is active:

- Reinforcement learning, or weakly supervised learning

- Attention mechanisms

- One-shot learning and knowledge transfer

- Multimodal learning

- Generative adversarial networks (GANs)

In a recent research work (https://arxiv.org/abs/1707.02968) from Google, the authors showed that the size of training data matters considerably. They used a data set of 300 million images classified into 18,291 categories and trained several DL architectures: AlexNet, VGG, ResNet 50, ResNet 101, and Inception-ResNet v2. They proved that even simpler architectures gain considerable accuracy by using more training data. You can find more information at https://research.googleblog.com/2017/07/revisiting-unreasonable-effectiveness.html.

These are the other conclusions:

- A large data set helps in representation learning and is used for pretraining models.

- Performance increases linearly with orders of magnitude of training data. Even at 300 million images, no saturation was observed.

- Capacity is crucial. Large and deep networks are
  necessary to accommodate the complexities in the data.
  For ResNet-50, the gain on the COCO object detection
  benchmark is much smaller (1.87 percent) compared to
  (3 percent) when using ResNet-152 (see Figure 11-1).

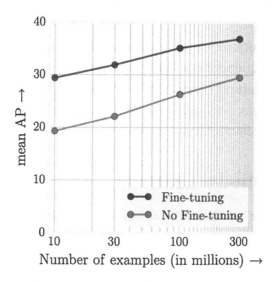

Figure 11-1. *Importance of data size in training DL models
(source:* `https://research.googleblog.com/2017/07/revisiting-`
`unreasonable-effectiveness.html`)

11.1.1 Attention

Attention mechanisms are key for text, image annotation, and video
processing because they allow you to process inputs of variable
(potentially unlimited) size by learning masks on where the input
layer should focus. Attention mechanisms are mainly used for text or
for combinations of text and images (like visual V&A), with CNNs and
LSTM. The paper "Attention Is All You Need" (`https://arxiv.org/`
`abs/1706.03762`) describes how the authors replaced an RNN with

a mechanism (the Transformer) entirely on attention to draw global dependencies between input and output. They reduced the number of discrete ingredients that go into the network, swapping out typical recurrent and convolutional mapping layers with ones that use attention instead. "The authors stated that we plan to extend the Transformer to problems involving input and output modalities other than text and to investigate local, restricted attention mechanisms to efficiently handle large inputs and outputs such as images, audio and video. Making generation less sequential is another research goal of ours."

For a simple example of how to implement an attentive mechanism in a CNN using Keras, see `www.danvatterott.com/blog/2016/09/20/attention-in-a-convolutional-neural-net/`.

11.1.2 Multimodal Learning

Multimodal learning, which is the ability to learn from multiple sources (text, image, video, etc.), is an active area of research and will remain so in the future.

Being able to aggregate structured and unstructured information in a unified distributed representation results in a powerful framework and puts us a step closer to solving the symbol grounding problem. For instance, according to [ARDK16], given only triples (question, world, answer) as training data, the model learned to assemble neural networks from an inventory of neural models and simultaneously learned weights for these modules so that they could be composed into novel structures. They extended a compositional question-answering approach to complex, continuous world representations like images. In other words, they replaced a fixed network topology with a dynamic one, thus adapting the computation performed for each problem, using more complex networks for harder questions, which is very efficient for small data sets.

The work of Quoc Le et al. (`https://arxiv.org/abs/1511.04834`) with gradient descent has also lots of disruptive potential as it allow the neural network to learn to create new programs. This approach represents a paradigm shift in the way we conceive computer programming, from a discrete discrete/symbolic approach to a fully differentiable continuous alternative.

A recent paper (`http://people.csail.mit.edu/yusuf/see-hear-read/paper.pdf`) from MIT combining sound, image, and text has an interesting approach and generates impressive results in classifying objects and entities using cross-modal data.

Google has published a paper called "One Model To Learn Them All" (`https://arxiv.org/pdf/1706.05137.pdf`) where it uses a single model for a number of disparate data sources spanning multiple domains. The model is trained concurrently on ImageNet, translation tasks, image captioning, speech recognition, and English parsing. The model contains convolutional layers, attention mechanisms, and sparsely gated layers. The authors observed that tasks with less data benefit largely from joint training with other tasks, while performance on large tasks degrades only slightly. This work definitely puts us closer to a general algorithm capable of solving any task.

11.1.3 One-Shot Learning

One-shot learning, or zero-shot learning, is also an exciting area of research. In a recent work from DeepMind (`https://arxiv.org/abs/1605.06065`), the team tried to capture the human ability to encounter a new concept (with one or few examples) and generalize to create new versions of the concept. The core solution was a method to describe the probabilistic process by which an observed data point (e.g., a handwritten "8") can be generated. The authors used a deep neural network to specify this probabilistic process and showed that their models were able to generate written characters and faces from a few observations.

One-shot learning is a particularly complex task for a machine, while a trivial one for a human. The problem relies in the fact that DL models typically rely on gradient-based optimization to tune weights for each neuron in the network, which requires lots of data and iterative passes through the net.

In the paper "One shot learning with memory-augmented neural networks" (https://arxiv.org/abs/1605.06065), Google DeepMind developed a network able to learn a new behavior by drawing valid inferences from small amounts of data. The authors used a two-tiered learning (*metalearning*) approach and showed that neural networks with memory are capable of metalearning applied to the Omniglot classification task (1,600 classes with only a few examples per class). The network performs better than the state-of-the-art ones and can even outperform humans. It does this by slowly learning a useful representation of raw data and then uses external memory to rapidly bind new information.

Learning the large number of parameters in CNN requires very large training data sets. Several authors, like Timothy Hospedales (www.eecs.qmul.ac.uk/tmh/), have dedicated extensive research efforts to techniques called *zero-shot learning*. In a recent work (https://arxiv.org/abs/1603.06470), the authors used CNNs for face recognition using a human face synthesis method that swaps the facial components of different face images to generate new faces. They achieved state-of-the-art face recognition performance on the data sets Linear Faces in the Wild (LFW) and CASIA NIR-VIS2.0. In the future, you will apply this technique to more applications of face analysis.

In the paper "One Shot Imitation Learning" (https://arxiv.org/pdf/1703.07326.pdf), the authors proposed a new method for imitation learning, learning from a very few demonstrations and being able to generalize to new situations in the same context. Their metalearning framework uses a neural network that takes as input one demonstration and the current state and outputs an action with the goal that the resulting sequence of states and actions matches as closely as possible with the second demonstration; see http://bit.ly/one-shot-imitation.

In a recent work (https://arxiv.org/pdf/1611.03199.pdf) from a group at Stanford, the authors explored a set of techniques to extend the applicability of DL when large amounts of training data are not available. They demonstrate how one-shot learning can be used to significantly lower the amounts of data required to make meaningful predictions in drug discovery applications. They used an architecture named *residual LSTM embedding* that, when combined with graph convolutional neural networks, significantly improves the ability to learn meaningful distance metrics over small molecules. Their models are open source in a library called DeepChem (http://deepchem.io/).

11.1.4 Reinforcement Learning and Reasoning

Most active reinforcement learning research is related to an agent's learning environment with a shared model or to interacting and learning from one another in the same environment, such as learning to navigate 3D environments like mazes or city streets for autonomous driving. Inverse reinforcement is learning the goal of a task (e.g., learning to drive or endowing nonplayer video game characters with human-like behaviors) from observed behaviors.

In the recent work "Hierarchical Deep Reinforcement Learning: Integrating Temporal Abstraction and Intrinsic Motivation DeepMind" (http://arxiv.org/pdf/1604.06057.pdf), the authors used curiosity to drive agents to achieve some success in the challenging Atari game *Montezuma Revenge*.

Model-free learning methods beyond Q-learning are also very active and are described at https://github.com/karpathy/paper-notes/blob/master/vin.md.

A recent work (https://www.ncbi.nlm.nih.gov/pmc/articles/PMC5299026/) showed that encoding models using CNNs and RNNs could be used for predicting brain activity in response to sensory stimuli, thus modeling how sensory information is represented in the brain.

They investigate the plausibility of recurrent neural networks models to "represent internal memories and for nonlinear processing of arbitrary feature sequences to predict feature-evoked response sequences as measured by functional magnetic resonance imaging," finding that they vastly outperform ridge regression models.

The video at `https://www.youtube.com/watch?v=eKaYnXQUb2g` from Sergey Levine is an excellent resource to understand the theory and improvements in control theory made possible by DL and summarizes some recent results.

One of the drawbacks of DNNs is their difficulty in explicitly extracting a hierarchical structure, as in graphical Bayesian models. ANNs make sophisticated predictions from unstructured data, like images and text, but with little interpretable structure. Structured models for image understanding that are sufficiently expressive to capture the complexity of data and amenable to tractable inference are difficult.

A recent work by Hinton shows how to overcome these difficulties by combining structured with unstructured learning, going beyond other unstructured deep generative methods, like VAEs, that cannot be easily interpretable [EHW+16]. Structured generative methods have largely been incompatible with deep learning, and therefore inference has been hard and slow (e.g., via MCMC). Hinton used a mix of structured probabilistic models and deep networks for scene interpretation via learned, amortized inference. The model imposes structure on its representation through appropriate partly or fully specified generative models, rather than supervision from labels; see `www.cs.toronto.edu/%20hinton/absps/AttendInferRepeat.pdf`. The proposed framework crucially allows for reasoning about the complexity of a given scene (the dimensionality of its latent space).

Relational reasoning is a central component of GAI but has proven very hard to solve by an ANN. Recently Google proposed a project to deal with the hard problem of relational reasoning. Its work (`https://arxiv.org/abs/1706.01427`) proposes an interesting solution. Google tested a model on three tasks: visual question answering (VQA) on a data set called CLEVR, achieving state-of-the-art (superhuman) performance; text-based question answering using the bAbI suite of tasks; and complex reasoning about dynamic physical systems. Google proved that convolutional networks do not have a general capacity to solve relational questions but can gain this capacity when augmented with relational networks.

In two recent papers (`https://deepmind.com/blog/agents-imagine-and-plan/`), DeepMind described a new family of approaches for imagination-based planning. It also introduced architectures that provide new ways for agents to learn and construct plans to maximize the efficiency of a task. These architectures are efficient, robust to complex, and imperfect models, and they can adopt flexible strategies for exploiting their imagination. The agents they introduce benefit from an "imagination encoder," a neural network that learns to extract any information useful for the agent's future decisions but ignores that which is not relevant. DeepMind tested the proposed architectures on multiple tasks, including the puzzle game sokoban and a spaceship navigation game.

11.1.5 Generative Neural Networks

Although not new, generative neural networks (GNNs) are becoming an active area of research. Deep generative models are a powerful approach to unsupervised and semisupervised learning where the goal is to discover the hidden structure within data without relying on external labels.

Generative models have applications in probability density estimation, image denoising and inpainting, data compression, scene understanding, representation learning, 3D scene construction, semisupervised classification, and hierarchical control.

There are three main types of generative models: fully observed models, latent variable models, and transformation models. Each one has a specific inference mechanism. These algorithms include autoregressive distribution estimators, variational auto-encoders, and generative adversarial networks. Examples of deep generative models using latent variables include deep belief networks, variational auto-encoders, and memoryless and amortized inference.

Generative models have, in principle, a richer explanatory capability than discriminative models.

- They are able to represent latent (hidden) structures in the data as well as its invariants, for instance, the concept of light intensity, rotation, bright, or layout in 3D objects.

- They can image the world as "it could be" rather than as "it is presented."

- They have the capability to express more than simple associations between inputs and outputs.

- They can detect surprising, but plausible, events in the data.

Generative models can be used for imputation, for instance, image in-painting (occlusion, patch removal), 3D generation, one-shot learning, and representation learning (for control).

All generative networks share the idea of using latent variables to represent the observed data, and they will continue to be very relevant in near future.

11.1.6 Generative Adversarial Neural Networks

Generative adversarial neural networks (GANs) is an active area of research. See the repository at https://github.com/nashory/gans-awesome-applications for a list of interesting applications of GANs.

GANs are particularly useful for style transfers and for use as generative models. Another advantage is that they can estimate the probability density by avoiding computation of the normalization factor in the partition function.

With GANs it's possible to do the following:

- Simulate training data

- Handle missing data (image inpainting, semisupervised learning)

- Accommodate multiple correct answers for a single input

- Generate realistic images

- Do simulation by prediction

- Solve hard inference problems

- Learn useful embeddings

- Control the latent space to represent interpolation (pose, age, etc.)

The drawback of these models is that they are unstable and hard to train. OpenAI published a detailed blog post with some tricks on how to solve some of the problems of training GANs and make them more stable for image generation. The authors presented new architectural features and training procedures for GANs, including semisupervised learning and the generation of human-realistic images. They trained the models with other goals rather than assigning a high likelihood to test data or learning well without labeled data. They achieved state-of-the-art results in semisupervised classification on MNIST, CIFAR-10, and SVHN. The model generated MNIST samples that humans cannot distinguish from real data and generated CIFAR-10 samples that yield a human error rate of 21.3 percent.

Creative-oriented applications like Photoshop potentially could allow artists to conjure up photos based only on high-level descriptions. For example, the artist could ask the application to draw a bedroom with modern furniture, large windows, afternoon sunlight, and two kids. A generative network, having been trained on a large corpus of bedroom photos and interior decoration magazines, would be able to create such a picture in seconds. After reviewing the first render, the artist then could ask for larger windows, a different color of paint on the walls, and so on. Because neural networks understand images at different layers of abstraction, at the object level, they have the ability to make these changes and enable a complete workflow.

Hyland et al. proposed a GAN for generating real-valued medical time-series generation with recurrent conditional GANs (`https://arxiv.org/pdf/1706.02633.pdf`). This is an interesting approach as medical data is hard to get access to because of regulatory issues.

The GAN approach is powerful because it is applicable to models for which evaluating the likelihood or the gradient are intractable; all that is required is a generative process that, given a random seed, generates a sample data object. In particular, the GAN approach avoids the computationally costly step of inference that is required in, for example, the expectation maximization algorithm. A recent work from Arakaki and Barello Capturing (`https://arxiv.org/pdf/1707.04582.pdf`) used GANs to fit the parameters of the response of selectivity of networks of biological neurons, thus avoiding building an explicit inference model with a predefined likelihood and prioris.

11.1.7 Knowledge Transfer and Learning How to Learn

Learning from a few examples and being able to generalize quickly is one of the most notorious features of human intelligence. Any artificial intelligence agent should be able to learn and adapt quickly from only a few examples and should continue to adapt as more becomes available. This kind of fast and flexible learning is challenging since the agent must integrate its prior experience with a small amount of new information, while avoiding overfitting to the new data. Furthermore, the form of prior experience and new data will depend on the task. As such, for the greatest applicability, the mechanism for learning to learn (or metalearning) should be general to the task and the form of computation required to complete the task.

Finn et al. proposed a very efficient algorithm for metalearning capable of rapidly adapting to new tasks from a previous trained network (https://arxiv.org/pdf/1703.03400.pdf). For example, a robot trained to walk can be quickly retrained to run.

Some promising new algorithms like the one proposed by Lake, Salakhutdinov, and Tenenbaum [LST15] will help a problematic side of DNNs, namely, their difficulty to learn from a few examples and to transfer knowledge so that they can incorporate new knowledge based on just a couple of observations. The authors called it a *Bayesian program learning* (BPL) framework, and it works by generating a unique program for every class using latent concepts. The software was capable not only of mimicking the way children acquire the ability to read and write but, rather, the way adults, who already know how, learn to recognize and then re-create handwritten characters.

Long et al. [LCWJ15] also proposed an interesting architecture to deal with knowledge transfer, called a *deep adaptation network* (DAN), that generalizes CNNs to the domain adaptation scenario by enhancing feature transferability in the task-specific layers of the deep neural network by explicitly reducing the domain discrepancy. The hidden representations of all the task-specific layers are embedded to a reproducing kernel Hilbert space where the mean embeddings of different domain distributions can be explicitly matched. They achieved state-of-the-art results in KT from images of different sources.

Esmali et al. [EHW⁺16] recently put forward a scheme to capture the hierarchical structure images through a variational inference in latent spaces. They treated inference as an iterative process, implemented as a recurrent neural network that attends to one object at a time, and learned to use an appropriate number of inference steps for each image. This allows for capturing a scalable visual representation by taking advantage of iterativity and also is scalable by implementing a recurrent inference network, thus capturing the dependencies between latent variables in the posterior, for instance accounting for the fact that parts of the scene have already been explained.

11.2 When Not to Use Deep Learning

Sometimes deep learning can be more of a hindrance than an asset. DL contains flexible models, with a multitude of architecture and node types, optimizers, and regularization strategies. Depending on the application, the model might have convolutional layers. (How wide and deep should be the layers? What are the sizes of the filters, and how many are there? Is the pooling operation max or average?). Or it might have a recurrent structure. (Is it unidirection or bidirectional? Is it LSTM or GRU?) It might be deep or with just a few hidden layers. (How many units does it have?) It might use rectifying linear units or other activation functions. It might or might not have dropout. (In what layers? With what fraction?). The weights should probably be regularized (l1, l2 or something else). What loss function should be applied?

This is only a partial list; there are many other details that may affect the performance of the network (regularization, transfer functions, loss functions, optimizers) and lots of hyperparameters to tweak and architectures to explore. Google recently boasted that its AutoML pipeline can automatically find the best architecture, which is impressive, but it still requires more than 800 GPUs churning full-time for weeks, something out of reach for almost anyone else. The point is that training deep nets carries a big cost, in both computational and debugging time. Such expense doesn't make sense for lots of day-to-day prediction problems and the ROI of tweaking a deep net to them.

Even when there's plenty of budget and commitment, there's no reason not to try alternative methods first even as a baseline. You might be pleasantly surprised that a SVM or XGBoost is really all you need.

11.3 News

This section highlights some news in the field of AI and important developments.

- A recent blog post (`https://blog.openai.com/deep-reinforcement-learning-from-human-preferences/`) from OpenAI presents a learning algorithm that uses small amounts of human feedback to navigate in complex RL environments. The algorithm needed 900 bits of feedback from a human evaluator to learn to backflip—a seemingly simple task that is easy to judge but challenging to specify.

- See the blog post at `https://medium.com/@pavelkordik/recent-developments-in-artificial-intelligence-b64286daa06b` for a nice tutorial on recent developments in DL.

- Super-resolution image processing is a new research area. Ledig et al. presented a technique (`https://arxiv.org/abs/1609.04802`) based on GAN, called the super-resolution (SRGAN), for achieving photorealistic natural images for 4x upscaling factors.

- Still in image super-resolution, Dahl et al. presented (https://arxiv.org/abs/1702.00783) a pixel-recursive super-resolution model that synthesizes realistic details into images while enhancing their resolution. Using a PixelCNN architecture, the model was able to represent a multimodal conditional distribution by modeling the statistical dependencies among the high-resolution image pixels, conditioned on low-resolution input.

- There are several recent techniques for image inpainting, which means filling a segment occulted from the image. See, for instance, "Image Inpainting with Perceptual and Contextual Losses using a DCGAN: Deep Convolutional Generative Adversarial Network" (http://arxiv.org/pdf/1607.07539v1.pdf).

- As mentioned, DL machines are essentially black boxes. The recent work "Why should I trust you" (https://arxiv.org/abs/1602.04938) is a very interesting paper in making DL machines more explainable and transparent in terms of features learned from the data. See also www.myaooo.com/wp-content/uploads/2017/08/understanding-hidden-memories-camera.pdf on how to make LSTM interpretable.

- Deep learning has also been applied to event spatial-temporal data [DDT+16]; see also https://www.mpi-sws.org/manuelgr/pubs/rmtpp.pdf. Based on the observed sequence of events, the authors could predict future events. Accurately estimating when a clinical event might occur can effectively facilitate patient-specific care and prevention to reduce the potential future risks. See also this work on spatial temporal predictions: https://arxiv.org/pdf/1706.06279.pdf.

11.4 Ethics and Implications of AI in Society

As computer algorithms become more complex and machines start making more complex and high-impact decisions—eventually life or death ones—some serious ethical questions will inevitably arise. Who should be accountable for these decisions if, for instance, a medical treatment proposed by the algorithm goes wrong or a self-driving car crashes into a group of pedestrians to save the driver?

The big problem is that the complexity of the software often means that it is impossible to work out exactly why an AI system does what it does. The recent experiment with the Microsoft Twitter bot, named Tay, demonstrated how well-intentioned technology can be twisted through interactions with humans. Tay was engineered to learn from interactions with Twitter users. In China, where the experiment was first launched, the bot was successful. But in the United States, the bot become sexist, racist, and xenophobe (https://www.theverge.com/2016/3/24/11297050/tay-microsoft-chatbot-racist). Exploring the bot's naïve "behavior" of pleasing the users, they soon exploited this weakness to intentionally persuade the bot of things like the deniable of the holocaust. This experiment puts in perspective the importance of socialization and the difficulty in incorporating ethics in robots.

A new Google research group was recently created to study how people interact with AI, called the People + AI Research Initiative (PAIR). The goal of the group is to make it easier for people to interact with AI systems and to ensure these systems do not display bias or are obtuse to the point of being unhelpful. PAIR will bring together AI researchers and engineers; domain experts such as designers, doctors, and farmers; and everyday users. You can find more information about the group at https://www.blog.google/topics/machine-learning/pair-people-ai-research-initiative/.

DeepMind created the DeepMind Ethics & Society (`https://deepmind.com/applied/deepmind-ethics-society/`) to address the implications of AI in society. On its blog it stated, "Technology is not value neutral, and technologists must take responsibility for the ethical and social impact of their work. In a field as complex as AI this is easier said than done, which is why we are committed to deep research into ethical and social questions, the inclusion of many voices, and ongoing critical reflection."

Here are some other noteworthy resources:

- China is using image and voice recognition technology to replace cards to retrieve money from ATMs; see `www.scmp.com/news/china/money-wealth/article/1813322/china-develops-cash-machines-facial-recognition-feature-curb`.

- The piece at `www.wired.co.uk/article/creating-transparent-ai-algorithms-machine-learning` explores the notion of algorithmic accountability and if algorithms could ever be made free from human bias.

- Nick Bostrom published a working paper entitled "Strategic Implications of Openness in AI Development" (`www.nickbostrom.com/papers/openness.pdf`) with some considerations on the importance of keeping AI open source.

- The authors of a high-profile study on the social dilemma of autonomous vehicles have released Moral Machines (`http://moralmachine.mit.edu/`). The platform will crowdsource human opinions on how machines should make decisions when faced with moral dilemmas as well as scenarios of moral consequence. The experiment asks some tough questions. Give it a try!

- The recent book *Weapons of Math Destruction* (https://www.amazon.co.uk/Weapons-Math-Destruction-Increases-Inequality/dp/0553418815) points to some very important issues on the flip side of machine learning and AI. See also a book raising some concerns on the implications of AI in society: *Our Final Invention*.

- Concerning algorithm bias, Kate Crawford launched the initiative Artificial Intelligence Now (https://artificialintelligencenow.com/), a research initiative working across disciplines to understand the social and economic implications of artificial intelligence. Algorithms that may conceal hidden biases are already routinely used to make vital financial and legal decisions. Most of these algorithms are proprietary and do not lend themselves to interpretation. They may decide, for instance, who gets a job interview, who gets granted parole (https://www.technologyreview.com/s/603763/how-to-upgrade-judges-with-machine-learning/), and who gets a loan.

- With the availability of more sophisticated neural networks that are able to generate very realistic content, text, image, or even videos (see, for example, the fake videos at https://www.youtube.com/watch?v=9Yq67CjDqvw%20list=PLTlqgr7kVS33DF-R5E9MsyVon9h_zCYgc%20index=3), detecting fake content is becoming very hard. For instance, researchers from the University of Chicago have trained a neural network to generate convincing fake restaurant reviews. Some authors claim that fake news played a decisive factor in 2016 U.S. elections.

- Social media news is a double-edged sword. On the one hand, it is low cost, offers easy access, and offers a rapid dissemination of information. On the other hand, it can spread "fake news," or low-quality news with intentionally false information. The extensive spread of fake news has the potential for extremely negative impacts on individuals and society. In a recent publication (`https://arxiv.org/abs/1708.01967`), the authors review methods for fake news detection on social media.

One major implication of AI is the fact that it will make it ever harder to separate real content from generated (fake). In a recent work (`http://grail.cs.washington.edu/projects/AudioToObama/siggraph17_obama.pdf`), a team from the University of Washington developed an algorithm capable of generating a realistic video of a person. They applied a recurrent neural network trained on hours of Barack Obama weekly address footage. Then, they used this network to generate realistic videos with fake content with impressive quality, which was very hard for humans to distinguish. Unlike prior work, they didn't require the subject to be scanned or a speech database to contain videos of many people saying predetermined sentences. Everything was learned from existing footage. See `https://www.youtube.com/watch?v=MVBe6_o4cMI`.

11.5 Privacy and Public Policy in AI

As neural networks reach human-level accuracy in image processing, serious implications will be raised in terms of privacy. For instance, the moment it's possible to identify individuals from omnipresent videos cameras, allowing governments or companies to track everyone on the streets, we may be closer to an Orwellian dystopia than we ever imagined.

The IBA Global Employment Institute, which offers HR guidance for global companies, released a report (https://drive.google.com/drive/folders/0Bxx383wVJ39Pb1p1eGhERTBGVDQ) on the impact of AI on legal, economic, and business issues, such as changes in the future labor market, company structures, working time, remuneration, working environment, forms of employment, and labor relations.

An independent report (https://www.gov.uk/government/publications/growing-the-artificial-intelligence-industry-in-the-uk/recommendations-of-the-review) on AI in the United Kingdom was published in September 2017 to advise the government. The report recommends facilitating data sharing via established data trusts, using public funding for data creation and sharing, and creating 300 new master's degree and 200 PhD degree programs for ML (growing to 1,600 PhDs by 2025), among other initiatives. It states that research and commercialization are huge opportunities for the UK technology industry. AI could increase the annual growth rate of the GVA in 2035 from 2.5 percent to 3.9 percent.

Satya Nadella, Microsoft CEO, outlines three key tenets of his vision for developing AI: augment human abilities and experiences instead of replacing us; work to earn a user's trust by solving privacy, transparency, and security; and technology should be inclusive and respectful of all users. However, others such as Elon Musk, Tesla CEO, raise questions about the need to regulate AI with the risk of being out of control.

Miles Brundage has published an exhaustive document called "A Guide to Working in AI Policy and Strategy" (https://80000hours.org/articles/ai-policy-guide/). He states, "We need answers to AI policy and strategy questions urgently because i) implementing solutions could take a long time, ii) some questions are better addressed while AI is less advanced and fewer views/interests on the topic are locked-in and iii) we don't know when particular AI capabilities will be developed, and can't rule out the possibility of surprisingly sudden advances."

11.6 Startups and VC Investment

DL represents a huge opportunity for startups and investors. In a recent review by the Economist (`www.economist.com/news/special-report/21700761-after-many-false-starts-artificial-intelligence-has-taken-will-it-cause-mass`), Nathan Benaich stated, "In 2015 a record $8.5 billion was spent on AI companies, nearly four times as much as in 2010, according to Quid, a data-analysis company. The number of investment rounds in AI companies in 2015 was 16% up on the year before, when for the technology sector as a whole it declined by 3%."

Funding for artificial intelligence startups continues its upward trend in 2017, with investment hitting new highs; see `https://techcrunch.com/2017/07/11/inside-the-q2-2017-global-venture-capital-ecosystem/` (see Figure 11-2). Venture, corporate, and seed investors have put an estimated $3.6 billion into AI and machine learning companies in the first half of 2017, according to CrunchBase data. That's more than they invested in all of 2016, marking the largest recorded sum ever put into the space in a comparable period.

Global Investment Into AI & Machine Learning

Dollar Volume Is Calculated From Rounds Of Known Size, Count Is All Rounds; Excludes PE

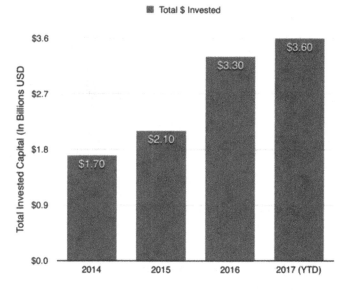

Figure 11-2. *Investment in AI from 2014 to mid-2017 (source: CrunchBase https://techcrunch.com/2017/07/15/vcs-determined-to-replace-your-job-keep-ais-funding-surge-rolling-in-q2/)*

According to a CrunchBase report, equity deals to startups in artificial intelligence—including companies applying AI solutions to verticals such as healthcare, advertising, and finance as well as those developing general-purpose AI technology—increased nearly sixfold, from roughly 70 in 2011 to nearly 400 in 2015 (see Figure 11-3).

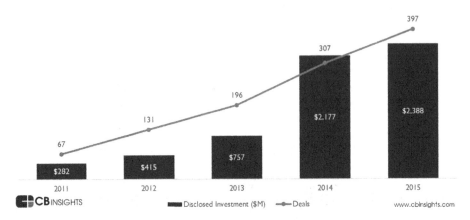

Figure 11-3. *Investment in AI-based startups (source: CrunchBase Insights)*

The 65 percent annual growth in funding to startups using artificial intelligence in 2014 was driven by four mega-rounds of more than $100 million raised by Avant, sales startup InsideSales.com, medical diagnostics company Butterfly Network, and deep learning startup Sentient Technologies.

Element.ai raised $102 million in series A funding; investors include Microsoft, Nvidia, and Intel Capital, all of which have their own AI ambitions. The company wants to democratize the access of AI to companies through easy-to-deploy solutions.

Google launched recently Gradient Ventures (`https://gradient.google/`) to invest in AI startups. Gradient Ventures will invest in 10 to 15 deals in 2018 and will typically commit $1 million to $8 million in each. Portfolio companies will have the opportunity to receive advanced AI training and engineering help from Google.

Healthcare is the leading industrial application of deep learning, according to CrunchBase Insights, raising $ 1.8 billion across 270 deals since 2012. The annual revenue for medical image analysis in healthcare alone will increase to $1.5 billion worldwide in 2025 from less than $100,000 in 2016, according to market research firm Tractica.

11.7 The Future

Truly foundational technologies—such as the steam engine, electricity, the transistor, or the Internet—have a huge impact on the world because they enable creation of new industries, products, and processes.

Deep learning is one of the most important foundational technologies to emerge since the Internet. In just a few years, it has moved from academia to production, powering vision, speech, robotics, healthcare, and various services used by billions of people worldwide. According to ARK Research, deep learning–based companies could create more than $17 trillion in new market capitalization over the next 20 years.

Deep learning, while only five years old as of 2017, is growing at a remarkable rate in use cases, startup formation, market adoption, and revenues. Despite its progress to date, new capabilities such as memory networks and generative networks could make deep learning far more powerful, possibly providing a bridge to artificial general intelligence. In such a scenario, deep learning could make even the Internet look small.

The impact of AI-driven automation in society will be tremendous as it can displace whole sectors of activity. For instance, roughly 4 million truck drivers in the United States alone are at risk of seeing their jobs being replaced by self-driving trucks.

This applies not only to low-skilled professions but also highly skilled ones. General practitioners are also at risk as machines will soon compete against pathologists and radiologists. Personal assistants may soon provide a more accurate diagnosis than an average family doctor. Even though machines cannot yet hold a conversation, current technologies already take orders in natural language and might be fully conversational in the near future.

With the combination of big data, advanced learning algorithms, and fast GPUs and TPUs, the future of deep learning is as bright as you may imagine. The implications in society will be huge, and many industries will be shackled to the foundation.

The following are some areas for future research in DL.

Although DL today can outperform doctors at diagnosing bone fracture, lung cancer, or skin cancer, these models still fail when presented with very atypical data (corner cases) and when integrating disparate sources of data, thus giving inaccurate results for unseen cases. Also, CNNs are easy targets of adversarial examples, which can make them very vulnerable. Further research is necessary to bridge these gaps and integrate more data (like genomics) so that these algorithms fulfill their potential.

To decode the mechanism of life, genetics research still needs to bridge the "genotype-phenotype divide." Genomic and phenotype data abounds. Unfortunately, the state of the art in meaningfully connecting this data results in a slow, expensive, and inaccurate process. To close the loop, you need systems that can determine intermediate phenotypes called *molecular phenotypes*, which function as stepping stones from genotype to disease phenotype. For this, machine learning is indispensable.

CNNs have reached human-level accuracy in image recognition tasks, segmentation, and object detection. However, despite all the progress, ANN remains far inferior to human brains in terms of energy efficiency (the brain consumes only 20 watts, while a single Titan-X GPU consumes 200 watts). Despite efforts from a Google TPU processor dedicated to deep learning, more efficient computational hardware is definitely needed.

Attention mechanisms as well as information feedback loops (from top down and bottom up) are also a promising avenue. There are some interesting ideas inspired by the human visual system, like the CortexNet (https://arxiv.org/abs/1706.02735) and the Feedbacknet (http://feedbacknet.stanford.edu/). These models are not only bottom-up feed-forward connections, but also they model the top-down feedback and lateral connections that are present in human visual cortex.

ANNs still struggle to grasp what humans take for granted: common sense. We don't realize how hard is to teach a machine to develop the capability to understand simple scenarios that are very easy for humans, such as that gravity is always pushing objects down, and therefore water flows downhill.

A solution to this problem is simply more data. To circumvent this difficulty, a large library for a human-like visual understanding of the world was recently created (`https://medium.com/twentybn/learning-about-the-world-through-video-4db73785ac02`). It contains two video data sets with 256,591 labeled videos to teach machines visual common sense. The first data set allows machines to develop a fine-grained understanding of basic actions that occur in the physical world. The second data set of dynamic hand gestures enables robust cognition models for human-computer interaction.

Recurrent networks are clearly superior to feed-forward models. More effective ways to train (including nondifferentiable models) are an important path of research. Evolutionary algorithms are a promising avenue.

11.7.1 Learning with Less Data

DL requires data-intensive algorithms and requires many human annotations. An AI algorithm that classifies cats and dogs will not be able to identify a rare dog species if not fed with images of that species.

Another major challenge is incremental data. In this example, if you are trying to recognize cats and dogs, you might train your AI with a number of cat and dog images of different species when you first deploy. While new species might be more similar to others, this may require complete re-training and re-assessment. Can you make the ANN more adaptable to these small changes?

11.7.2 Transfer Learning

The learning is transferred from one task to the other within the same algorithm in *transfer learning*. Algorithms trained on one task (the source task) with a larger data set can be transferred with or without modification as part of an algorithm trying to learn a different task (the target task) on a (relatively) smaller data set.

Using parameters of an image classification algorithm as a feature extractor in different tasks such as object detection is a simple application of transfer learning. In contrast, it can also be used to perform complex tasks. The algorithm Google developed to classify diabetic retinopathy better than doctors was made using transfer learning.

11.7.3 Multitask Learning

In *multitask learning*, multiple learning tasks are solved at the same time while exploiting commonalities and differences across domains. Sometimes learning two or more tasks together (also called *multimodal learning*) can improve precision.

An important aspect of multitask learning that is seen in real-world applications is that when training any task to become bulletproof, you need to respect data coming from many domains (also called *domain adaptation*). An example in the cat and dog use cases is an algorithm that can recognize images of different sources (say VGA cameras and HD cameras or even infrared cameras). In such cases, an auxiliary loss of domain classification (where the images came in from) can be added to any task, and then the machine learns such that the algorithm keeps getting better at the main task (classifying images into cat or dog images) but purposely gets worse at the auxiliary task (this is done by backpropagating the reverse error gradient from the domain classification task). The idea is that the algorithm learns discriminative features for the main task but forgets features that differentiate domains.

11.7.4 Adversarial Learning

Adversarial learning as a field evolved from the research work of Ian Goodfellow. The most popular applications of adversarial learning are the generative adversarial networks (GANs) that can be used to generate high-quality images; there are other applications, though.

The domain adaptation game can be made better using the GAN loss. The auxiliary loss here is a GAN system instead of pure domain classification, where a discriminator tries to classify which domain the data came from and a generator component tries to fool it by presenting random noise as data. This works better than plain domain adaptation (which is also more erratic than code).

11.7.5 Few-Shot Learning

Few-shot learning is a study of techniques that make deep learning algorithms (or any machine learning algorithms) learn with fewer examples compared to a traditional algorithm. *One-shot learning* is basically learning with one example of a category; inductively, k-shot learning means learning with k examples of each category.

Few-shot learning as a field is seeing an influx of papers in all major deep learning conferences, and there are now specific data sets to benchmark results on, just like MNIST and CIFAR for normal machine learning. One-shot learning is seeing a number of applications in certain image classification tasks such as feature detection and representation.

There are multiple methods that are used for few-shot learning, including transfer learning, multitask learning, and metalearning as all or part of the algorithm. There are other ways such as having clever loss function, using dynamic architectures, or using optimization hacks. Zero-shot learning uses a class of algorithms that claims to predict answers for categories that the algorithm has not even seen; basically they are algorithms that can scale with a new type of data.

11.7.6 Metalearning

Metalearning has become an active area in deep learning recently, most commonly using the technique for hyperparameter and neural network optimization, finding good network architectures, using few-shot image recognition, and using fast reinforcement learning. Refer to the recent work at `https://deepmind.com/blog/population-based-training-neural-networks/` from Google.

This is referred to as full automation for deciding both parameters and hyperparameters such as the network architecture. Despite all the hype around them, metalearners are still algorithms; in other words, they are pathways to scale machine learning with increasingly complex and varied data.

11.7.7 Neural Reasoning

Neural reasoning is a step above pattern recognition, where algorithms are moving beyond the idea of simply identifying and classifying text or images. Neural reasoning is solving more generic questions in text analytics or visual analytics.

This new set of techniques appeared after the release of Facebook's bAbi data set or the recent CLEVR data set. The techniques that decipher relations and not just patterns have immense potential to solve not just neural reasoning but also multiple other hard problems including few-shot learning problems.

All the techniques mentioned help solve training with less data in some way or the other. While metalearning would provide architectures that just mold the data, transfer learning is taking knowledge from some other domains to compensate for less data. Few-shot learning is dedicated to the problem as a scientific discipline. Adversarial learning can help enhance the data sets.

Domain adaptation (a type of multitask learning), adversarial learning, and (sometimes) metalearning architectures help solve problems arising from data diversity. Metalearning and few-shot learning help solve problems of incremental data.

Neural reasoning algorithms have immense potential to solve real-world problems when incorporated as metalearners or few-shot learners.

APPENDIX A

Training DNN with Keras

This appendix will discuss using the Keras framework to train deep learning and explore some example applications on image segmentation using a fully convolutional network (FCN) and click-rate prediction with a wide and deep model (inspired by the TensorFlow implementation).

Despite their massive size, successful deep artificial neural networks can exhibit a remarkably small difference between training and test performance; see https://blog.acolyer.org/2017/05/11/understanding-deep-learning-requires-re-thinking-generalization/. In a blog post (https://beamandrew.github.io/deeplearning/2017/06/04/deep_learning_works.html), Andrew Beam explains why it's possible to apply very large neural networks even if you have small data sets without the risk of overfitting.

A.1 The Keras Framework

Keras.io is an excellent framework to start deploying a deep learning model. The author, Francois Chollet, has created a great library, following a minimalist approach and with many hyperparameters and optimizers already preconfigured. You can run complex models in less than ten lines of code using Theano, TensorFlow, and CNTK backends.

© Armando Vieira, Bernardete Ribeiro 2018
A. Vieira and B. Ribeiro, *Introduction to Deep Learning Business Applications for Developers*,
https://doi.org/10.1007/978-1-4842-3453-2

A.1.1 Installing Keras in Linux

Keras is pretty straightforward to install. The first step is to install Theano or TensorFlow. Installing TensorFlow is easy with Pip. Be careful with the version you install, though. If you use a GPU, you have to choose a compatible installation that will run Cuda. There are some obvious dependencies like Numpy or less obvious ones like hdf5 to compress files. See the full instructions for a Linux installation at `www.pyimagesearch.com/2016/11/14/installing-keras-with-tensorflow-backend/`.

A.1.2 Model

Models in Keras are defined as a sequence of layers. A network is a stack of layers forming a network topology. The input layer needs to have the same dimensions as the input data. This can be specified when creating the first layer with the *input_dim* argument.

Finding the best network architecture (number of layers, size of layers, activation functions) is done mostly by trial and error. Generally, you need a network large enough to accommodate the complexity of the problem but one that is not too complex.

Fully connected layers are defined using the `Dense` class. You can specify the number of neurons in the layer as the first argument.

The network weights should be initialized to a small random number generated from a uniform distribution. The initialization method can be specified as an `int` argument. The activation function is also specified as an argument. If you are unsure about these initializations, simply use the defaults.

A.1.3 The Core Layers

A neural network is composed of a set of (mostly sequential) layers that are connected with each other. These are the most common layers:

- Input

- Dense

- Convolution1D and convolution2D

- Embedding

- LSTM

A neural network works with tensors. Before you perform computation, you need to convert your data (as a Numpy array of a Pandas data frame) into a tensor. The input layer is the entry point of a neural network.

The dense layer is the most basic (and common) type of layer. It has as arguments the number of unities and the activation function. The rectifier linear unit (ReLU) activation function is the most common one. The convolution layers (1D or 2D) are mostly used for text and images and the required parameters are the number of filters and the kernel size. The embedding layer is very useful for text data as they can convert a very high dimensional data into a denser representation - they require two parameters `input_dim` and `output_dim`. The LSTM layer is very useful to learn temporal or sequential data - the only required parameter is the number of units - careful since these networks with these layers are very computational intensive and they overfit easily.

Some other common activation functions are tanh, softmax, and argmax.

The following is a simple example of a Keras model to classify data (the response variable is the last column of the file `xxx.csv`, either 0 or 1). In this example, you will train a classifier, minimize the cross entropy over 150 epochs, and print the predictions. The data is assumed to be normalized. As the activation function in the last layer, you are using `sigmoid`, but normally softmax should be used. It is assumed that input data is contained in the initial X_dim columns - parameter that should be provided.

```python
from keras.models import Sequential
from keras.layers import Dense
import numpy as np
# load a dataset
dataset = np.loadtxt("xxx.csv", delimiter=",")
# split into input (X) and output (Y) variables
X = dataset[:,0:X_dim]
Y = dataset[:,X_dim]
# create model
model = Sequential()
model.add(Dense(12, input_dim=X_dim, init='uniform',
activation='relu'))
model.add(Dense(5, init='uniform', activation='relu'))
model.add(Dense(1, init='uniform', activation='sigmoid'))
# Compile model
model.compile(loss='binary_crossentropy', optimizer='adam',
    metrics=['accuracy'])
# Fit the model
model.fit(X, Y, epochs=150, batch_size=10, verbose=2)
# calculate predictions
predictions = model.predict(X)
# round predictions
rounded = [round(x[0]) for x in predictions]
print(rounded)
```

A.1.4 The Loss Function

Keras comes with the most common loss functions, including these basic ones:

- Cross entropy and binary cross entropy for classification problems

- Categorical cross entropy

- Mean Square Error (MSE) for regression problems

Building a personalized loss function is quite straightforward. An example is provided in the code of the FCN later in this chapter to weight the cross entropy to account for imbalanced categorical data, using the `binary_crossentropy_2d_w()` function. Care should be taken because loss functions have to be fully differentiable. For instance, you cannot use `if`, `then`, `else`.

A.1.5 Training and Testing

Normally you specify the metrics of interest by calling the `compile` method. For instance, you can compile this model using the Adam optimizer with a learning rate of 0.001, minimizing the binary cross entropy loss and displaying the accuracy.

```
model.compile(Adam(0.001), loss='binary_crossentropy',
metrics='accuracy')
```

To display all metrics from training a model, just use this:

```
history=model.fit(X_train,Y_train,epochs=50)
print(history.history.keys())
```

A.1.6 Callbacks

Keras can register a set of callbacks when training neural networks.

The default callback tracks the training metrics for each epoch, including the loss and the accuracy for training and validation data.

An object named history is returned from a call to the fit() function. Metrics are stored in the form of a dictionary in the history member of the object returned.

The following is an example using a checkpoint to save the weights (in the file weights.hdf5) of the best model:

```
from keras.callbacks import ModelCheckpoint
checkpointbest = ModelCheckpoint(filepath='weights.hdf5',
verbose=1, save_best_only=True)
model.fit(x_train, y_train, epochs=20, validation_data=
(x_test, y_test), callbacks=[checkpointbest])
```

A.1.7 Compile and Fit

After the model is defined, it can be compiled; only at this point is the computational graph effectively generated. Compiling uses the numerical libraries from the Keras backend such as Theano or TensorFlow. The backend automatically chooses the best way to represent the network for training and makes predictions for running on hardware, such as a CPU or GPU and single or multiple. You can run models on a CPU, but a GPU is advisable if you are dealing with large image data sets because it will speed up the training by an order of magnitude.

Compiling requires additional properties for training the network for finding the best set of weights connecting the neurons. You must specify the loss function to use to evaluate the network, the optimizer used to search through different weights for the network, and any optional metrics you would like to collect and report during training.

For classification, you typically use logarithmic loss, which for a binary classification problem is defined in Keras as `binary_crossentropy`. For optimization, the gradient descent algorithm `adam` is commonly used.

```
model.compile(loss='binary_crossentropy', optimizer='adam',
metrics ['accuracy'])
```

Other common optimizers include Adadelta, SGD, and Adagrad.

To train, or fit, the model on data, you call the `fit()` function on the model. The training process will run for a fixed number of iterations through the data set called *epochs*, which is specified through the epochs argument. You can also set the number of instances that are evaluated before a weight update in the network is performed, called the *batch size*, using the `batch_size` argument.

A.2 The Deep and Wide Model

Wide and deep models can be jointly trained using linear models and deep neural networks. The wide component consists of a generalized linear model, and the cross-product interaction is modeled as a neural network with embedding layers (see Figure A-1).

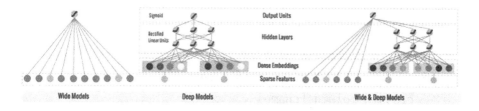

Figure A-1. *Wide and deep neural network model*

The following code, in Python 2.7, is the Keras implementation of the code originally presented in TensorFlow. To run it, you need to download the adult data set from `http://mlr.cs.umass.edu/ml/machine-learning-databases/adult/adult.data`. It was provided by Javier Zaurin (`https://github.com/jrzaurin/Wide-and-Deep-Keras`).

First you will do the imports and define some functions to be used later.

```python
# to run : python wide_and_deep.py -method method
# example: python wide_and_deep.py -method deep
import numpy as np
import pandas as pd
import argparse
from sklearn.preprocessing import StandardScaler
from copy import copy

from keras.models import Sequential
from keras.layers import Dense
from keras.optimizers import Adam
from keras.layers import Input, concatenate, Embedding,
Reshape, Merge, Flatten, merge, Lambda
from keras.layers.normalization import BatchNormalization
from keras.models import Model
from keras.regularizers import l2, l1_l2

def cross_columns(x_cols):
    """simple helper to build the crossed columns in a pandas
    dataframe
    """
    crossed_columns = dict()
    colnames = ['_'.join(x_c) for x_c in x_cols]
    for cname,x_c in zip(colnames,x_cols):
        crossed_columns[cname] = x_c
    return crossed_columns

def val2idx(DF_deep,cols):
    """helper to index categorical columns before embeddings.
    """ DF_deep = pd.concat([df_train, df_test])
    val_types = dict()
    for c in cols:
```

```
        val_types[c] = DF_deep[c].unique()

    val_to_idx = dict()
    for k, v in val_types.iteritems():
        val_to_idx[k] = o: i for i, o in enumerate(val_
        types[k])

    for k, v in val_to_idx.iteritems():
        DF_deep[k] = DF_deep[k].apply(lambda x: v[x])

    unique_vals = dict()
    for c in cols:
        unique_vals[c] = DF_deep[c].nunique()

    return DF_deep,unique_vals

def embedding_input(name, n_in, n_out, reg):
    inp = Input(shape=(1,), dtype='int64', name=name)
    return inp, Embedding(n_in, n_out, input_length=1,
        embeddings_regularizer=l2(reg))(inp)

def continous_input(name):
    inp = Input(shape=(1,), dtype='float32', name=name)
    return inp, Reshape((1, 1))(inp)
```

Then you define the wide model.

```
def wide():

    target = 'cr'

    wide_cols = ["gender", "xyz_campaign_id", "fb_campaign_id",
    "age", "interest"]
    x_cols = (['gender', 'age'],['age', 'interest'])

    DF_wide = pd.concat([df_train,df_test])
```

```
# my understanding on how to replicate what layers.crossed_
column does One
# can read here: https://www.tensorflow.org/tutorials/linear.
crossed_columns_d = cross_columns(x_cols)

categorical_columns =
    list(DF_wide.select_dtypes(include=['object']).columns)
wide_columns = wide_cols + crossed_columns_d.keys()

for k, v in crossed_columns_d.iteritems():
    DF_wide[k] = DF_wide[v].apply(lambda x: '-'.join(x),
    axis=1)

DF_wide = DF_wide[wide_columns + [target] + ['IS_TRAIN']]
dummy_cols = [
    c for c in wide_columns if c in categorical_columns +
        crossed_columns_d.keys()]
DF_wide = pd.get_dummies(DF_wide, columns=[x for x in
dummy_cols])

train = DF_wide[DF_wide.IS_TRAIN == 1].drop('IS_TRAIN',
axis=1)
test = DF_wide[DF_wide.IS_TRAIN == 0].drop('IS_TRAIN', axis=1)

# sanity check: make sure all columns are in the same order
cols = ['cr'] + [c for c in train.columns if c != 'cr']
train = train[cols]
test = test[cols]

X_train = train.values[:, 1:]
Y_train = train.values[:, 0]
X_test = test.values[:, 1:]
Y_test = test.values[:, 0]
```

```
# WIDE MODEL
wide_inp = Input(shape=(X_train.shape[1],),
dtype='float32', name='wide_inp')
w = Dense(1, activation="sigmoid", name = "wide_model")
(wide_inp)
wide = Model(wide_inp, w)
wide.compile(Adam(0.01), loss='mse', metrics=['accuracy'])
wide.fit(X_train,Y_train,nb_epoch=10,batch_size=64)
results = wide.evaluate(X_test,Y_test)

print " Results with wide model:
```

Then you define the wide model.

```
def deep():
    DF_deep = pd.concat([df_train,df_test])
    target = 'cr'
    embedding_cols = ["gender", "xyz_campaign_id",
    "fb_campaign_id", "age", "interest"]
    deep_cols = embedding_cols + ['cpc','cpco','cpcoa']
    DF_deep,unique_vals = val2idx(DF_deep, embedding_cols)
    train = DF_deep[DF_deep.IS_TRAIN == 1].drop('IS_TRAIN',
    axis=1)
    test = DF_deep[DF_deep.IS_TRAIN == 0].drop('IS_TRAIN', axis=1)

    n_factors = 5
    gender, gd = embedding_input('gender_in', unique_vals[
                                'gender'], n_factors, 1e-3)
    xyz_campaign, xyz = embedding_input('xyz_campaign_id_in',
    unique_vals[
                                        'xyz_campaign_id'], n_
                                        factors, 1e-3)
```

```
fb_campaign_id, fb = embedding_input('fb_campaign_id_in',
unique_vals[
                                    'fb_campaign_id'], n_
                                    factors, 1e-3)
age, ag = embedding_input('age_in', unique_vals[
                            'age'], n_factors, 1e-3)
interest, it = embedding_input('interest_in', unique_vals[
                                'interest'], n_factors,
                                1e-3)

# adding numerical columns to the deep model
cpco, cp = continous_input('cpco_in')
cpcoa, cpa = continous_input('cpcoa_in')

X_train = [train[c] for c in deep_cols]
Y_train = train[target]
X_test = [test[c] for c in deep_cols]
Y_test = test[target]

# DEEP MODEL: input same order than in deep_cols:
d = merge([gd, re, xyz, fb, ag, it], mode='concat')
d = Flatten()(d)
# layer to normalise continous columns with the embeddings
d = BatchNormalization()(d)
d = Dense(100, activation='relu',
    kernel_regularizer=l1_l2(l1=0.01, l2=0.01))(d)
d = Dense(50, activation='relu',name='deep_inp')(d)
d = Dense(1, activation="sigmoid")(d)
deep = Model([gender, xyz_campaign, fb_campaign_id, age,
interest,
            cpco, cpcoa], d)
```

```
deep.compile(Adam(0.001), loss='mse', metrics=['accuracy'])
deep.fit(X_train,Y_train, batch_size=64, nb_epoch=10)
results = deep.evaluate(X_test,Y_test)

print " Results with deep model:
```

Then you compose the wide and deep model using some cross-tabular columns.

```
def wide_deep():

    target = 'cr'
    wide_cols = ["gender", "xyz_campaign_id", "fb_campaign_id",
    "age", "interest"]
    x_cols = (['gender', 'xyz_campaign'],['age', 'interest'])

    DF_wide = pd.concat([df_train,df_test])

    crossed_columns_d = cross_columns(x_cols)

    categorical_columns =
        list(DF_wide.select_dtypes(include=['object']).columns)
    wide_columns = wide_cols + crossed_columns_d.keys()

    for k, v in crossed_columns_d.iteritems(): DF_wide[k] =
        DF_wide[v].apply(lambda x: '-'.join(x), axis=1)

    DF_wide = DF_wide[wide_columns + [target] + ['IS_TRAIN']]
    dummy_cols = [
        c for c in wide_columns if c in categorical_columns +
            crossed_columns_d.keys()]
    DF_wide = pd.get_dummies(DF_wide, columns=[x for x in
    dummy_cols])
```

```
train = DF_wide[DF_wide.IS_TRAIN == 1].drop('IS_TRAIN',
axis=1)
test = DF_wide[DF_wide.IS_TRAIN == 0].drop('IS_TRAIN', axis=1)

# sanity check: make sure all columns are in the same order
cols = ['cr'] + [c for c in train.columns if c != 'cr']
train = train[cols]
test = test[cols]

X_train_wide = train.values[:, 1:]
Y_train_wide = train.values[:, 0]
X_test_wide = test.values[:, 1:]

DF_deep = pd.concat([df_train,df_test])
embedding_cols = ['gender', 'xyz_campaign','fb_campaign_
id', 'age', 'interest']
deep_cols = embedding_cols + ['cpco','cpcoa']
DF_deep,unique_vals = val2idx(DF_deep,embedding_cols)
train = DF_deep[DF_deep.IS_TRAIN == 1].drop('IS_TRAIN',
axis=1)
test = DF_deep[DF_deep.IS_TRAIN == 0].drop('IS_TRAIN', axis=1)

n_factors = 5
gender, gd = embedding_input('gender_in', unique_vals[
                            'gender'], n_factors, 1e-3)
xyz_campaign, xyz = embedding_input('xyz_campaign_id_in',
unique_vals[
                                    'xyz_campaign_id'],
                                    n_factors, 1e-3)
fb_campaign_id, fb = embedding_input('fb_campaign_id_in',
unique_vals[
                                    'fb_campaign_id'], n_
                                    factors, 1e-3)
```

```
age, ag = embedding_input('age_in', unique_vals[
                          'age'], n_factors, 1e-3)
interest, it = embedding_input('interest_in', unique_vals[
                          'interest'], n_factors, 1e-3)

# adding numerical columns to the deep model
cpco, cp = continous_input('cpco_in')
cpcoa, cpa = continous_input('cpcoa_in')

X_train_deep = [train[c] for c in deep_cols]
Y_train_deep = train[target]
X_test_deep = [test[c] for c in deep_cols]
Y_test_deep = test[target]

X_tr_wd = [X_train_wide] + X_train_deep
Y_tr_wd = Y_train_deep # wide or deep is the same here
X_te_wd = [X_test_wide] + X_test_deep
Y_te_wd = Y_test_deep # wide or deep is the same here

#WIDE
wide_inp = Input(shape=(X_train_wide.shape[1],),
dtype='float32',
    name='wide_inp')

#DEEP
deep_inp = merge([ge, xyz, ag, fb, it, cp, cpa],
mode='concat')
deep_inp = Flatten()(deep_inp)
# layer to normalise continous columns with the embeddings
deep_inp = BatchNormalization()(deep_inp)
deep_inp = Dense(100, activation='relu',
         kernel_regularizer=l1_l2(l1=0.01, l2=0.01))
         (deep_inp)
```

```
deep_inp = Dense(50, activation='relu',name='deep_inp')
(deep_inp)

#WIDE + DEEP
wide_deep_inp = concatenate([wide_inp, deep_inp])
wide_deep_out = Dense(1, activation='sigmoid',
    name='wide_deep_out')(wide_deep_inp)
wide_deep = Model(inputs=[wide_inp, gender, age, xyz_
campaign,
                          fb_campaign_id,cpco, cpcoa],
                            outputs=wide_deep_out)
wide_deep.compile(optimizer=Adam(lr=0.001),loss='mse',
    metrics=['accuracy'])
wide_deep.fit(X_tr_wd, Y_tr_wd, nb_epoch=50, batch_size=80)
# wide_deep.optimizer.lr = 0.001
# wide_deep.fit(X_tr_wd, Y_tr_wd, nb_epoch=5, batch_
size=64)
results = wide_deep.evaluate(X_te_wd, Y_te_wd)

print " Results with wide and deep model:
```

The main module is finally assembled.

```
if __name__ == '__main__':

    ap = argparse.ArgumentParser()
    ap.add_argument("-method", type=str, default="wide_deep",
        help="fitting method")
    args = vars(ap.parse_args())
    method       = args["method"]

    df_train = pd.read_csv("train.csv")
    df_test = pd.read_csv("test.csv")
    df_train['IS_TRAIN'] = 1
    df_test['IS_TRAIN'] = 0
```

```
    if method == 'wide':
        wide()
    elif method == 'deep':
        deep()
    else:
        wide_deep()
```

A.3 An FCN for Image Segmentation

This section will provide the code for image segmentation using a fully convolutional network.

You will begin by doing some imports and setting some functions, as shown here:

```
import glob
import os
from PIL import Image
import numpy as np

from keras.layers import Input, Convolution2D, MaxPooling2D,
UpSampling2D, Dropout
from keras.models import Model
from keras import backend as K
from keras.callbacks import ModelCheckpoint
smooth = 1.

# define a weighted binary cross entropy function
def binary_crossentropy_2d_w(alpha):
    def loss(y_true, y_pred):
        bce = K.binary_crossentropy(y_pred, y_true)
        bce *= 1 + alpha * y_true
        bce /= alpha
        return K.mean(K.batch_flatten(bce), axis=-1)
    return loss
```

```
# define dice score to assess predictions
def dice_coef(y_true, y_pred):
    y_true_f = K.flatten(y_true)
    y_pred_f = K.flatten(y_pred)
    intersection = K.sum(y_true_f * y_pred_f)
    return (2. * intersection + smooth) / (K.sum(y_true_f) +
        K.sum(y_pred_f) + smooth)

def dice_coef_loss(y_true, y_pred):
    return 1 - dice_coef(y_true, y_pred)
```

Then you load the data and the respective masks. The transpose can be skipped if you use TensorFlow as the backend (because it assumes images are specified as width×height×channels). A low-resolution image is 640×480×3.

```
def load_data(dir, boundary=False):
    X = []
    y = []
    # load images
    for f in sorted(glob.glob(dir + '/image??.png')):
        img = np.array(Image.open(f).convert('RGB'))
        X.append(img)
    # load masks
    for i, f in enumerate(sorted(glob.glob(dir + '/image??_
    mask.txt'))):
        if boundary:
            a = get_boundary_mask(f)
            y.append(np.expand_dims(a, axis=0))
        else:
            content = open(f).read().split('')[1:-1]
            a = np.array(content, 'i').reshape(X[i].shape[:2])
            a = np.clip(a, 0, 1).astype('uint8')
            y.append(np.expand_dims(a, axis=0))
```

```
# stack data
X = np.array(X) / 255.
y = np.array(y)
X = np.transpose(X, (0, 3, 1, 2))
return X, y
```

Then you define the network used for training. You start with eight filters, and each time you do max pooling, it doubles: 16, 32, and so on.

```
# define the network model
def net_2_outputs(input_shape):
    input_img = Input(input_shape, name='input')

    x = Convolution2D(8, 3, 3, activation='relu',
        border_mode='same')(input_img)
    x = Convolution2D(8, 3, 3, activation='relu', border_
        mode='same')(x)
    x = Convolution2D(8, 3, 3, subsample=(1, 1),
        activation='relu', border_mode='same')(x)
    x = MaxPooling2D((2, 2), border_mode='same')(x)
    x = Convolution2D(16, 3, 3, activation='relu', border_
        mode='same')(x)
    x = Convolution2D(16, 3, 3, activation='relu', border_
        mode='same')(x)
    x = Convolution2D(16, 3, 3, subsample=(1, 1),
        activation='relu',
        border_mode='same')(x)
    x = MaxPooling2D((2, 2), border_mode='same')(x)
    x = Convolution2D(32, 3, 3, activation='relu', border_
        mode='same')(x)
    x = Convolution2D(32, 3, 3, activation='relu', border_
        mode='same')(x)
    x = Convolution2D(32, 3, 3, activation='relu', border_
        mode='same')(x)
```

```
    # up
    x = UpSampling2D((2, 2))(x)
    x = Convolution2D(16, 3, 3, activation='relu', border_
        mode='same')(x)
    x = UpSampling2D((2, 2))(x)
    x = Convolution2D(8, 3, 3, activation='relu', border_
        mode='same')(x)
    output = Convolution2D(1, 3, 3, activation='sigmoid',
        border_mode='same', name='output')(x)

    model = Model(input_img, output=[output])
    model.compile(optimizer='adam', loss='output':
        binary_crossentropy_2d_w(5))
return model
```

Next, you train the model.

```
def train():
    X, y = load_data(DATA_DIR_TRAIN.replace('c_type', c_type),
        boundary=False) # load the data

    print(X.shape, y.shape) # make sure it's the right shape
    h = X.shape[2]
    w = X.shape[3]
    training_data = ShuffleBatchGenerator(input_data='input': X,
        output_data='output': y, 'output_b': y_b) # generate
        batches for
        training and testing
    training_data_aug = DataAugmentation(training_data,
        inplace_transfo=['mirror', 'transpose']) # apply some data
        augmentation
    net = net_2_outputs((X.shape[1], h, w))
    net.summary()
```

```
model = net
model.fit(training_data_aug, 300, 1, callbacks=[ProgressBar
Callback()])
net.save('model.hdf5' )

# save predictions to disk
res = model.predict(training_data, training_data.nb_
elements)
if not os.path.isdir('res'):
    os.makedirs('res')
for i, img in enumerate(res[0]):
    Image.fromarray(np.squeeze(img) *
        255).convert('RGB').save('res/
for i, img in enumerate(res[1]):
    Image.fromarray(np.squeeze(img) *
        255).convert('RGB').save('res/
if __name__ == '__main__':
        train()
```

A.3.1 Sequence to Sequence

Sequence-to-sequence models (seq2seq) convert a sequence from one domain (e.g., sentences in English) to a sequence in another domain (e.g., the same sentences translated to French) or convert from past observations to a sequence of future observations (prediction).

When both sequences have the same length, a simple Keras LSTM is enough. In the general case of arbitrary lengths where the entire input sequence is required, an RNN layer will act as the encoder. It projects the input sequence into its own internal state (the context), and another RNN layer is trained as the decoder to predict the next elements of the target sequence. The encoder uses as the initial state the vectors from the encoder. The decoder learns to generate `targets[t+1...]` given `targets[...t]`, conditioned on the input sequence. The following example was created by F. Chollet and is available online at `https://blog.keras.io/a-ten-minute-introduction-to-sequence-to-sequence-learning-in-keras.html`:

```
from keras.models import Model
from keras.layers import Input, LSTM, Dense

encoder_inputs = Input(shape=(None, num_encoder_tokens))
encoder = LSTM(latent_dim, return_state=True)
encoder_outputs, state_h, state_c = encoder(encoder_inputs)
# We discard 'encoder_outputs' and only keep the states.
encoder_states = [state_h, state_c]

# Set up the decoder, using 'encoder_states' as initial state.
decoder_inputs = Input(shape=(None, num_decoder_tokens))
# We set up our decoder to return full output sequences,
# and to return internal states as well. We don't use the
# return states in the training model, but we will use them in
inference.
decoder_lstm = LSTM(latent_dim, return_sequences=True, return_
state=True)
decoder_outputs, _, _ = decoder_lstm(decoder_inputs,
                                initial_state=encoder_states)
decoder_dense = Dense(num_decoder_tokens, activation='softmax')
decoder_outputs = decoder_dense(decoder_outputs)

# Define the model that will turn
# 'encoder_input_data' 'decoder_input_data' into 'decoder_
target_data'
model = Model([encoder_inputs, decoder_inputs], decoder_outputs)

# Run training
```

```
model.compile(optimizer='rmsprop', loss='categorical_
crossentropy')
model.fit([encoder_input_data, decoder_input_data], decoder_
target_data,
        batch_size=batch_size,
        epochs=epochs,
        validation_split=0.2)

encoder_model = Model(encoder_inputs, encoder_states)

decoder_state_input_h = Input(shape=(latent_dim,))
decoder_state_input_c = Input(shape=(latent_dim,))
decoder_states_inputs = [decoder_state_input_h, decoder_state_
input_c]
decoder_outputs, state_h, state_c = decoder_lstm(
    decoder_inputs, initial_state=decoder_states_inputs)
decoder_states = [state_h, state_c]
decoder_outputs = decoder_dense(decoder_outputs)
decoder_model = Model(
    [decoder_inputs] + decoder_states_inputs,
    [decoder_outputs] + decoder_states)

def decode_sequence(input_seq):
    # Encode the input as state vectors.
    states_value = encoder_model.predict(input_seq)

    # Generate empty target sequence of length 1.
    target_seq = np.zeros((1, 1, num_decoder_tokens))
    # Populate the first character of target sequence with the
    start character.
    target_seq[0, 0, target_token_index['']] = 1.

    # Sampling loop for a batch of sequences
    # (to simplify, here we assume a batch of size 1).
```

```
stop_condition = False
decoded_sentence = "
while not stop_condition:
    output_tokens, h, c = decoder_model.predict(
        [target_seq] + states_value)

    # Sample a token
    sampled_token_index = np.argmax(output_tokens[0, -1, :])
    sampled_char = reverse_target_char_index[sampled_token_
    index]
    decoded_sentence += sampled_char

    # Exit condition: either hit max length
    # or find stop character.
    if (sampled_char == '' or
        len(decoded_sentence) > max_decoder_seq_length):
        stop_condition = True

    # Update the target sequence (of length 1).
    target_seq = np.zeros((1, 1, num_decoder_tokens))
    target_seq[0, 0, sampled_token_index] = 1.

    # Update states
    states_value = [h, c]

return decoded_sentence
```

A.4 The Backpropagation on a Multilayer Perceptron

In this section, we will consider a rather general neural network consisting of L layers (of course not counting the input layer). Let's consider an arbitrary layer, say ℓ, which has N_ℓ neurons, $X_1^{(\ell)}, X_2^{(\ell)}, ..., X_{N_\ell}^{(\ell)}$, each with a transfer function, $f^{(\ell)}$. Notice that the transfer function may be different from layer to layer. As in the extended Delta rule, the transfer function may be given by any differentiable function but does not need to be linear. These neurons receive signals from the neurons in the preceding layer, $\ell-1$. For example, neuron $X_j^{(\ell)}$ receives a signal from $X_i^{(\ell-1)}$ with a weight factor of $w_{ij}^{(\ell)}$. Therefore, you have an $N_{\ell-1}$ by N_ℓ weight matrix, $\mathbf{W}^{(\ell)}$, whose elements are given by $W_{ij}^{(\ell)}$, for $i=1,2,\dots,N_{\ell-1}$ and $j=1,2,\dots,N_\ell$. Neuron $X_j^{(\ell)}$ also has a bias given by $b_j^{(\ell)}$, and its activation is $a_j^{(\ell)}$.

To simplify the notation, you will use $n_j^{(\ell)}\left(=y_{in,j}\right)$ to denote the net input into neuron $X_j^{(\ell)}$. It is given as follows:

$$n_j^{(\ell)} = \sum_{i=1}^{N_{\ell-1}} a_i^{(\ell-1)} w_{ij}^{(\ell)} + b_j^{(\ell)}, j=1,2,\dots,N_\ell.$$

Thus, the activation of neuron $X_j^{(\ell)}$ is as follows:

$$a_j^{(\ell)} = f^{(\ell)}\left(n_j^{(\ell)}\right) = f^{(\ell)}\left(\sum_{i=1}^{N_{\ell-1}} a_i^{(\ell-1)} w_{ij}^{(\ell)} + b_j^{(\ell)}\right).$$

You can consider the zeroth layer as the input layer. If an input vector $\mathbf{x}$ has N components, then $N_0 = N$, and neurons in the input layer have activations $a_i^{(0)} = x_i, i=1,2,\dots,N_0$.

Layer L of the network is the output layer. Assuming that the output vector $\mathbf{y}$ has M components, you must have $N_L = M$. These components are given by $y_j = a_j^{(L)}, j=1,2,\dots,M$.

For any given input vector, the previous equations can be used to find the activation for each neuron for any given set of weights and biases. In particular, the network output vector $\mathbf{y}$ can be found. The remaining question is how to train the network to find a set of weights and biases for it to perform a certain task.

You will now consider training a rather general multilayer perceptron for pattern association using the BP algorithm. Training is carried out supervised, so you can assume that a set of pattern pairs (or associations), as in $\mathbf{s}^{(q)} : \mathbf{t}^{(q)}, q = 1,2,\ldots,Q$, is given. The training vectors $\mathbf{s}^{(q)}$ have N components, as shown here:

$$\mathbf{s}^{(q)} = \begin{bmatrix} s_1^{(q)} & s_2^{(q)} & \cdots & s_N^{(q)} \end{bmatrix},$$

Their targets, $\mathbf{t}^{(q)}$, have M components, as shown here:

$$\mathbf{t}^{(q)} = \begin{bmatrix} t_1^{(q)} & t_2^{(q)} & \cdots & t_M^{(q)} \end{bmatrix}.$$

Just like in the Delta rule, the training vectors are presented one at a time to the network during training. Suppose in time step t of the training process, a training vector $\mathbf{s}^{(q)}$ for a particular q is presented as input, $\mathbf{x}(t)$, to the network. The input signal can be propagated forward through the network using the equations in the previous section and the current set of weights and biases to obtain the corresponding network output, $\mathbf{y}(t)$. The weights and biases are then adjusted using the steepest descent algorithm to minimize the square of the error for this training vector:

$$E = \left\| \mathbf{y}(t) - \mathbf{t}(t) \right\|^2,$$

Here, $\mathbf{t}(t) = \mathbf{t}^{(q)}$ is the corresponding target vector for the chosen training vector $\mathbf{s}^{(q)}$.

This square error E is a function of all the weights and biases of the entire network since $\mathbf{y}(t)$ depends on them. You need to find the set of updating rules for them based on the steepest descent algorithm.

$$w_{ij}^{(\ell)}(t+1) = w_{ij}^{(\ell)}(t) - \alpha \frac{\partial E}{\partial w_{ij}^{(\ell)}(t)}$$

$$b_j^{(\ell)}(t+1) = b_j^{(\ell)}(t) - \alpha \frac{\partial E}{\partial b_j^{(\ell)}(t)},$$

Here, $\alpha(>0)$ is the learning rate.

To compute these partial derivatives, you need to understand how E depends on the weights and biases. First, E depends explicitly on the network output $\mathbf{y}(t)$ (the activations of the last layer, $\mathbf{a}^{(L)}$), which then depends on the net input into the L-th layer, $\mathbf{n}^{(L)}$. In turn, $\mathbf{n}^{(L)}$ is given by the activations of the preceding layer and the weights and biases of layer L. The explicit relation is as follows (for brevity, the dependence on step t is omitted):

$$E = \left\| \mathbf{y} - \mathbf{t}(t) \right\|^2 = \left\| \mathbf{a}^{(L)} - \mathbf{t}(t) \right\|^2 = \left\| f^{(L)}\left(\mathbf{n}^{(L)}\right) - \mathbf{t}(t) \right\|^2$$

$$= \left\| f^{(L)}\left(\sum_{i=1}^{N_{L-1}} a_i^{(L-1)} w_{ij}^{(L)} + b_j^{(L)} \right) - \mathbf{t}(t) \right\|^2.$$

It is then easy to compute the partial derivatives of E with respect to the elements of $\mathbf{W}^{(L)}$ and $\mathbf{b}^{(L)}$ using the chain rule for differentiation.

$$\frac{\partial E}{\partial w_{ij}^{(L)}} = \sum_{n=1}^{N_L} \frac{\partial E}{\partial n_n^{(L)}} \frac{\partial n_n^{(L)}}{\partial w_{ij}^{(L)}}.$$

Notice the sum is needed in the previous equation for the correct application of the chain rule. You now define the sensitivity vector for a general layer ℓ to have components.

$$s_n^{(\ell)} = \frac{\partial E}{\partial n_n^{(\ell)}} \quad n = 1, 2, \ldots, N_\ell.$$

This is called the sensitivity of neuron $X_n^{(\ell)}$ because it gives the change in the output error, E, per unit change in the net input it receives.

For layer L, it is easy to compute the sensitivity vector directly using the chain rule to obtain this.

$$s_n^{(L)} = 2\left(a_n^{(L)} - t_n(t)\right)\dot{f}^{(L)}\left(n_n^{(L)}\right), n = 1, 2, \ldots, N_L.$$

Here, $\dot{f}$ denotes the derivative of the transfer function f. You also know the following:

$$\frac{\partial n_n^{(L)}}{\partial w_{ij}^{(L)}} = \frac{\partial}{\partial w_{ij}^{(L)}}\left(\sum_{m=1}^{N_{L-1}} a_m^{(L-1)} w_{mn}^{(L)} + b_n^{(L)}\right) = \delta_{nj} a_i^{(L-1)}.$$

Therefore, you have this:

$$\frac{\partial E}{\partial w_{ij}^{(L)}} = a_i^{(L-1)} s_j^{(L)}.$$

Similarly, you have this:

$$\frac{\partial E}{\partial b_j^{(L)}} = \sum_{n=1}^{N_L} \frac{\partial E}{\partial n_n^{(L)}} \frac{\partial n_n^{(L)}}{\partial b_j^{(L)}},$$

In addition, since you have this:

$$\frac{\partial n_n^{(L)}}{\partial b_j^{(L)}} = \delta_{nj},$$

then you get the following:

$$\frac{\partial E}{\partial b_j^{(L)}} = s_j^{(L)}.$$

For a general layer, ℓ, you can write this:

$$\frac{\partial E}{\partial w_{ij}^{(\ell)}} = \sum_{n=1}^{N_\ell} \frac{\partial E}{\partial n_n^{(\ell)}} \frac{\partial n_n^{(\ell)}}{\partial w_{ij}^{(\ell)}} = \sum_{n=1}^{N_\ell} s_n^{(\ell)} \frac{\partial n_n^{(\ell)}}{\partial w_{ij}^{(\ell)}}.$$

$$\frac{\partial E}{\partial b_j^{(\ell)}} = \sum_{n=1}^{N_\ell} \frac{\partial E}{\partial n_n^{(\ell)}} \frac{\partial n_n^{(\ell)}}{\partial b_j^{(\ell)}} = \sum_{n=1}^{N_\ell} s_n^{(\ell)} \frac{\partial n_n^{(\ell)}}{\partial b_j^{(\ell)}}.$$

Since you have this:

$$n_n^{(\ell)} = \sum_{m=1}^{N_{\ell-1}} a_m^{(\ell-1)} w_{mn}^{(\ell)} + b_n^{(\ell)}, j = 1, 2, \ldots, N_\ell,$$

the you have the following:

$$\frac{\partial n_n^{(\ell)}}{\partial w_{ij}^{(\ell)}} = \delta_{nj} a_i^{(\ell-1)}$$

$$\frac{\partial n_n^{(\ell)}}{\partial b_j^{(\ell)}} = \delta_{nj},$$

and finally the following:

$$\frac{\partial E}{\partial w_{ij}^{(\ell)}} = a_i^{(\ell-1)} s_j^{(\ell)}, \frac{\partial E}{\partial b_j^{(\ell)}} = s_j^{(\ell)}.$$

Therefore, the updating rules for the weights and biases are as follows (now you put back the dependency on the step index t):

$$w_{ij}^{(\ell)}(t+1) = w_{ij}^{(\ell)}(t) - \alpha \, a_i^{(\ell-1)}(t) s_j^{(\ell)}(t)$$

$$b_j^{(\ell)}(t+1) = b_j^{(\ell)}(t) - \alpha \, s_j^{(\ell)}(t),$$

To use these updating rules, you need to be able to compute the sensitivity vectors $\mathbf{s}^{(\ell)}$ for $\ell = 1,2,\ldots,L-1$. From their definition, you have this:

$$s_j^{(\ell)} = \frac{\partial E}{\partial n_j^{(\ell)}} \quad j=1,2,\ldots,N_\ell,$$

You need to know how E depends on $n_j^{(\ell)}$. The key to computing these partial derivatives is to note that $n_j^{(\ell)}$ in turn depends on $n_i^{(\ell-1)}$ for $i=1,2,\ldots,N_{\ell-1}$, because the net input for layer ℓ depends on the activation of the previous layer, $\ell-1$, which in turn depends on the net input for layer $\ell-1$. Specifically, you have this for $j=1,2,\ldots,N_\ell$:

$$n_j^{(\ell)} = \sum_{i=1}^{N_{\ell-1}} a_i^{(\ell-1)} w_{ij}^{(\ell)} + b_j^{(\ell)} = \sum_{i=1}^{N_{\ell-1}} f^{(\ell-1)}\left(n_i^{(\ell-1)}\right) w_{ij}^{(\ell)} + b_j^{(\ell)}$$

Therefore, you have the following for the sensitivity of layer $\ell-1$:

$$s_j^{(\ell-1)} = \frac{\partial E}{\partial n_j^{(\ell-1)}} = \sum_{i=1}^{N_\ell} \frac{\partial E}{\partial n_i^{(\ell)}} \frac{\partial n_i^{(\ell)}}{\partial n_j^{(\ell-1)}}$$

$$= \sum_{i=1}^{N_\ell} s_i^{(\ell)} \frac{\partial}{\partial n_j^{(\ell-1)}} \left(\sum_{m=1}^{N_{\ell-1}} f^{(\ell-1)}\left(n_m^{(\ell-1)}\right) w_{mi}^{(\ell)} + b_i^{(\ell)} \right)$$

$$= \sum_{i=1}^{N_\ell} s_i^{(\ell)} \dot{f}^{(\ell-1)}\left(n_j^{(\ell-1)}\right) w_{ji}^{(\ell)} = \dot{f}^{(\ell-1)}\left(n_j^{(\ell-1)}\right) \sum_{i=1}^{N_\ell} w_{ji}^{(\ell)} s_i^{(\ell)}.$$

Thus, the sensitivity of a neuron in layer $\ell-1$ depends on the sensitivities of all the neurons in layer ℓ. This is a recursion relation for the sensitivities of the network since the sensitivities of the last layer L is known. To find the activations or the net inputs for any given layer, you need to feed the input from the left of the network and proceed forward to the layer in question. However, to find the sensitivities for any given layer, you need to start from the last layer and use the recursion relation going backward to the given layer. This is why the training algorithm is called *backpropagation*.

To compute the updates for the weights and biases, you need to find the activations and sensitivities for all the layers. To obtain the sensitivities, you also need $\dot{f}^{(\ell)}\left(n_j^{(\ell)}\right)$. That means that in general you need to keep track of all the $n_j^{(\ell)}$ as well.

In neural networks trained using the backpropagation algorithm, there are two functions often used as the transfer functions. One is the log-sigmoid function, shown here:

$$f_{logsig}(x) = \frac{1}{1+e^{-x}}$$

This is differentiable, and its value goes smoothly and monotonically between 0 and 1 for x around 0. The other is the hyperbolic tangent sigmoid function, shown here:

$$f_{tansig}(x) = \frac{1-e^{-x}}{1+e^{-x}} = \tanh(x/2)$$

This is also differentiable, but its value goes smoothly between -1 and 1 for x around 0. It is easy to see that the first derivatives of these functions are given in terms of the same functions alone.

$$\dot{f}_{logsig}(x) = f_{logsig}(x)\left[1 - f_{logsig}(x)\right]$$

$$\dot{f}_{tansig}(x) = \frac{1}{2}\left[1 + f_{tansig}(x)\right]\left[1 - f_{tansig}(x)\right]$$

Since $f^{(\ell)}\left(n_j^{(\ell)}\right) = a_j^{(\ell)}$, in implementing the neural network on a computer, there is actually no need to keep track of $n_j^{(\ell)}$ at all (thus saving memory).

References

[AAB+15]   Dario Amodei, Rishita Anubhai, Eric Battenberg, Carl Case, Jared Casper, Bryan Catanzaro, Jingdong Chen, Mike Chrzanowski, Adam Coates, Greg Diamos, Erich Elsen, Jesse Engel, Linxi Fan, Christopher Fougner, Tony Han, Awni Y. Hannun, Billy Jun, Patrick LeGresley, Libby Lin, Sharan Narang, Andrew Y. Ng, Sherjil Ozair, Ryan Prenger, Jonathan Raiman, Sanjeev Satheesh, David Seetapun, Shubho Sengupta, Yi Wang, Zhiqian Wang, Chong Wang, Bo Xiao, Dani Yogatama, Jun Zhan, and Zhenyao Zhu. Deep speech 2: End-to-end speech recognition in english and mandarin. *CoRR*, abs/1512.02595, 2015.

[AAL+15]   Stanislaw Antol, Aishwarya Agrawal, Jiasen Lu, Margaret Mitchell, Dhruv Batra, C. Lawrence Zitnick, and Devi Parikh. VQA: Visual Question Answering. In *International Conference on Computer Vision (ICCV)*, 2015.

[AG13]   G. Hinton A. Graves, A. Mohamed. Speech recognition with deep recurrent neural networks. *Arxiv*, 2013.

[AHS85]   David H. Ackley, Geoffrey E. Hinton, and Terrence J. Sejnowski. A learning algorithm for boltzmann machines. *Cognitive Science*, 9(1):147–169, 1985.

[AIG12] Krizhevsky A., Sutskever I., and Hinton G. Imagenet classification with deep convolutional neural networks. *Advances in Neural Information Processing Systems. Curran Associates*, 25:1106–1114, 2012. `http://papers.nips.cc/paper/4824-imagenet-classification-with-deep-convolutional-neural-networks.pdf`.

[AM15] E. Asgari, M. R. Mofrad. Continuous Distributed Representation of Biological Sequences for Deep Proteomics and Genomics. *PloS one*, 10(11):e0141287, 2015.

[AOS⁺16] Dario Amodei, Chris Olah, Jacob Steinhardt, Paul Christiano, John Schulman, and Dan Mané. Concrete problems in AI safety. *CoRR*, abs/1606.06565, 2016.

[ARDK16] Jacob Andreas, Marcus Rohrbach, Trevor Darrell, and Dan Klein. Learning to compose neural networks for question answering. *CoRR*, abs/1601.01705, 2016.

[AV03] N. P. Barradas A. Vieira. A training algorithm for classification of high-dimensional data. *Neurocomputing*, 50:461–472, 2003.

[AV18] Attul Sehgal Armando Vieira. How banks can better serve their customers through artificial techniques. In *Digital Markets Unleashed*, page 311. Springer-Verlag, 2018.

[BCB14] Dzmitry Bahdanau, Kyunghyun Cho, and Yoshua Bengio. Neural machine translation by jointly learning to align and translate. *CoRR*, abs/1409.0473, 2014.

[BLPL06] Yoshua Bengio, Pascal Lamblin, Dan Popovici, and Hugo Larochelle. Greedy layer-wise training of deep networks. In *Proceedings of the 19th International Conference on Neural Information Processing Systems*, NIPS'06, pages 153–160, Cambridge, MA, USA, 2006. MIT Press.

[BUGD⁺13] Antoine Bordes, Nicolas Usunier, Alberto Garcia-Duran, Jason Weston, and Oksana Yakhnenko. Translating embeddings for modeling multi-relational data. In C. J. C. Burges, L. Bottou, M. Welling, Z. Ghahramani, and K. Q. Weinberger, editors, *Advances in Neural Information Processing Systems 26*, pages 2787–2795. Curran Associates, Inc., 2013.

[CBK09] Varun Chandola, Arindam Banerjee, and Vipin Kumar. Anomaly detection: A survey. *ACM computing surveys (CSUR)*, 41(3):15:1–15:58, 2009.

[CCB15] KyungHyun Cho, Aaron C. Courville, and Yoshua Bengio. Describing multimedia content using attention-based encoder-decoder networks. *CoRR*, abs/1507.01053, 2015.

[CHY⁺14] Charles F. Cadieu, Ha Hong, Daniel L. K. Yamins, Nicolas Pinto, Diego Ardila, Ethan A. Solomon, Najib J. Majaj, and James J. DiCarlo. Deep neural networks rival the representation of primate IT cortex for core visual object recognition. *PLOS Computational Biology*, 10(12):1–18, 12 2014.

[CLN⁺16] Y. Chen, Y. Li, R. Narayan et al. Gene expression inference with deep learning. *Bioinformatics*, 2016(btw074).

[DCH⁺16] Yan Duan, Xi Chen, Rein Houthooft, John Schulman and Pieter Abbeel. Benchmarking Deep Reinforcement Learning for Continuous Control. *CoRR*, abs/1604.06778, 2016.

[DDT⁺16] Nan Du, Hanjun Dai, Rakshit Trivedi, Utkarsh Upadhyay, Manuel Gomez-Rodriguez, and Le Song. Recurrent marked temporal point processes: Embedding event history to vector. In *Proceedings of the 22Nd ACM SIGKDD International Conference on Knowledge Discovery and Data Mining*, KDD'16, pages 1555–1564, New York, NY, USA, 2016. ACM.

REFERENCES

[DHG⁺14]   Jeff Donahue, Lisa Anne Hendricks, Sergio Guadarrama, Marcus Rohrbach, Subhashini Venugopalan, Kate Saenko, and Trevor Darrell. Long-term recurrent convolutional networks for visual recognition and description. *CoRR*, abs/1411.4389, 2014.

[Doe16]   Carl Doersch. Tutorial on variational autoencoders. *CoRR*, 2016.

[E12]   Dumbill E. What is big data? an introduction to the big data landscape. *In Strata*, 2012. Making Data Work. O'Reilly, Santa Clara, CA O'Reilly.

[EBC⁺10]   Dumitru Erhan, Yoshua Bengio, Aaron Courville, Pierre-Antoine Manzagol, Pascal Vincent, and Samy Bengio. Why does unsupervised pre-training help deep learning? *J. Mach. Learn. Res.*, 11:625–660, March 2010.

[EHW⁺16]   S. M. Ali Eslami, Nicolas Heess, Theophane Weber, Yuval Tassa, Koray Kavukcuoglu, and Geoffrey E. Hinton. Attend, infer, repeat: Fast scene understanding with generative models. *CoRR*, abs/1603.08575, 2016.

[Elm90]   Jeffrey L. Elman. Finding structure in time. *Cognitive Science*, 14(2):179–211, 1990.

[FF15]   Ralph Fehrer and Stefan Feuerriegel. Improving decision analytics with deep learning: The case of financial disclosures. 2015. https://arxiv.org/pdf/1508.01993v1.pdf.

[FG16]   Basura Fernando and Stephen Gould. Learning end-to-end video classification with rank-pooling. *ICML*, 2016. http://jmlr.org/proceedings/papers/v48/fernando16.pdf.

[GBC16]   Ian Goodfellow, Yoshua Bengio, and Aaron Courville. *Deep Learning*. MIT Press, 2016. www.deeplearningbook.org.

[GBWB13] Xavier Glorot, Antoine Bordes, Jason Weston, and Yoshua Bengio. A semantic matching energy function for learning with multi-relational data. *CoRR*, abs/1301.3485, 2013.

[GEB15] Leon A. Gatys, Alexander S. Ecker, and Matthias Bethge. A neural algorithm of artistic style. *CoRR*, abs/1508.06576, 2015.

[GLO+16] Yanming Guo, Yu Liu, Ard Oerlemans, Songyang Lao, Song Wu, and Michael S. Lew. Deep learning for visual understanding. *Neurocomput.*, 187(C):27–48, April 2016.

[GMZ+15] Haoyuan Gao, Junhua Mao, Jie Zhou, Zhiheng Huang, Lei Wang, and Wei Xu. Are you talking to a machine? dataset and methods for multilingual image question answering. pages 2296–2304, 2015.

[GPAM+14] Ian Goodfellow, Jean Pouget-Abadie, Mehdi Mirza, Bing Xu, David Warde-Farley, Sherjil Ozair, Aaron Courville, and Yoshua Bengio. Generative adversarial nets. In Z. Ghahramani, M. Welling, C. Cortes, N. D. Lawrence, and K. Q. Weinberger, editors, *Advances in Neural Information Processing Systems 27*, pages 2672–2680. Curran Associates, Inc., 2014.

[GR06] Hinton GE and Salakhutdinov RR. Reducing the dimensionality of data with neural networks. *Science 313(5786): 504–507*, 2006.

[GVS+16] Shalini Ghosh, Oriol Vinyals, Brian Strope, Scott Roy, Tom Dean, and Larry Heck. Contextual LSTM (CLSTM) models for large scale NLP tasks. *CoRR*, abs/1602.06291, 2016.

[HDFN95] G. E. Hinton, P. Dayan, B. J. Frey, and R. M. Neal. The wake-sleep algorithm for unsupervised neural networks. *Science*, 268:1158–1161, 1995.

REFERENCES

[Hin02]   Geoffrey E. Hinton. Training products of experts by minimizing contrastive divergence. *Neural Comput.*, 14(8):1771–1800, August 2002.

[HKG+15]   Karl Moritz Hermann, Tomáš Kočiský, Edward Grefenstette, Lasse Espeholt, Will Kay, Mustafa Suleyman, and Phil Blunsom. Teaching machines to read and comprehend. In *Proceedings of the 28th International Conference on Neural Information Processing Systems*, NIPS'15, pages 1693–1701. MIT Press, Cambridge, MA, USA, 2015.

[HOT06]   G. E. Hinton, S. Osindero, and Y. W. Teh. A fast learning algorithm for deep belief nets. *Neural computation*, 18(7):1527–1554, 2006.

[HS97]   Sepp Hochreiter and Jürgen Schmidhuber. Long short-term memory. *Neural Comput.*, 9(8):1735–1780, November 1997.

[HSL+16]   Gao Huang, Yu Sun, Zhuang Liu, Daniel Sedra, and Kilian Q. Weinberger. Deep networks with stochastic depth. *CoRR*, abs/1603.09382, 2016.

[HZRS15]   Kaiming He, Xiangyu Zhang, Shaoqing Ren, and Jian Sun. Deep residual learning for image recognition. *CoRR*, abs/1512.03385, 2015.

[J15]   Schmidhuber J. Deep learning in neural networks: An overview. *Neural Networks*, 61, 2015.

[Jor90]   Michael I. Jordan. Attractor dynamics and parallelism in a connectionist sequential machine. In Joachim Diederich, editor, *Artificial Neural Networks*, pages 112–127. IEEE Press, Piscataway, NJ, USA, 1990.

[KFF17]   A. Karpathy and L. Fei-Fei. Deep visual-semantic alignments for generating image descriptions. *IEEE Transactions on Pattern Analysis and Machine Intelligence*, 39(4):664–676, 2017.

[KZS+15]   Ryan Kiros, Yukun Zhu, Ruslan Salakhutdinov, Richard S. Zemel, Antonio Torralba, Raquel Urtasun, and Sanja Fidler. Skip-thought vectors. *CoRR*, abs/1506.06726, 2015.

[LBD+89]   Y. LeCun, B. Boser, J. S. Denker, D. Henderson, R. E. Howard, W. Hubbard, and L. D. Jackel. Backpropagation applied to handwritten zip code recognition. *Neural Comput.*, 1(4):541–551, December 1989.

[LBP+16]   B. Lee, J. Baek, S. Park et al. deepTarget: End-to-end Learning Framework for microRNA Target Prediction using Deep Recurrent Neural Networks. *arXiv preprint arXiv*, 1603.09123, 2016.

[LCWJ15]   Mingsheng Long, Yue Cao, Jianmin Wang, and Michael I. Jordan. Learning transferable features with deep adaptation networks. *ICML*, 2015. `http://jmlr.org/proceedings/papers/v37/long15.pdf`.

[LFDA16]   Sergey Levine, Chelsea Finn, Trevor Darrell, and Pieter Abbeel. End-to-end training of deep visuomotor policies. *Journal of Machine Learning Research*, 17:1–40, 2016. `https://arxiv.org/abs/1504.00702`.

[LM14]   Quoc V. Le and Tomas Mikolov. Distributed representations of sentences and documents. *CoRR*, abs/1405.4053, 2014.

[LST15]   Brenden M. Lake, Ruslan Salakhutdinov, and Joshua B. Tenenbaum. Human-level concept learning through probabilistic program induction. *Science 350.6266*, pages 1332–1338, 2015.

[M13]   Grobelnik M. Big data tutorial. *European Data Forum*, 2013. `www.slideshare.net/EUDataForum/edf2013-big-datatutorialmarkogrobelnik`.

[Mac03]   D.J.C. MacKay. *Information Theory, Inference and Learning Algorithms*. Cambridge University Press, 2003.

[MBM⁺16] Volodymyr Mnih, Adrià Puigdomènech Badia, Mehdi Mirza, Alex Graves, Timothy P. Lillicrap, Tim Harley, David Silver, and Koray Kavukcuoglu. Asynchronous methods for deep reinforcement learning. *CoRR*, abs/1602.01783, 2016. http://arxiv.org/abs/1602.01783.

[MKS⁺15] Volodymyr Mnih, Koray Kavukcuoglu, David Silver, Andrei A. Rusu, Joel Veness, Marc G. Bellemare, Alex Graves, Martin A. Riedmiller, Andreas Fidjeland, Georg Ostrovski, Stig Petersen, Charles Beattie, Amir Sadik, Ioannis Antonoglou, Helen King, Dharshan Kumaran, Daan Wierstra, Shane Legg, and Demis Hassabis. Human-level control through deep reinforcement learning. *Nature*, 518(7540):529–533, 2015.

[MLS13]   Tomas Mikolov, Quoc V. Le, and Ilya Sutskever. Exploiting similarities among languages for machine translation. *CoRR*, abs/1309.4168, 2013.

[MVPZ16] Polina Mamoshina, Armando Vieira, Evgeny Putin, and Alex Zhavoronkov. Applications of deep learning in biomedicine. *Molecular Pharmaceutics*, 13(5):1445–1454, 2016.

[MXY⁺14] Junhua Mao, Wei Xu, Yi Yang, Jiang Wang, and Alan L. Yuille. Explain images with multimodal recurrent neural networks. *CoRR*, abs/1410.1090, 2014.

[MZMG15] Ishan Misra, C. Lawrence Zitnick, Margaret Mitchell, and Ross B. Girshick. Learning visual classifiers using human-centric annotations. *CoRR*, abs/1512.06974, 2015.

[NSH15]   Hyeonwoo Noh, Paul Hongsuck Seo, and Bohyung Han. Image question answering using convolutional neural network with dynamic parameter prediction. *CoRR*, abs/1511.05756, 2015.

[O'N03]   Cathy O'Neil. *Weapons of Math Destruction*. Penguin, 2003.

[PBvdP16]   Xue Bin Peng, Glen Berseth, and Michiel van de Panne. Terrain-adaptive locomotion skills using deep reinforcement learning. *ACM Trans. Graph.*, 35(4):81:1–81:12, July 2016.

[RG09]   Salakhutdinov R and Hinton GE. Deep Boltzmann Machines. *JMLR*, 2009.

[RMC15]   Alec Radford, Luke Metz, and Soumith Chintala. Unsupervised representation learning with deep convolutional generative adversarial networks. *CoRR*, abs/1511.06434, 2015. http://arxiv.org/abs/1511.06434.

[SA08]   Saratha Sathasivam and Wan Ahmad Tajuddin Wan Abdullah. Logic learning in hopfield networks. *CoRR*, abs/0804.4075, 2008.

[SGS15]   Rupesh Kumar Srivastava, Klaus Greff, and Jürgen Schmidhuber. Highway networks. *CoRR*, abs/1505.00387, 2015.

[SHM⁺16]   David Silver, Aja Huang, Christopher J. Maddison, Arthur Guez, Laurent Sifre, George van den Driessche, Julian Schrittwieser, Ioannis Antonoglou, Veda Panneershelvam, Marc Lanctot, Sander Dieleman anc Dominik Grewe anc John Nham, Nal Kalchbrenner, Ilya Sutskever, Timothy Lillicrap, Madeleine Leach, Koray Kavukcuoglu, Thore Graepel, and Demis Hassabis. Mastering the game of go with deep neural networks and tree search. *Nature*, 529:484–503, 2016.

[SKM84]   R. Snow, P. Kyllonen, and B. Marshalek. The topography of ability and learning correlations. In *Advances in the Psychology of Human Intelligence*, pages 47–103, June 1984.

[SMB10]   Dominik Scherer, Andreas Müller, and Sven Behnke. Evaluation of pooling operations in convolutional architectures for object recognition. In *Proceedings of the 20th International Conference on Artificial Neural Networks: Part III*, ICANN'10, pages 92–101, Berlin, Heidelberg, 2010. Springer-Verlag.

[SMGS15]   Marijn F. Stollenga, Jonathan Masci, Faustino Gomez, and Juergen Schmidhuber. Deep networks with internal selective attention through feedback connections. *NIPS*, 2015. https://papers.nips.cc/paper/5276-deep-networks-with-internal-selective-attention-through-feedback-connections.pdf.

[Smo86]   Paul Smolensky. Chapter 6: Information processing in dynamical systems: Foundations of harmony theory. In David E. Rumelhart and James L. McLelland, editors, *Parallel Distributed Processing: Explorations in the Microstructure of Cognition, Volume 1: Foundations*, volume 1, pages 194–281. MIT Press, 1986.

[SSB+15]   Iulian Vlad Serban, Alessandro Sordoni, Yoshua Bengio, Aaron C. Courville, and Joelle Pineau. Hierarchical neural network generative models for movie dialogues. *CoRR*, abs/1507.04808, 2015.

[SSN+15]   S. K. Sønderby, C. K. Sønderby, H. Nielsen et al. Convolutional LSTM Networks for Subcellular Localization of Proteins. *arXiv preprint arXiv*, 1503.01919, 2015.

[SSS+15]   Basu Saikat, Ganguly Sangram, Mukhopadhyay Supratik, DiBiano Robert, Karki Manohar, and Nemani Ramakrishna. Deepsat: A learning framework for satellite imagery. In *Proceedings of the 23rd SIGSPATIAL International Conference on Advances in Geographic Information Systems*, SIGSPATIAL '15, pages 37:1–37:10, New York, NY, USA, 2015. ACM.

[SsWF15]   Sainbayar Sukhbaatar, arthur szlam, Jason Weston, and Rob Fergus. End-to-end memory networks. In C. Cortes, N. D. Lawrence, D. D. Lee, M. Sugiyama, and R. Garnett, editors, *Advances in Neural Information Processing Systems 28*, pages 2440–2448. Curran Associates, Inc., 2015.

[SVL14]   Ilya Sutskever, Oriol Vinyals, and Quoc V. Le. Sequence to sequence learning with neural networks. In *Proceedings of the 27th International Conference on Neural Information Processing Systems*, NIPS'14, pages 3104–3112, Cambridge, MA, USA, 2014. MIT Press.

[SZ16]   Falong Shen and Gang Zeng. Weighted residuals for very deep networks. *CoRR*, abs/1605.08831, 2016.

[ULVL16]   Dmitry Ulyanov, Vadim Lebedev, Andrea Vedaldi, and Victor S. Lempitsky. Texture networks: Feed-forward synthesis of textures and stylized images. *CoRR*, abs/1603.03417, 2016.

[vdOKV+16] Aäron van den Oord, Nal Kalchbrenner, Oriol Vinyals, Lasse Espeholt, Alex Graves, and Koray Kavukcuoglu. Conditional image generation with pixelCNN decoders. *CoRR*, abs/1606.05328, 2016.

[VKFU15]   Ivan Vendrov, Ryan Kiros, Sanja Fidler, and Raquel Urtasun. Order-embeddings of images and language. *CoRR*, abs/1511.06361, 2015.

[VLBM08]   Pascal Vincent, Hugo Larochelle, Yoshua Bengio, and Pierre-Antoine Manzagol. Extracting and composing robust features with denoising autoencoders. In *Proceedings of the 25th International Conference on Machine Learning*, ICML '08, pages 1096–1103, New York, NY, USA, 2008. ACM.

[VTBE14]   Oriol Vinyals, Alexander Toshev, Samy Bengio, and Dumitru Erhan. Show and tell: A neural image caption generator. *CoRR*, abs/1411.4555, 2014.

[VXD⁺14]   Subhashini Venugopalan, Huijuan Xu, Jeff Donahue, Marcus Rohrbach, Raymond J. Mooney, and Kate Saenko. Translating videos to natural language using deep recurrent neural networks. *CoRR*, abs/1412.4729, 2014.

[Wes16]   Jason Weston. Dialog-based language learning. *CoRR*, abs/1604.06045, 2016.

[WS98]   M. Wiering and J. Schmidhuber. HQ-learning. *Adaptive Behavior*, 6(2):219–246, 1998.

[WWY15]   Hao Wang, Naiyan Wang, and Dit-Yan Yeung. Collaborative deep learning for recommender systems. In *Proceedings of the 21th ACM SIGKDD International Conference on Knowledge Discovery and Data Mining*, KDD '15, pages 1235–1244, New York, NY, USA, 2015. ACM.

[WZFC14]   Zhen Wang, Jianwen Zhang, Jianlin Feng, and Zheng Chen. Knowledge graph embedding by translating on hyperplanes. In Carla E. Brodley and Peter Stone, editors, *AAAI*, pages 1112–1119. AAAI Press, 2014.

[YAP13]   Bengio Y, Courville A, and Vincent P. Representation learning: A review and new perspectives. pattern analysis and machine intelligence. *IEEE Transactions*, 35(8):1798–1828, 2013.

[YZP15]   Kaisheng Yao, Geoffrey Zweig, and Baolin Peng. Attention with intention for a neural network conversation model. *CoRR*, abs/1510.08565, 2015.

[ZCLZ16]   Shuangfei Zhai, Yu Cheng, Weining Lu, and Zhongfei Zhang. Deep structured energy based models for anomaly detection. In *Proceedings of the 33rd International Conference on International Conference on Machine Learning – Volume 48*, ICML'16, pages 1100–1109. JMLR.org, 2016.

[ZCSG16]   Ke Zhang, Wei-Lun Chao, Fei Sha, and Kristen Grauman. *Video Summarization with Long Short-Term Memory*, pages 766–782. Springer International Publishing, Cham, 2016.

[ZKZ⁺15]   Yukun Zhu, Ryan Kiros, Richard S. Zemel, Ruslan Salakhutdinov, Raquel Urtasun, Antonio Torralba, and Sanja Fidler. Aligning books and movies: Towards story-like visual explanations by watching movies and reading books. *CoRR*, abs/1506.06724, 2015.

[ZT15]   J. Zhou, O. G. Troyanskaya. Predicting effects of noncoding variants with deep learning-based sequence model. *Nature methods*, 12(10):931-4, 2015.

Index

A

Actor-critic algorithm (A3C), 147–148, 150, 190

Adversarial auto-encoder (AAE), 72, 228

Aggressive regularization techniques, 82

AI assistants
  Amy, 243
  definition, 241
  Google's Smart Reply, 243
  messaging bots, 242, 243
  text based, 242
  voice based, 242
  voice interaction, 241

AIX, 191

Anomaly detection
  conditional variational auto-encoder, 210
  data analysis, 208
  DSEBM, 210
  fake reviews, 213
  fraud prevention, 211–212
  generative adversarial networks, 210
  models, 208
  PCA, 208
  SAEs, 210
  supervised learning, 209
  unbalanced data sets, 210
  unsupervised techniques
    clustering, 210
    density-based methods, 209
    kernel methods, 210
    variational auto-encoder, 210

Apache Institute, 30

Apocalypse scenario, 17

Applications
  anomaly detection, 208
  big data, 231
  forecast, 216
  machine learning, 207
  medicine and biomedical
    crowdsourcing symptoms, 221
    drug discovery, 228
    medical image processing, 222
    omics, 225–227
  security and prevention, 214
  user experience, 230–231
  voice recognition, 230

Artificial intelligence (AI)
  challenges, 4
  history, 3
  research fields, 4

© Armando Vieira, Bernardete Ribeiro 2018
A. Vieira and B. Ribeiro, *Introduction to Deep Learning Business Applications for Developers*,
https://doi.org/10.1007/978-1-4842-3453-2

S

Printed in the United States
By Bookmasters